POLITICAL DECISION-MAKING PROCESSES

The Jossey-Bass/Elsevier
International Series

 Elsevier Scientific Publishing Company

Amsterdam

POLITICAL DECISION-MAKING PROCESSES

Studies in National, Comparative and International Politics

Edited by

DUSAN SIDJANSKI

Jossey-Bass Inc., Publishers

San Francisco · Washington 1973

POLITICAL DECISION-MAKING PROCESSES: STUDIES IN NATIONAL,
COMPARATIVE AND INTERNATIONAL POLITICS
Edited By Dusan Sidjanski

For the United States of America and Canada:

Jossey-Bass, Inc., Publishers
615 Montgomery Street
San Francisco, California 94111

For all other areas:

Elsevier Scientific Publishing Company
335 Jan van Galenstraat
Amsterdam, The Netherlands

Library of Congress Catalogue Card Number 72-97434

International Standard Book Number ISBN 0-87589-179-9

Manufactured in The Netherlands

FIRST EDITION

Code 7322

Contributors

CHADWICK F. ALGER	Ohio State University, Columbus, Ohio
ROBERT W. COX	International Institute for Labour Studies and Graduate Institute of International Studies, Geneva, Switzerland
ALEXANDER J. GROTH	University of California at Davis
HAROLD K. JACOBSON	University of Michigan, Ann Arbor, Michigan
SANJEEVA NAYAK	Southampton College, Long Island University, Brookville, New York
ROBERT PRESTHUS	York University, Downsview, Canada
CHARLES ROIG	Centre National de la Recherche Scientifique, Paris, France
DUSAN SIDJANSKI	University of Geneva, Switzerland
PAOLO URIO	University of Geneva, Switzerland
LARRY L. WADE	University of California at Davis

Contents

Introduction: Decision-Making Approaches

DUSAN SIDJANSKI

This volume contains the reports presented to a group of specialists at the VIIIth World Congress of the International Political Science Association (Munich, September 1970). The problem of decision-making — the phenomenon of choice, of determination — has always been a subject of philosophical enquiry. Its study has now become a feature common to various social sciences, and an approach which students of experimental psychology or group dynamics, as well as economics, econometry or management science, all make use of to some extent. [1] The angle may vary, the approach may be macro- or micro-political, but always the basic questions arise: Who are the men who make the decisions? How were they chosen, and by whom? They fulfill to be sure, the roles assigned to them by institutions, but how do their personal make-ups, preferences, or background relate to the choices they make? These questions illustrate points of interest common to different disciplines. They show how the decision-making approach can serve as a rallying point for many branches of learning, affording wide scope for multidisciplinary collaboration.

This relatively new approach is increasingly popular in political science. It regards the political apparatus as a machine for generating projects, for making choices at the level of society as a whole, and for carrying them out. The dramatic impact of the decisional method is not, however, confined to this aspect but embraces also the factors that influence the implementation of a decision. Decisions compel individuals and groups to take positions and to act. Decisions, and especially important ones, bring to light the various forces which gave them birth. As in the turning points or crises of a man's life, when he is challenged to show his mettle by his deeds, a decision of importance forces groups and leaders to show where they stand – in other words, to choose. At such times the gap between proclaimed objectives and actual behaviour shows up vividly. An acute crisis or a decisive turn of events exposes the nature of man or of social forces; general – and hence generous – programmes may then reveal their motivations and underlying designs. The actors often drop their masks. While these occasions are not very frequent, the fact remains that a decision is a focal point around which the actions and reactions of the social actors are plotted. Whereas other approaches rely on a sector-by-sector method of analysis, here institutions, groups, leaders – in short, all the relevant factors – are involved together in the decision-making process. Their acts or pressures are no longer presented as one-way processes emanating from a group or factor and directed towards the apparatus, but become integral parts of a complex game where everyone in turn acts and is influenced.

"Decision-making is a process", as defined by Richard C. Snyder, "which results in the selection from a socially defined, limited number of problematical, alternative projects of one project intended to bring about the particular future state of affairs envisaged by the decision-makers." [2] In Snyder's analytical model – whose complexity sometimes makes it inapplicable – enquiry is focused on both the decision-making unit or nucleus and the persons responsible. For example, in the case of the invasion of Korea, which he analyzes, the major decisions throughout the week were made by an ad hoc decisional unit. Thus, the U.S. National Security Council does not loom large in the process regardless of the fact that it might be considered a natural agency. Nor was a permanent group in the State Department involved. Relationships among decision-makers during the week were mostly informal, and communication was predominantly oral and face-to-face. This suggests that a multidimensional crisis decision which requires top-level authority necessitates the formation of a key group which can escape organizational formality and normal procedures. The pressure of the situation results in the *invention* of a special decisional unit. As shown above, the decision-makers acted with remarkable speed.

This relatively informal, high-level organizational process minimized the problem of coordination among roles and agencies. No involved processes of clearance and compromise were necessary. President Truman's leadership, viewed as an independent organizational variable, determined the membership of decisional units (except the first one) and the allocation of power and responsibility within the decision-making group. [3]

In politics, the decision centre and the moment when the decision is made are not always the same as the place and time formally defined. For example many decisions appear as outputs of parliaments. In fact, it is well known that these often amount to a mere endorsement of decisions already made elsewhere — by groups, parties, or executives. Thus, it is not an easy task to locate the real decisional units. In practice, the operation of pressure groups in particular makes it easier to locate the real decision centres on which their influences and pressures are in effect concentrated. At a later stage, the decisions's implementation gives the actual measure of its effectiveness. In other words, analysis must be concerned both with the making of the decision and with its implementation, particularly as the latter may throw light on earlier stages of the process, insofar as the decision-makers behave in accordance with their expectations as to how the decision is likely to be implemented. For instance, in Switzerland, certain economic groups accepted the "anti-cartel" legislation in the hope that its moderate or "reasonable" application would temper the severity of the text. This relationship is, of course, no secret. Important as that side is, however, we shall confine our attention to one aspect, namely the first phase, i.e. participation in the decision-making process. However, the distinction that we propose between open and closed decisions concerns both their making and implementation.

In addition to the many advantages which this approach is generally credited with, we believe that it has the merit of bringing together other approaches used in political science: all political

3

institutions can be looked upon as top-level decision centres and all political parties and pressure groups as autonomous decision centres in a polyarchical society, while the leaders — as the persons who actually take the decisions — participate in or influence their formation. In short, these various elements — focal points of decision, pressures, influences, roles played, and positions taken — centre around the idea of the decision viewed in terms of its components. While reintroducing the dynamic and evolutionary factor, the decision-making process brings all of these elements into play in an attempt to capture dynamic reality.

So many advantages imply some risks. The few drawbacks mentioned here as examples will, it is hoped, temper the excess of uncritical enthusiasm and give a more balanced picture of the value and significance of the method. First of all, it need hardly be recalled that political life is not made up exclusively of decisions. It is, therefore, risky to concentrate wholly on decisions or on exceptional conflict situations at the expense of imperceptible but lasting changes. These being difficult to discern and, like minor or day-to-day decisions, wholly unspectacular, it is understandable that the study of a revolution should be found more tempting than that of an uneventful historic process. But it is certainly true that, as with pathological cases in medicine, the study of turbulent times is conducive to an understanding of normal or peaceful phases, even if it does not explain them entirely. But the problem here is more complex: Political decisions are often based on attitudes — diffuse and implicit factors — as much as on rules — explicit and unequivocal procedures. [4] In this context, "rules" and "procedures" may be replaced by "decisions" and "explicit acts", and what we are saying is that such decisions and explicit acts are by no means the sole reflection of political reality. C. Wright Mills actually considers the absence of decisions to be just as significant as their existence.

"The power elite is composed of men whose positions enable them to transcend the ordinary environments of ordinary men and women; they are in positions to make decisions having major consequences. Whether they do or do not make such decisions is less important than the fact that they do occupy such pivotal positions: their failure to act, their failure to make decisions, is

4

itself an act that is often of greater consequence than the decisions they do make". [5]

Exclusive concentration on decisions overlooks a wide fringe of political reality. A crisis situation and the feverish atmosphere associated with it, mass demonstrations, the pressures of public opinion, the flavour or climate of a period, and imperceptible changes − all of these are essential political factors, even though they are not always reflected in decisions. As Jean Meynaud observes, decisional analysis can give a fragmented picture of political events. If carried to extremes, or simply isolated from other methods, the decisional approach can only result in dissecting and breaking down the political process, magnifying the active, the perceptible, and the striking at the expense of other relevant factors, and giving, in effect, a mere caricature of political reality. The political fabric is really made up of a succession of clean breaks − i.e. decisions − alternating, combining or coexisting with imperceptible trends, which together with the decisions, contribute in different degrees to shaping or colouring political life. A decision, therefore, can be studied only within the context of a political process where its true proportions can be clearly seen and where it can be analyzed in association with the less perceptible attitudes and developments which link it to reality. Such are, briefly stated, the merits as well as the shortcomings of a dramatic methodological approach whose guiding thread, woven around a nexus of actions, runs through the various sectors of political life. This vantage point affords a more complete picture than could be provided by any single or sectoral approach, situated as it is at the crossroads where wills, forces, factors, and influences intersect and on which the spotlight of analysis can be focused most vividly.

However, in spite of the positive and enriching contribution of the decisional approach, its progress so far has been largely restricted to the pragmatic level and has lacked theoretical support. While such authors as David Easton and Karl Deutsch have tried to develop a conceptual framework (the former through his "system analysis of politics" and the latter through the application of cybernetic concepts), both of them − however valuable their contribution has undoubtedly been − stress processes or channels of communication at the expense of an overall theory covering both procedure and substance.

5

There is a further problem, not yet wholly solved: there are as many ways of accounting for political decisions as there are authors. The time, therefore, may well have come to attempt a classification of decisions based on a full inventory and classified arrangement of all the categories suggested in the literature. The following is an example of a few *criteria for classifying decisions.*

1) *Necessity and opportuneness.* (*a*) according to degree of necessity, necessary versus optimal decisions — as regards the decision-making process. (*b*) according to degree of opportuneness, opportune versus inopportune decisions.

2) *The time factor.* (*a*) degree of urgency, urgent versus nonurgent decisions. (*b*) degree of speed, prompt versus slow decisions.

3) *Motivations and choice.* (*a*) type of motivation, economically, ideologically or power-motivated decisions. (*b*) degree of rationality, rational versus irrational decisions. (*c*) degree of intervention, intervention — system based on finality — versus retroaction — system based on causation. (*d*) extent of choice, closed (i.e. yes-or-no) decisions versus progressive decisions.

4) *Nature and content.* (*a*) degree of complexity, complex versus simple decisions. (*b*) decisional field, public sector versus private sector — autonomy of subsystems.

5) *Weight of decisions.* (*a*) degree of importance, important or vital decisions versus minor decisions. (*b*) impact of the decision, fundamental versus derivative decisions.

6) *Effects.* (*a*) degree of generality, general versus particular decisions. (*b*) degree of reversibility, reversible versus irreversible decisions. (*c*) degree of compulsion, compulsory (imperative) versus optional (indicative) decisions. (*d*) degree of fidelity, conformity versus nonconformity of the effect. (*e*) degree of implementation, implemented versus nonimplemented decisions. (*f*) degree of social change, decisions resulting in reform — revolutionary or reformist decisions — versus administrative ones.

7) *Decision-making process.* (*a*) degree of information, public versus secret decisions. (*b*) degree of participation, closed, mixed or open decisions.

This last criterion cuts across the previous six, which it also supplements by introducing the concept of extent and nature of participation. Thus, for example, decisions whether necessary or optional, urgent or non-urgent, ideologically or economically motivated, can all be classified as closed or open. Taking into account the growing importance of the aspect of participation in decision-making, we shall give some more details on this last distinction.

By closed decisions we mean those which are made and implemented solely by or within public authorities or official circles, without any outside participation. In contrast, open decisions are the result of a process in which the authorities responsible consult elements representing the various social forces or informed elites.

Thus the decision-making process is said to be closed when the authorities, excluding all interested parties and persons not members of the official apparatus, take the decision themselves; instead of seeking advice or having consultations outside government circles, they withdraw among themselves to do their own thinking. As for the implementation of a decision, it is said to be closed when it is imposed by the authorities alone, without help from other forces, as in the case of forced implementation. This underscores the close relationship between the making and implementation of a decision: the more dependent its implementation on wide mass participation, and the more it tends to exceed the authorities' means of enforcement, the more the authorities try to associate the masses or their representatives with the preparation and making of the decision, so as to secure in advance the widest possible measure of active support. This, of course, does not mean — aside from exceptional cases — that closed decisions eliminate the pressure of groups entirely; on the contrary, they stimulate them insofar as their results may affect the interests of such groups, but, as a rule, a closed decision is one taken and implemented in a self-contained circuit. One of the most significant examples is the set of U.S. decisions related to its intervention in Vietnam. [6] On the other hand, decision-making and implementation are open whenever the authorities consult interested or representative groups, *independent* experts, certain sectors of the population — or indeed the whole population as in the referendum in France on Algeria — in the various stages of preparation and implementation. As a rule, when implementation requires the effective and willing support of groups or citizens — as in the case of the measures to cope with an overheated economy in Switzerland, or the *indicative* plan in France — the decision is the outcome of a more or less lengthy process of preparation, with extensive consultations, aimed at securing the loyal support of those mainly affected. This, however, is not uniformly true. A decision may be closed in its formative stages, like a conventional war declaration, but open at the stage of implementation, when the active participation of the population is needed under penalty of national collapse, as it is under conditions of *democratized* warfare. Nuclear warfare, on the other hand, being the affair of a small army of specialists, depends on closed decisions, both in its preparation and its practice. The majority of the people can only react passively to the consequences of an airtight decision in which they have had no part and whose implementation lies solely in the hands of the supreme national authority. Thus the effects of technical progress in modern societies are not all in the same direction: depending on the area in which it operates — e.g. economic policy or use of nuclear weapons — it can have opposite effects by accelerating the trend towards one or the other of these two types of decision-making.

The distinction between open and closed decisions is not the same as that between public and secret ones. In fact, open decisions in which external groups participate are often secret, and nearly always they are limited to a fairly small circle of people; they are secret in the sense that they are withheld from the public and the press. Hence, the term *Anonymous Empire* is used by Finer to define the decision-making apparatus: a mechanism at once complex, secretive and powerful through which cooperation — sometimes degenerating into symbiosis — takes place between governments and parliaments on the one hand, and pressure groups on the other (particularly professional associations). Jean Meynaud has drawn attention to the interpretation of these two factors in the government process in Switzerland, [7] which far from constituting an exceptional case typifies a widespread present-day trend in western democracies. This is not to say that all open decisions are the work of anonymous bodies: some are made by official institutions such as economic councils and state planning systems.

As for closed decisions, while they are almost invariably secret and impenetrable, there are exceptions. For example, in the case of the accession of various countries to the partial nuclear-test-ban treaty, the first phase is closed and secret, while the second — without which the decision remains incomplete — is, even though confined to the closed institutional circuit of parliaments, nevertheless public.

This first approximation to a distinction between closed and open decisions can obviously be neither rigid nor categorical. The line separating the two is sinuous and often blurred; it may indeed be imperceptible. In practice concrete decisions may be located at any point along a continuous line separating the two extreme positions. Apart from a very few clear-cut cases, most decisions are part closed and part open, and the mix can vary depending on the stage reached in the process. Thus, a decision which is initially closed can become open at a later stage. Similarly, closed decision-making can be followed by open implementation, in which all parties concerned will be associated to a greater or lesser extent. Nevertheless we can consider that, by and large, no decision exhibiting any degree of *openness* should be considered as closed. This suggests that a single decision ought to be classified according to whether the closed or open element in a decision is the more important — *closed, open* and *mixed* decisions.

Applied to studies contained in this volume, this criterion may give rise to some of the following comments. By definition, two studies escape this kind of classification: the general approach of Charles Roig, and the analysis of education policy outcomes by Groth and Wade. The latter does not focus on the process, and therefore excludes the participation factor. The two studies on international organizations (by Alger and by Cox and Jacobson) are principally devoted to processes involving official actors and representatives. Alger's analysis is dedicated essentially to decision outputs of official bodies; Cox and Jacobson's report analyzes the participation or the influence of nonofficial actors, such as national and international pressure groups which may be associated with the decision-making. Even if Presthus' article does not go into the various forms of the process, it gives valuable information on the atmosphere in which interaction between pressure groups and Canadian M.P.s takes place. The study on Ghanaian elites distinguishes between governing and nongoverning elites, a distinction which could be compared to closed and open decision-making, even if the cut does not correspond entirely. The case of national defense in Switzerland fits perfectly the category of closed decision-making which tends to associate some external actors.

The papers collected here illustrate the variety of research approaches covered by the blanket title *Analysis of Political Decisions*. Their common objective, of course, constitutes a unifying principle, but they vary widely in their vantage points and in the manner in which they tackle problems of political decision-making. Even so, the full range of possible approaches is not covered, since neither the mathematical dimension nor the content analysis technique are represented in this collective work; it does afford a fair sample of the wealth of viewpoints found in the literature. Nor, in the absence of an overall theory of decision-making, do these various approaches constitute a coherent whole; they remain separate efforts in spite of their common object.

The purpose of Charles Roig's study is to raise the basic conceptual issues. He begins by making a distinction between Snyder's conception, which he describes as *intra-systemic*, based on observation of decision-makers operating within a system and reflecting or summing up the influence of various factors, and the analysis suggested by Easton, whose decision-making system reproduces at the level of the overall political process the idea of a black box into which inputs are fed and out of which come outputs constituting decisions, all within the framework of an environment. In reality, as it turns out, these two approaches supplement each other and constitute in effect, as Roig points out, a system of interaction. It is also worth pointing out that these interactions weave and unfold around the decision, which is the common, central point of interest.

This paper's chief contribution lies in the reasoned distinction it makes between the historic and the systematic method. In the former case, the stress is on *chronological* sequence — the process as it can actually be observed. A more or less systematic analysis of the system is nevertheless possible through the use of certain techniques, e.g. content, actors, phases of the process, and outcome. The *systematic* method, on the other hand, relies on logical sequence, the three stages of decision-making being (1) knowledge (information retained, scientific and nonscientific knowledge), (2) the formalities (methods and objectives of forecasting, follow-

10

ed by norms), and (3) implementation (real objectives and means and real behaviour patterns). The final phase is that of control (validity, ideological, and routine) which completes the loop. Each of these two models must be clearly understood if confusion is to be avoided and the two combined.

This general theoretical study of decision-making is followed by three national case studies — an empirical one by Robert Presthus on "Interest Groups and the Canadian Parliament", a study by Sanjeeva Nayak entitled "An Analytical Model of Hegemonical Tension among Ghanaian Elites" (1957–1966), and one by Paolo Urio on "Decision-Making in National Defence in Switzerland".

The originality of Presthus' research project lies in his having carried out some 2,200 interviews with random sampling in Canada and the United States with pressure group executives, legislators, and higher civil servants. The interviews of the sample of 140 M.P.s in Ottawa permitted testing various hypotheses related to interaction theory, legitimacy, and influence of pressure groups (labour, professional, educational, social-recreational, etc). The first finding concerns personal contacts, which are extensive among all parties: 70 percent of the M.P.s see pressure group representatives frequently (twice a week) or occasionally (twice a month). Concerning the functions of pressure groups, two appear as privileged: mobilizing public opinion and providing information. While the latter is, of course, usual, the former is somewhat surprising. What is meant, in fact, is not so much resorting to public opinion as a means of pressure, as giving expression to it — albeit in a fragmentary way — and channelling it.

Another significant finding disclosed by the study is that a large majority of M.P.s do not regard the activities of lobbyists as a form of improper pressure, but only half of them consider lobbying as healthy for democracy. The data generally fail to support the hypothesis that interaction and legitimacy are positively associated, but do confirm the association between legitimacy and perceived influence. This last finding may well reflect the M.P.s' desire to justify or legitimate the influence exerted on them by pressure groups. Overall, Presthus' research findings confirm the importance of pressure groups in the Canadian political process.

Nayak's approach is focused on political power and elites in Ghana. The elites are perceived as divided into governing and nongoverning elites, who aspire and attempt to replace the ruling elite. His study is thus concerned not with the decision-making process but with the men who make the decisions and wield political power. The model comprises concentric circles of different elites which operate in groups, and its centre of gravity is Nkrumah and his people's party. The principle that governs Nayak's classification is the proximity of each elite group to the commanding heights of the polity. The United Party, immediate competitor and presumed successor, occupies the second circle. The auxiliaries of the governing elite (Trade Union Congress, student organization, farmer's council, Ghanaian women and young pioneers) are placed in the third circle. Their objective is to crush the common enemy, the United Party. This party includes among its supporters, traditional rulers, entrepreneurs, voluntary associations, and religious groups. They are placed in the outer circle. After describing the context and ideological tendencies, Nayak analyzes the pattern of hegemonical tension among the various components of the model and the actual evolution of the process. Having neutralized the UP, the CPP then concentrated on other political parties. When, by 1960, Nkrumah surmised that the opposition was no longer a threat, he reorganized his strategy to deal with the groups in the outer circle. After having established its control over traditional rulers, the government attacked intellectuals and the university, entrepreneurs and the agricultural sector. In 1965, Nkrumah finally set out to tame the police and the army. The latter, especially, had a number of grievances against the CPP and resisted the efforts of the party to politicize it. The conflict with these two forces was what, in all probability, provoked the coup d'etat in 1966. Thus Nayak analyzes the struggle for political power among Ghanaian elites.

Urio's study is concerned with a field of enquiry quite different from rational decision-making. In Switzerland advanced techniques are now applied to the choice of combat aircraft as a result of the Mirage crisis, which led not only to the strengthening of parliamentary control and to reform of the Department of Defence, but also to the revision of the decision-making process and techniques. The process was subdivided into seven main phases, from the definition of the conception of national defence and general planning to the choice, upkeep, and inspection. It appears clearly from Urio's article that the actual process is in keeping with modern techniques of analysis and evaluation, and that it applies methods such as PERT, system and tree analysis, operational research, and cost-efficiency analysis. Nevertheless, it is interesting to note that despite the use of these techniques, it has not yet been possible to take a decision which could meet the general consensus. Their use leaves a margin for political choice but also for political controversy. The effect has been to bring out into the open the whole problem of a nonprofessional parliament, whose members are no longer able to master and control complex decision-making processes, and to pose squarely the question of thorough reform of the parliament and its working methods. Recently, despite the publication of a technical report recommending the purchase of the U.S. Corsair instead of the French Mirage-Milan, the Federal Council decided, after some hesitation, to postpone its choice of a combat plane. Political and budgetary considerations as well as concern for the inflationary rate weighed more heavily in the balance than "rational" choice criteria.

The second series of articles consists of international studies, including a comparative survey by Alexander J. Groth and L.L. Wade on "Educational Allocations and Political Regimes"; a general report on "Decision-Making in International Organizations" by R.W. Cox and H.K. Jacobson; and finally a further specialized analysis on "Decision-Making in Public Bodies of International Organizations: ILO, WHO, WMO, UN" by Chadwick F. Alger.

Unlike the other articles, the Groth and Wade study focuses on decision outputs in education: while levels of economic development impose some constraints upon what particular societies might achieve in terms of educational outcomes, the type of political regime heavily influences the variance between the possible minimal and maximal outcomes.

Their classification of political systems includes four categories: Affluent Democracies (15 countries), Poorer Democracies (15), Communist systems (11), and Autocracies (26). In order to compare the outcomes of their policies, the authors adopted a quantitative measure expressed by school enrollment and a qualitative one conceived as a student/teacher ratio. The analysis of the first indicator confirms that, to the extent that economic development is associated with educational enrollments, the associations are closer in the poorer nations regardless of political system. Thus, in

13

the poorest group of nations — the Autocracies — educational policy outcomes and economic development are strongly associated at every level of education. Enrollments in the Poorer Democracies and Communist countries are moderately associated with per capita national income. The association is weak to slightly negative at all levels in the Affluent Democracies. In general, the analysis suggests that the influence of political, rather than economic differences, seems to be overwhelming. Apparently the resource constraint is not always the controlling element in public policy development.

From the qualitative student/teacher comparisons, it appears that the Communist countries actually outperform the Affluent Democracies in pre-primary education and equal them in primary: they are also in a better position than Poorer Democracies at the same level of economic development. At the secondary level, Poorer Democracies provide 1 teacher for 17 students and show a better level of educational quality than the Affluent Democracies. And while Autocracies (20.5) again rank last among the four systems, they are only marginally below the Communist states (21.9). It may be recalled that enrollments at the secondary level in Poorer Democracies exceed those of the Communist states. Judging from enrollment ratios, the authors observe that secondary education in all but the wealthiest nations remains an elite activity. At the third or advanced level, there is no significant difference among any of the types of political systems. The authors propose two explanations: the nature of higher education, or more likely, the elitist character of higher education in all types of political systems.

The variability of student/teacher ratios is least in the Communist states at the primary and secondary level, pointing out once again the relatively similar structure of public choices in those states. The variability is next lowest in the Affluent Democracies. A rough summary index relating resource constraints to educational quality is moderate in all systems (Poorer Democracies 0.43, Communist states 0.55; and Autocracies 0.42), except the Affluent Democracies (0.08). This moderate relationship between economic development and student/teacher ratios suggests, according to the authors, that national political systems have considerable autonomy, over and above resource constraints, in providing one aspect of quality education. Public choice seems to be highly dependent upon political and other noneconomic factors. National decision-makers appear to have substantial latitude in which to shape policy and are not as tightly confined by resource constraints as is sometimes suggested.

From analytical study we move toward synthetic presentations of approaches, typologies, and hypotheses on decision-making in international organizations. The paper written by Cox and Jacobson contains a wealth of suggestive observations. In addition to a definition of two ideal types of organizations — forum organization and service organization — they propose a taxonomic analysis. In order to be able to consider patterns of decision-making and the distribution of influence, it is useful to classify decisions by issue-areas.

The taxonomy of decisions in international organizations proposed by Cox and Jacobson divides them into seven categories: *representational* decisions affect membership; *symbolic* ones constitute tests of alignment of opinions; *boundary* decisions concern the organization's external relations; *programmatic* decisions are related to the strategic allocation of the organization's resources among different types and fields of activity; *rule-creating* decisions define norms bearing upon matters within the substantive scope of the organization; *rule-supervising* ones concern the application of approved rules by those subject to them; and *operational* decisions relate to the provision of services by the organization or the use of its resources in accordance with approved rules, policies or programs. Patterns of interaction among actors within international organizations may be described — as the authors do for eight agencies — for each of these decision-types.

Having pointed out some differences between international and national bodies Cox and Jacobson note their preference for a broad definition of international organization: a system of interaction including all of those who directly participate in decisions taken within the framework of the organization, and in addition all officials and individuals who in various ways actively determine the positions of the direct participants. This definition includes national elements or forces, government departments, and interest groups; it also includes other subsystems, such as the International Chamber of Commerce or multinational corporations. Finally, the

15

actors — as conceived in this study — are individuals who participate directly in the decisions of the international organization. An actor's capacity to exercise influence depends primarily on his position and his personal attributes. Starting from these basic concepts, the authors propose a multi-approach analysis of coalitions, voting, and many important variables. The environment is considered to be composed of a number of relevant variables; for example, it is assumed that there is some relationship between the power of a state in international affairs generally and its power in international organizations. The second major variable is the distribution of states according to their economic and political characteristics. The types of politics — competitive, mobilizing and authoritarian — are significant, as well as the patterns of conflicts and alignments on major world political and ideological issues. In addition, as each organization has a specific environment so, it may be argued, has each issue-area or even — at the limit — each decision. The result of such a set of analyses should be a description and an explanation of the structure of influence in international organization.

Chadwick Alger presents some preliminary findings from his quantitative research on decision-making in ILO, WHO, WMO, and the UN for three selected years — 1955, 1960, and 1965 — dealing with 5147 decisions. The decisions are subdivided into five categories by subject — administrative, budget-finance, elections and appointments, procedural, and program; and in three categories relating to discussion — no discussion, agreement, and some disagreement.

Some general findings could be pointed out. In the UN procedural decisions represent more than half. Program decisions are much more numerous in service organizations, with the exception of WMO. The percentage of decisions made without discussion gradually increased over the three years, with 69 percent in 1955, 74 percent in 1960, and 76 percent in 1965. When debate does take place it is highly concentrated on program issues (57 percent); it seems plausible that discussion can be avoided if the decisions are well prepared by informal negotiations. The same can be assumed regarding voting procedure: of the 5147 decisions, 4027 were made without voting (78 percent). Decision-making without voting increased from 73 percent in 1955, to 78 percent in 1960, and 84 percent in 1965. Roll call voting seldom occurs in the three specialized agencies; it also represents only 14.6 percent of decisions taken in the General Assembly and 21.8 percent in the Security Council where all votes are automatically roll call votes. Their limited number suggests that difficulties may arise in relation to roll call votes and that there is a need to complete this analysis by coding positions taken in debates.

The author concludes that there is an increasing trend towards consensual decision-making in international organizations. Voting is avoided, due generally to the preparatory work of groups and committees and to a good system of informal communications and negotiations.

The study presented by Alger is a good example of a way in which the decision-making process can be analyzed by using quantitative techniques, in combination with other approaches.

NOTES

[1] Cf. D.W. Miller and M.K. Starr, *The Structure of Human Decisions* (Englewood Cliffs, New Jersey: Prentice-Hall, 1967). This work constitutes a survey of various aspects of the decision-making approach.

[2] R.C. Snyder, H.W. Bruck and B. Sapin, *Foreign Policy Decision Making: An Approach to the Study of International Politics* (New York: The Free Press of Glencoe, 1962), p. 90.

[3] R.C. Snyder and G.D. Paige, "U.S. Decision to Resist Aggression in Korea" in Snyder, *Foreign Policy Decision Making,* pp. 242, 243.

[4] François Bourricaud, "Science politique et sociologie" (*Revue française de science politique,* 8, 2, June 1958), p. 261.

[5] C. Wright Mills, *The Power Elite* (New York: Galaxy Book, Oxford University Press, 1959), pp. 3, 4.

[6] *The Pentagon Papers* (New York: Bantam Books, Inc., 1971).

[7] Jean Meynaud, *Les organisations professionnelles en Suisse* (Lausanne: Payot, 1963). The author takes into consideration primarily open decisions, and examines only those closed decisions which were influenced by the pressure of professional groups.

Some Theoretical Problems in Decision-Making Studies

CHARLES ROIG*

Over the past thirty-odd years the tools of analysis in the social sciences have developed so fast that the proliferation of new concepts and approaches evokes the whims of fashion more than it does any real enrichment of our ability to explain social phenomena. In part, this is because epistemological and methodological reflection has failed to keep pace with the new techniques as they have evolved. The gaps in social science theory, lack of interest in a pursuit which is less rewarding than, say, natural science theory or pure empirical research, the shaky foundations of the sociology of knowledge (which all too often ignores the contributions which linguistics, for example, could make), these are some of the reasons for the social scientist's quandary in having to cope with a growing range of heterogeneous facts and concepts.

It seems generally agreed that a general or limited theory is the social sciences' most pressing need. But what do we mean by a *theory*? And can it be anything better than a mere transposition of mechanistic, biological, or cybernetic models? If in attempting an answer we can take the matter even one step — however modest

* Centre National de la Recherche Scientifique, Paris, and Department of Political Science, University of Geneva.

and tentative — beyond the mere repetition of a hackneyed axiom, this paper will have served its purpose.

Among the concepts or approaches which will be discussed, two have achieved unique prominence. They are *decision-making* (or the decisional process or approach) and the *system* (or systems analysis or systemic approach). Their confrontation lends itself, I think, to fruitful epistemological and methodological inquiry by making it possible to outline certain relationships and open certain avenues which have so far been overlooked (except by a few writers) very often because of the artificial separation of academic disciplines.

Some Characteristics of the Decisional Approach in Political Science

For the purpose of this paper, I shall recapitulate some of the characteristics of decision-making studies in political science, without laying any claim to exhaustiveness. Nor shall I attempt to define the *decision,* the whole object of the paper being to show how complex a problem this really is.

The Decisional Approach as a Discipline

It may be useful to stress at the outset the disciplinary individuality of the decisional approach as it emerges from the writings of political scientists.

As Dusan Sidjanski sees it, decision-making studies "constitute a new phase in political science", following the institutional phase, the group approach, and the study of the ruling class and the leaders. "What these three approaches have in common", he writes, "is that they are partial and static". One of the advantages of the decisional approach, as quoted from Sidjanski, is that it "weaves together the other approaches used in political science". Basic to the argument is the concept of the decision centre, which can account for institutions as well as parties, pressure groups, and individuals. The decision is thus the central idea, which can be apprehended "from the angle of its various components". [1]

Richard C. Snyder, in another important study on the same

subject, expresses it this way: "I shall argue that if a sound conceptual framework can be constructed, decision-making analysis will be appropriate for *any* area of political science where there is an interest in policy-formation or judgment of some kind".[2]

These statements underscore explicitly the link between the decisional approach and the emergence of a differentiated discipline. More often than not, however, the link will be implicit, though always decisive in orienting investigation.

The Study of Sequential Processes

The feature of the decisional approach most commonly stressed in the literature is its dynamic character implied by the sequential order of the events analysed: "Relatively speaking, dynamic analysis is *process* analysis. By process is meant here, briefly, *time* plus *change* — change in relationships and conditions. Process analysis concerns a sequence of events, i.e., behavioral events". [3]

This dynamic character of decision-making studies differentiates them from more static approaches such as structural-functional analysis, while on the other hand relating them to other process analysis techniques such as the study of the interaction of individuals, groups, states, etc. These, however, describe and measure only the *how* of phenomena, whereas decision-making analysis makes it possible to explain *why*.

Passing mention may be made of the rather hasty manner in which Snyder tends to identify *dynamic* with sequence, process, time plus change, etc. We shall deal later with the problem of the relationship between time and action, which is not quite that simple.

Decision and Environment

In Snyder's writings, the role of environment is decidedly understressed, as the following passage illustrates: "Every group of decision-makers functions in a larger setting. Setting is felt, analytically, to be more satisfactory than environment, which has certain explicit connotations in psychology and has ambiguous connotations otherwise. Setting refers to a set of categories of *potentially relevant factors and conditions* which may affect the action of decision-makers". [4]

The *setting* is later described as variable and determined mainly by the attitudes, perceptions, and plans of the decision-makers. Methodologically, it is useful mainly in limiting the number of nonpolitical factors to be taken into account. The author then distinguishes the social from the political institutional setting, the latter being by far the more important.

In short, the environment in the decisional approach may be little more than a backdrop against which the actors/decision-makers stand out as the focal points.

On the other hand, David Easton considers the environment as an inevitable, if not central, concept of decision-making analysis, owing to the interplay of inputs and outputs.

> Inputs will serve as *summary-variables* that concentrate and mirror everything in the environment that is relevant to political stress. Thereby this concept serves as a powerful tool.

Concerning outputs:

> In a comparable way, the idea of outputs helps us to organize the consequences flowing from the behaviour of the members of the system rather than from actions in the environment. Our primary concern is, to be sure, with the functioning of the political system. In and of themselves, at least for understanding political phenomena, we would have no need to be concerned with the consequences that political actions have for the environmental system ...
> But the fact is that the activities of the members of the system may well have some importance with respect to their own subsequent actions or conditions. To the extent that this is so, we cannot entirely neglect those actions that do flow out of the system into its environment. [5]

Outputs are composed of the actions and decisions of the political authorities in relation to the environment. Political science, however, is not concerned with all their effects upon the latter, but only with those which later influence decisions through the action of inputs emanating from the environment. To conceptualize this selective process Easton proposes the term *feed-back loop.*

In stating the problem of the environment as they do, the authors I have just quoted reveal what to my mind is their main preoccupation, namely to identify that which in the decision-making area is properly political and thus narrow down the field of political science investigation. The answers given by Snyder and Easton really reflect two decisional approaches. One (Snyder's) can be described as *intra-systematic* since it is confined to a *deci-*

sional field consisting of one or more actors and the factors they take into account. The other (Easton's) can be called *extra-systemic* in that it brings in certain elements of the environment. In both cases, the conceptualization is so vague and tentative as to afford no clue to the epistemological and methodological problem involved.

Decision-Making and Rationality

The concept of rationality is a source of vagueness and confusion and has been deliberately shunned by most theorists of political decision-making. Snyder refers to the *rationalization* of the motives invoked by decision-makers only as a warning to students of political science not to be misled. This unduly subjectivist point of view is an oversimplification — perhaps indeed a rationalization of the very type cautioned against.

From a more general point of view, there seems to be an opposition between two levels of decision-making as Snyder defines it. In one definition, he asserts that "all political decisions are formulated and executed in a decisional context, regardless of their level in other respects or of their place in the state-structure"; but the indications he goes on to give on organizational decision-making hint clearly at some degree of rationality, albeit limited, for example in the choice of one among several courses of action equally capable of bringing about the ends sought by the decision-maker.

Further on, however, the author lapses into a search for variables accounting not for the decision taken but for the behaviour of the decision-maker — sphere of competence, communication and information, and above all motivation.

This attitude is fairly widespread among political scientists, who dismiss the problem of rationality by identifying it with any theory of decision-making based on a normative approach and directed toward the choice of that decision which is best in principle. [6] But even though widespread this attitude is not the only possible one; indeed influential theorists, while criticising the theory of decisional rationality inherited from economic analysis, have constructed models in which rational planning is integrated with other variables limiting its scope, such as information, which can be incomplete, the cognitive faculties or the motivations of the protagonists, which are fallible, and so on ...[7]

23

Briefly stated, the weakness of political theory in dealing with the problem of rationality lies in its being confused with the normative approach, thus making it possible to reject both on grounds of *positivism*, allegedly the guarantor of the *empirical* value of research.

The Underlying Models in Decision-Making Studies

I shall now attempt to show, in the light of some of its characteristics, that the decisional approach leads to the formulation of a vague and unstable conceptual framework because it encompasses two terminologies and two logical models which should in reality be differentiated both epistemologically and methodologically. These are, on the one hand, an historical model and, on the other, a systemic one, both with their own logic.

Positivism and the Logical Model

The element of positivism running through the entire decisional approach is a determination to analyse the decision *as it is* (or *as it was made*), shunning any normative element or pre-existing theoretical model (in contrast with, for example, the rational decision models used by economists). It is important to show that this is an epistemological fallacy and that such decision-making studies are in fact based on a preconceived framework which largely predetermines the interpretation of the empirical data.

In decision-making studies, the concept of decision fulfils a threefold purpose corresponding in effect to three levels of increasingly abstract and theoretical analysis.

(1) The decision is significative of concrete, specific reality, often embodied in a formally defined action. On this level, the positivist and empirical option is confirmed.

(2) The decision defines what can be called a *decisional field* or *field of action,* composed of the whole cast of actors who take a more or less direct part in the process of elaboration. At this level, nonempirical considerations assume importance; for example, the decisional field must be defined in *political* terms to avoid encroaching on allied disciplines and the information

available must be sufficient to widen the *field* as far as possible even though its reliability can never be formally proved. [8]

(3) The decision, viewed as a process, describes the totality of interactions between protagonists. It thus appears successively as a gamble, a compromise, a formal act, a consequence, etc. and each of these terms implies a type of relation which can be formalized and studied in itself, independently of the concrete decision which is the original subject of enquiry.

In terms of the threefold function just described, the decision appears as a sort of focal point chosen *a posteriori* and lending coherence and empirical content to a study concerned essentially with protagonists and their relations, i.e. with a system of interaction. Ultimately, it might be more appropriate to speak of a plan of research rather than of a theory, and indeed the often used term *approach* reflects the existence of this twilight zone. The positivist tendency is based on a doctrinal rather than methodological emphasis on the first of the three levels of analysis distinguished above, at the expense of the other two. The reasons given are sometime obscure and indeed incomprehensible.

Thus Snyder has the greatest difficulty in offering methodological support for his distinction between decision-making and the interactions of the protagonists, as illustrated by the following passage:

> Earlier I made a distinction between two kinds of process analysis: *interaction* and *decision-making*. This may save some misunderstanding on the present point. Interaction process analysis does not require – and indeed would be handicapped by – a separation of decision-makers into official and nonofficial groups or a boundary line between governmental and nongovernmental decision-making. But the limitation here is that interaction analysis per se cannot answer the *why* questions of decision-making activity...
>
> I have become convinced that when one shifts to decision-making analysis, it is far less troublesome methodologically to *account* only for the behavior of official decision-makers and to relate them to decision-makers outside of government by some other scheme than one which requires that *both* groups be regarded as actors *in the same social system* – which means accounting for the behavior of both according to formal rules of action analysis. [9]

This passage – apart from being flavoured with individualism in that it presents decision-making analysis as the most suitable method for the study of actors on the political scene — puts forward in essence two main arguments:

(1) Decisional analysis provides the answer to the *why* of actions which interaction analysis cannot account for. So far as the meaning, or content, of this *why* can be discerned (the author offers no clue), the difference would seem to lie in the method rather than in the basic principles postulated at the beginning of the inquiry. In the case of interaction analysis, as Snyder sees it, interacting elements (individuals or groups) are considered apart from any possible output. This, it may be noted, is an assertion and nothing more. In the case of decision analysis, on the other hand, the output is given at the outset since it provides a definition of the actors and their relations. It can thus be considered *a priori* as the answer to the *why* of their actions. The pitfalls of Snyder's doctrine are self-evident and it is, moreover, specious in that the answers cannot but be known beforehand. That, at least, is how I understand it in the absence of other explanations from the author.

(2) Decisional analysis, it is further argued, accounts more readily for the existence of public decision-makers as against private ones because interaction analysis requires that all the actors belong to the same social system. This again is no more than an assertion. It is common knowledge that one of the problems of social systems analysis is precisely to draw up subsystems or networks of subsystems wherever needed as analytical tools. True, the existence of a subsystem of public actors and one of private actors is not postulated in advance, but who would dare to carp on grounds of methodological orthodoxy?

I have commented at some length on Snyder's analyses, because I think they have the merit of bringing out sharply the shortcomings, inconsistencies, and ambiguities of a certain type of decisional approach. Most other authors prefer to ignore them or to treat them separately.

Edward Banfield, in his study on decision-making in the Chicago city government, explains in a appended "note on the conceptual scheme" the three central concepts — politics, planning and public interest — which have enabled him to select, organize and interpret the empirical data. [10] It is surprising that this capital information is given only in a note at the end of the volume —

after the facts have been set out in a completely positive spirit. As it is, they show that the facts have been *selected* as a part of a preconceived conceptual scheme and in order to prove an underlying thesis.

American political science affords many other examples of this. I shall conclude by mentioning Robert Dahl's study on New Haven because of the controversy it aroused between those who hold a pluralistic theory of political power and those who hold an elitist one; it had at least the merit of calling attention to the doctrinal and ideological dimensions of decisional analyses. [11] But in saying this we have not, of course, exhausted by any means the store of epistemological and methodological lessons to be drawn from the decisional approach.

The Problem of Time

In my view, the studies on decision-making quoted above aim (consciously or otherwise) at an impossible synthesis between two methods, each with its own postulates and logic. These are the historic (or historiographic) method and the systems method, and ignorance of their specific characters and constraints has led to regrettable ambiguities and confusions.

The historic method can easily be confused with historicism, giving an illusion of positivity. This illusion, of which historians are very much aware, should give political scientists pause for reflection since more often than not decision-making studies are of an essentially historic nature. As Dusan Sidjanski interestingly observes:

> The observer also confronts problems familiar to the historian: how to reconstitute *ex post facto* and without distorting it the process which, following a multiplicity of by-ways and detours, finally culminates in the decision? His progress is all the more hesitant for his having to travel backwards and relive the actual process in reverse. He is in the same position as the historian to whom the outcome of the battle is known in advance ... [12]

This, to my mind, reveals not a mere similarity but an actual identity of method. It shows that the decision analyst, just like the historian, is imprisoned within the temporal framework of one-dimensional linear historic time, oriented from past to present. So

it is not a matter of similarity but of one and the same methodological problem facing researchers involved with the different
phases of history (see Fernand Braudel [13]).

In decision-making terms, this means considering the various
phases in the actors' moves and in the development of their environmental conditions. It must be recognized that conceptualization in this area has not gone far enough, despite a few worthwhile
efforts; and yet it is an absolute prerequisite for success. [14]

At present, the study of any decision-making process necessarily
entails the application of the historic method to an object whose
embodiment is the decision. A major consequence is the *unique-
ness* of the event accounted for and the epistemological impossibility of extending the explanation to a class of events. This is something which any careful historian will guard against, but which
political scientists, prone to generalizations, indulge in freely.

Is there a logical method for integrating history into decisional
analysis as an independent variable, thus avoiding the constraints
imposed on the historian? Haroun Jamous tries to answer this
question by differentiating three types of elements which help to
account for a decision, namely the decision itself, the socio-historical conditions, and the personality of the reformer. [15] These elements are linked by a "certain chain of causality" which the author characterizes as follows: "The socio-historical conditions
described have, with a strong element of probability, shaped the
reformer's choice and determined the form and nature of the decision". He adds: "This proposition constitutes a synoptic conclusion of the study, but also takes the form of an inducted hypothesis which further investigation could substantiate".

What is interesting here is the significance and explanatory value
attributed to the adjective *historic,* and the author's hope of
generalizing the explanation. From a purely conceptual point of
view, however, that significance and value are demonstrably ambiguous, and in any case the historical reference adds nothing to
the theory's explanatory potential. In the first place, there are
three categories of elements and not only one present at the
historical moment, since decision and the reformer's personality
intervene in quite the same way as social conditions. From the
point of view of language, the adjective *historic* adds nothing.

It is possible, however, to regard the adjective as expressing a deliberate choice of the researcher, assuming that he is going to choose, from within the entire range of possible social conditions, those with an historic dimension as explanatory variables in his model. If such a choice is indeed possible, we must then find out what he means by *socio-historic conditions.* What is referred to, in short, is the process by which groups aware of malfunctions in an aging organization work out alternative options able to meet the needs of society as a whole and hence likely to be well received by those in authority. It will be clear from the foregoing that these socio-historical conditions reflect not an historic analysis but a dynamic formalized model based on a certain sequential order. This model comes very close ultimately to the models of social innovation conceptualized in the last few years in the framework of systems analysis. [16]

In the intellectual exercise just described, therefore, it is necessary to separate the logical construction which can be generalized because it is nontemporal from the empirical data which can be seen as forming part of history (like any other known fact). A model is a logical construction, implicitly or explicitly, and hence amenable to generalization — something which strictly historical explanation will not allow. We must be quite clear on this point, since it lies at the very root of the shortcomings of decisional analysis.

The historic method itself implies a model based on *time,* which I have defined as linear, one-dimensional, and oriented in *chronological* time, in which the chronological sequence is assumed to coincide with an order of causality. This assumption makes it possible to reconstitute a decisional process, taking an historically-situated decision (that is, a dated one) as its point of departure, or, in other words, to reverse the chronological process, always assuming that the time period reconstituted by the analyst coincides with that lived through by the decision-maker. This is the fundamental principle on which the soundness of decision-making studies in political science depends. The method flowing from it is legitimate provided that the student is aware of its limitations, the first being the logical impossibility of generalizing the results; for while such a generalization can have a heuristic value it can never be a substitute for a demonstration. Secondly, and above all, the motivations and reasons attributed to the actors can be no more than *inferences* made by the political scientist on extremely fragile bases. When the actions took place, the actors' setting was not that of historic time, but another one which can be defined by the trilogy *past-present-future,* or again *experience-possibilities-fulfilment.* Historic positivism is unable to reconstitute this more complex time framework except through resort to other terminologies relying on psychological or psychoanalytical explanations or, more simply, on the assumed interests of the actors.

The point is that historic positivism is no more than a *convention,* as normative and as limited in its usefulness as any other convention designed to advance knowledge. That being so, and given the impossibility of reducing the two time concepts to common terms, another convention is needed in order to move from the historic (or historiographic) model to the systems model, whose principles can be deduced *a contrario* from those underlying the historic model.

Here the historic time dimension disappears. Time is no longer seen as linear, nor as a chronological framework for human actions. Instead it is treated as a variable, most frequently quantitative, which varies with other variables in functions which constitute many systems and which can be reflected in graphs—exponential, logistic, cyclic, etc.

The decision itself disappears as an independent, historically-localized element. It is replaced by formalized components or, at least, by a set of complex relationships which are a *logical* prerequisite to the undertaking of action. The decision-maker himself is superseded by a *rationality* component which takes his place in determined conditions (particularly where a stable order of preference can be established among the various objectives contemplated). Similarly, as we shall see later, the *environment* component becomes something more than a mere setting or a backdrop commanding only lip service.

For the time being, I shall confine myself to the concept of time in systems analysis as applied to decisions and stress its specific nature, based on convention. The two figures below reproduce its many components, it being understood that there are many forms of systems analysis relying on many variants.

These figures are deliberately conceived in broad terms. "State of affairs" can refer either to the system or to the environment, or

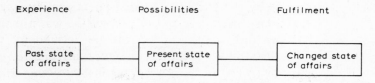

Fig. 1. Basic scheme.

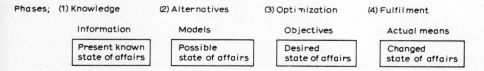

Fig. 2. Decisional phases.

both at once. The system, as we shall see, is not a constant defined once and for all, but a dynamic and variable concept.

The basic figure purports to synthesize the decision-maker's time framework mentioned earlier. Briefly stated, time as here understood is not directed from the past to the present but from the stage of possibility to that of fulfilment.

The figure illustrating the decisional phases sets out the operations which a decision implies, and which can lend themselves to individual treatment or to formalization as the case may be. I refer of course to *logical*, not chronological phases, which can be applied separately (for example in taxonomies).

The typology of decisions established by Thompson and Tuden illustrates this by relating two variables, namely the decision-makers' assessment of existing causal relationships (Phase 1: Knowledge) and their preferences among possible alternatives (Phase 3: Optimization). [17] Either of these variables can assume two values according to whether the decision-makers agree or disagree. This may be illustrated as follows:

It can be seen that each cell defines a given type of decision, as well as form of organization which the authors regard as the most suitable for bringing about the corresponding type of decision.

While the problem of time is essential to an understanding of the principles underlying decision-making studies, that of environment helps to reintroduce a measure of unity in decision-making

31

Preferences among possible alternatives
(Phase 3)

		Agreement	Disagreement
Assessment of causal relationships (Phase 1)	Agreement	Computational (Expertise, Bureaucracy)	Compromise (Negotiation, Representation)
	Disagreement	Judgmental (Majority vote)	Inspirational (Charisma)

Fig. 3.

theory, particularly in regard to the opposition between *normative rationality* and *empiricism* often encountered in the literature.

The Problem of Environment

Study of the problem of environment provides a key to the definition of system models as applied in decision-making studies.

It will be recalled that the most elaborate attempt in this direction in political science has been made by David Easton, who ascribes to the decision — viewed as an output in a political system — a tangible effect on the environment, which in turn influences the political system through the operation of inputs. The link between decision-output and effect-input is illustrated by a feedback loop. Two features of Easton's model are, I think, worth stressing. The first is the danger inherent in the simple transposition of a conceptual framework — here cybernetics and control by feedback — in the study of complex and heterogeneous phenomena — here political. The use of terms like outputs, inputs, and feedbacks can be misleading insofar as they rely on mere semantic analogies with no explanatory value. [18]

Easton's model, however, has the merit of drawing attention to the relationship between decision and environment, even if it views that relationship purely in terms of a feedback loop based on a sequential (output-feedback-input) type of relationship. This provides the starting point for a different definition of the problem based on a simple awareness of the fact that the environment is not a *terra incognita* of moderate interest to the political scientist, but a place of uncertainties for the decision-maker, whose time framework is inevitably oriented from the stage of possibilities to that of fulfilment. Thus stated, the problem, far from being peripheral, is central to every decision-making theory by showing that the sole object of rational decision analyses is to formalize these relations of uncertainty by reference to certain probabilist features of the environment. These analyses tend towards a *formalization of environmental data* which can serve to determine options rather than to build up a normative theory of rational decision-making.

Viewed in this light, each of the three models of rational decision — linear programming, statistical decision, games theory — can be considered as a formalization of a specific type of environment.

The writings of F.E. Emery and E.L. Trist provide an interesting starting point for a typology of environments made up of ideal types of "causal texture, approximations of which can be assumed to exist in the real world". [19] The same can be said of formalized environment models.

These authors go on to define a first type of environment as "placid and randomized", meaning by this that it is made up of events distributed in a haphazard way (as in the model underlying the statistical decision). The second type of environment is "placid and clustered"; events being regrouped in series but nevertheless amenable to separate treatment (linear programming is applicable to this kind of environment). The third is the "disturbed-reactive" environment, made up of a multiplicity of concurrent systems (the games theory deals with some of these problems). Finally, the fourth is the "turbulent field" type. Its dynamic properties are determined not only by the interaction among organizations, as in the preceding case, but also by the "field" itself, or the "terrain", taken as a whole. In this last instance formalization assumes a new and different form which, as we shall see, is in effect institutionalization.

The stress laid on the decisional implications of these analyses (hence their assimilation to normative theories) does not make them any less valuable to the political scientist concerned primarily with decision-making theory. The table below aims at summing up a theory of decisional environment based on two variables, namely, the nature of the environment (stable or dynamic) and its effects (specific or diffuse).

TABLE 1

		Effects of the Environment	
		Specific	Diffuse
Nature of the environment	Stable	Clustered (Linear programming)	Randomized (Statistical decision)
	Dynamic	Disturbed-reactive (Games theory)	Turbulent fields (Institutionalization)

This typology is of course tentative and incomplete. It does, however, highlight some important aspects of decision-making.

The first of these is linked to the concept of *uncertainty,* which I regard as central to decisional analysis. James D. Thompson's study on rationality-uncertainty throws fresh conceptual light on the subject: "Just as complete uncertainty or randomness is the antithesis of purpose and organization, complete certainty is a figment of the imagination; but the tighter the norms of rationality, the more energy the organization will devote to moving toward certainty". [20] I shall have more to say about Thompson's writings, but even now his basic concept seems worth bearing in mind. Rationality is the antithesis of uncertainty which in varying degree typifies all human actions. The norms of rationality are the principles of action which can narrow the area of uncertainty.

The problem of *norms* is another unresolved aspect of decisional theory; the concept has many connotations which often seem mutually incompatible. The foregoing table illustrating types of environment suggests a deep-rooted opposition between on the one hand, the types of norms which linear programming, statistical decision, and game theory can be held to imply, and on the other, those implied by institutionalization, the latter being more akin to norms in the legal or social sense.

This opposition emerges sharply in Emery and Trist's interpretation of human reactions in a turbulent field environment. In such an environment social values assume decisive importance "as coping mechanisms that make it possible to deal with persisting areas of relevant uncertainty. Unable to trace out the consequences of their actions as these are amplified and resonated through their extended social fields, men in all societies have sought rules, sometimes categorical, such as the Ten Commandments to provide them with a guide and a ready calculus..." [21]

Through systems analysis the problem of norms can be stated in conceptual and epistemological terms. A starting point is provided by Thompson's distinction between *technical rationality,* which is based on instrumental and economic criteria in closed systems, and *organizational rationality,* which concerns the insertion of a technology into an environment and raises much wider problems.

> One or more technologies constitute the core of all purposive organizations. But this technical core is always an incomplete representation of what the organization must do to accomplish desired results. Technical rationality is a necessary component but never alone sufficient to provide *organizational rationality,* which involves acquiring the inputs which are taken for granted by the technology, and dispensing outputs which again are outside the scope of the core technology. [22]

Based on this distinction (which would of course require further elaboration), it may be considered that norms are of two kinds: those linked with technical rationality, which are more exacting and closer to complete certainty, and those inherent in organizational rationality, which are less exact and more akin to uncertainty. The norms embodied in the four types of decisional environment I have described are of the latter type.

It can then be postulated that in each of these types of environment there are two normative levels defining two categories of norms: first, those which, generally speaking, determine the rules of the game and the validity of the calculations. In other words, these norms define a closed system within which uncertainty tends to be eliminated or narrowed down. They form the basis for developing quantified models, fundamental rules for the games theory, or constitutional or constituent norms in the context of institutionalization. They may be termed *fundamental norms.*

The second category of norms are those which govern the strategy of the actors and can be called *strategic norms* in the sense that given the fundamental norms which define the rules of the game, the actors have the possibility of behaving in a manner that will either maximize the gains or advantages or minimize the losses or penalties.

The function of organizational norms in all cases is to maximize the chances that the actors' behaviour will conform to a subjacent — and most frequently an implicit — model. In statistical terms, the function of the norms is to maximize the chances that the distribution of behaviours will conform to the normal law (Gauss' s-curve) with as little variance as possible, the aim or ideal being, of course, a collective one by reference to which all the organizational norms can be defined. The actors themselves may or may not adopt a given attitude, their actual behaviour being *independent* of the norms, which are not necessarily conformed to. Statistical behavioural distribution can thus be different from normal distribution.

Thus, from a normative point of view, the games theory is not fundamentally different from the bureaucratic institution described by Max Weber. It must take account both of the norms defining the rules of the game in a closed system (fundamental norms) and of those which are imposed upon actors having a choice between different strategies, having regard to the strategies of other actors. *Logically* speaking, an assessment of likely gains or losses will induce the actors to adopt certain strategies and reject others: if they accept this *logic,* they behave *rationally.* In Weberian bureaucracy too there are fundamental norms defining the bureaucratic order (for example, the conditions for entering and leaving it), but there are also those which reward or penalize certain forms of bureaucratic behaviour and constitute incentives to behave rationally taking into account the behaviour of other bureaucrats — superiors, equals, or inferiors.

In the two cases I have just mentioned, the combined effect of fundamental and strategic norms is to reduce the uncertainty concerning the actors' behaviour by bringing it into closer conformity with a pre-established model and thus making it in principle more *foreseeable* and more *coherent* (the strategies of the actors being linked).

To sum up, what I have just tried to demonstrate is the inability of historiographic, positivist models to account for the complexity of the decision-maker's actual situation when making his decision. In such models (including Easton's, despite the many types of environment which he distinguishes), the environment is a *chaos,* an absolute unknown, a *black box* in the cybernetic sense — implying an actual reversal of Easton's terminology. The models of systems analysis, on the other hand, do fuller justice to the actual situation of the decision-maker whose strategy is directed mainly at reducing the margin of uncertainty. This principle provides the starting point for a conceptual elaboration whose logic and orientation I have tried to suggest in broad outline, though fully aware of all that remains to be done.

The Basic Concepts of Systems Analysis

Some of the terms above have epistemological implications which I have already alluded to, for example when I used the term "closed system", which conversely raises the problem of "open" systems. A number of authors, including political scientists, have made a worth-while contribution in this field and developed useful concepts, two of which I shall now discuss.

Open System, Closed System

In *Organizations in Action,* Thompson briefly outlines the theory of organization and in so doing notes the existence of two main *strategies,* according to the literature. One is the *closed system* strategy, which treats the organization as a determinate system by reducing it to a few controllable variables, including in some cases the elimination of outside influences. The examples he gives are bureaucracy and scientific management, characterized by the pursuit of a goal and its efficient attainment. The other is the *open system* strategy, which assumes the impossibility of controlling all the variables in a system and the inevitability of some degree of uncertainty and surprise. Examples quoted are the unofficial organization, which stresses feelings, clans, unofficial social controls, etc.... and the organization, viewed as conditioned by the environment. The first strategy is focused on the "quest for certainty", the second on "the expectation of the uncertain".

Thompson's argument is that in organizations both elements are present, but at different levels. "We will conceive of complex organizations as open systems, hence indeterminate and faced with uncertainty, but at the same time as subject to criteria of rationality and hence needing determinateness and certainty". [23]

Organizational dynamics are thus based on three distinct operations. One aims at eliminating uncertainty and tends to constitute a technical core conceived of as a closed system able to control a limited number of variables. Another consists of the transfer of the uncertainty born of interaction with the environment to another level of organization which the author describes as *institutional*. Finally, at the level of management, mediation occurs between the two previous levels; it is here that the crucial decisions are made — decisions affecting the very life of the organization, torn between the quest for certainty at its technical core level and the need for flexibility which alone can enable it to adjust properly on the other levels.

This conception defines the organizational framework of the decision, which has to contend with three types of constraint. The first springs from the incompleteness and uncertainty of the knowledge on the basis of which the decision must be made. The second is that organizational goals are established through coalition behaviour patterns. The image of the all-powerful boss at the top of an organizational pyramid is a mere symbol, with little relevance to the realities of complex organizations. The only boss is the man who can lead a coalition. The third type of constraint results from contradictory preferences regarding the aims to be pursued.

Thompson puts forward the interesting idea that the formation and dissolution of coalitions are the tools through which the organization can reduce the area of uncertainty by treating it as internal conflict.

> Potential for conflict within the dominant coalition increases with inter-dependence of the members and the areas they represent, and as external forces require internal compromise on outcome preferences. Potential for conflict also increases with the variety of professions incorporated in the organization.
> When such forces result in a wide distribution of power and therefore in a large dominant coalition, coalition business is conducted by an inner circle. Without such an inner circle, such an organization is immobilized. When power is widely dispersed, compromise issues can be ratified but cannot be decided by the dominant coalition in toto. [24]

The inference is that conflicts which spring from uncertainty are themselves regulated by coalitions on the one hand, by a concentration of power on the other, under penalty of paralyzing the organization.

This brief summary makes no claim to reproduce Thompson's thinking in anything approaching its fullness, but merely to pinpoint those elements which best typify the problems involved in the systems analysis approach to decision-making. And here one need emerges immediately, with striking clarity: that of overcoming, in any major decision, the fundamental opposition between such terms as closed or open, uncertainty and rationality, knowledge and action.

Logic and Action

The value of Eugene J. Meehan's [25] epistemological studies is that they stress the fundamental relationships between the *system* as a logical construction, and *action* viewed as a way of controlling the environment. Meehan makes a distinction between analysis based on deductive paradigm (as in physics and chemistry) and that based on systems paradigm in which a finite logical system is linked with empirical description, thereby avoiding the as—yet unsolved problem of induction.

This will be made clearer by the following passage:

> Reasoned and intentional control over the environment, as distinguished from activity that may influence the environment in unpredictable ways, requires a way of structuring the relations among events that will allow the user to foresee with some confidence the consequences of altering those relations. The instrument that makes this possible is the *system*. Systems are formal logical structures, sets of variables and the rules governing their interactions. One of the basic elements in any explanation, therefore, will be a system. However, since explanations must have objects, must be relevant to something in human experience, each explanation will also involve a *description* which contains the events to be explained. Construed as a process, explanation is the application of a logical system to a description. [26]

Again, in characterizing systems as logical structures, stress is laid on their closed and finite nature, without which they could have no logical or cognitive implications. Such systems must be wholly calculable with all the variables (these being mere formal symbols with meaning only in terms of the calculations) assumed to be known. Only at a later stage — that at which the phenomenon is actually explained — do these symbols acquire an empirical content.

The closed and finite nature of logical systems, however, raises a problem in the analysis of a real situation in which everything in one way or another is linked to everything else as is the case in the empirical world, which is by definition *open*.

In tackling this problem, Meehan uses a strictly epistemological approach by stressing the morphological identity of system and reality — a postulate which has been formulated in more precise terms by Ross Ashby, a cybernetics expert. The degree of identity between logical construction and empirical situation is, however, always imperfect, and criteria must be developed in order to assess it.

Lastly, and above all, Meehan advocates the use of *conceptual frameworks* which can be open in the sense that they are not finite and can encompass not only closed systems but also incomplete and imperfect ones. In my view conceptual frameworks form the mainstay of most social sciences, and it is, I think, in these terms that the problem of their significance should be looked at.

Dynamic Perspective

As a starting point for the dynamic model which I propose to outline, I shall take the opposition between closed, determinate and predictable systems and open, indeterminate and unpredictable ones. In essence, I am keeping to the line of thought developed by Thompson and Meehan.

Closed systems are intellectual constructions in which all the elements are perceived and understood in a context of logically necessary and numerically limited reactions. Formalized and quantified models are the most elaborate form of closed system. But we shall see that the *closedness* of a system is always relative and in a sense *conventional,* so that there is really scope for development in any direction.

Open systems are much more ambiguous when the concept is applied to abstract data, with ill-defined spatial limits. (The concept of the open system as defined, for example, by biologists cannot be so applied, since it refers to exchanges across the boundaries of a spatially defined system.) The first question which arises, therefore, is how to define an open system if it is to be applied to nonmaterial phenomena constituted by symbols. Thompson's answer is not really satisfactory. There is no reason to assume that informal groups in organizations are not at least as *formalizable* as formal ones. Indeed, the theory of organizations as it has developed suggests the reverse. This may be due to terminological confusion concerning the word *formal* as used in this theory. As for the alleged dependence of organizations on their environment and their lack of autonomy, viewed as an obstacle to their plans, this reflects a statement of fact rather than any theoretical approach.

Meehan's answer, identifying openness with empirical reality, is tantamount to saying that there are no open systems, and that nature exists independently as a complex of interrelations impenetrable to man except through the construction of closed and more or less concordant systems. On the other hand, the idea of the conceptual framework opens up a line of thought which can be fruitful if it is taken to mean the human capacity to verbalize the nonverbal world — even without a full understanding of its complexity, and even without closing it through a logical process.

In this case, it can be posited that open systems are *terminological systems or systems of words,* with all the connotations, motivations, and rhetorical patterns which this implies. These terminological systems are as *real* as material ones and have their own principles which govern their operation. The concept of *closed* or *shut* is irrelevant here inasmuch as such systems can encompass the most general and the most sweeping phenomena, there being nothing which language cannot express *in terms* of the universe, of divine creation, of humanity or of history, just as much as *in terms* of mechanics or psychology. The very concept of openness could not exist but for this variety of terminological levels in language. It thus becomes clear that the relationship between language and action is central to the systems theory and that a lot of work remains to be done in this field, which has scarcely been touched upon by linguistics, sociology of language, or symbolics. [27]

To return to Thompson and Meehan, it seems correct to assume, as they do, that the human capacity to act through a process of organization or decision is somehow conditioned by the capacity to convert the uncertainty of open systems into the certainty of closed ones. This, however, seems one possibility among a variety of conversion processes.

The first is the cognitive one as outlined by Meehan, the closed system thus being a *logical* one. Jean Piaget, whose epistemological work is of crucial importance in this field, defines this system by reference to three main characteristics: totality, conversions, and self-regulation. [28] The *closedness* of a system (or of a structure) gives individuals a "sense of logical necessity" which influences their behaviour. [29]

It is worth noting that the cognitive processes which give birth to logical systems are at the same time social processes. They determine patterns of behaviour and belief, since the rules are felt to be necessary. They also determine patterns of organization in so far as causal relationships can be injected into human activities with a fair degree of certainty, as is often the case in the world of production (we come back here to Thompson's "technical rationality").

Another feature of logical systems is that they are unstable and evolving. There is no hard and fast frontier between closed and open systems: the proliferation of logical systems tends to displace it continually. This might be termed the principle of *growing extension* of logical systems, by which knowledge as a prerequisite for action is conditioned.

To show how this principle operates, we may tentatively distinguish two main elements: (1) The quest for certainty (and precision), on which effective action depends, necessarily takes place at the expense of the amount of information processed (Windelband's principle); (2) Less information means a less valid system (or model), entailing the need for another system covering a wider field of information. A causal, cyclic link can be established between these two elements, albeit with possible breaks either because information is lacking or because its cost is felt to be too high.

A second process is the socio-linguistic one. Symbols and key-terms are also verbal means through which the elements of reality can be closed (or perhaps it would be better to say circumscribed). This flows logically from the properties of language: any terminology is selective, acting as a screen in relation to the real world, which it provides with a means not only of verbalizing but also of interpreting.

The prospects thus opened are tremendous. Myths, ideas, symbols, and words are powerful agents in crystallizing terminological systems, and their impact on social activities is unquestionable. The need here (and especially in political science) is for appropriate conceptual elaboration.

A third process which is worth mentioning is the traditional one, in the sense that it operates by reference to the previous ones. No one will dispute its importance in the area of human behaviour, nor does it imply any idea of immobility; it refers, rather, to a pattern of action in which change is brought about by trial and error, based upon the resultant verbalized experience.

Decisional Channelling

The figure given below is an attempt to synthesize the elements which have hitherto been presented in an analytical form. It defines mainly the patterns of decisional channelling which can serve as a basis for a classification of decisions in the systems

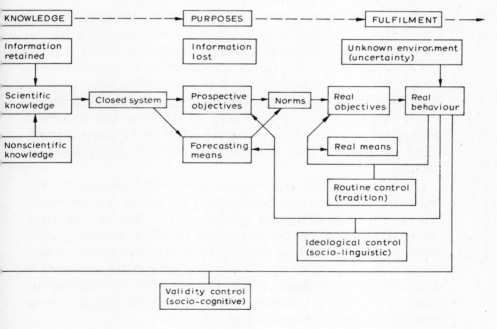

Fig. 4.

approach I have attempted to define. This graphic representation of decisional channelling calls for some explanation and comment.

(1) The figure illustrates the essential phases of decision-making, showing in columns the various elements of analysis which must be taken into account because they determine the outcome of the phase.

In the *knowledge* phase, *closed systems* which embody the possible options available are determined by information retained but also by its processing, which in turn depends on scientific (empirical–logical) as well as nonscientific (doctrinal or ideological) elements. This is the very problem which modern epistemology is attempting to solve.

The *aims* column characterizes the abstract, essentially *verbal,* nature of its contents. The future is here made *present*; while it embodies scientific elements, the ideological and motivational elements are dominant.

One essential characteristic of this phase is that it can ignore contradictions insofar as it is concerned with the principles embodied in charters, constitutions, economic plans, etc.

Finally, lost information is a liability which jeopardizes scientific forecasts without, however, affecting the terminological systems which reflect deep-seated, social motivations.

The *fulfilment* column marks the transition to concrete reality. What is noteworthy here is that lost information is no longer a mere liability but becomes a factor of uncertainty determining actual behaviour in the same way as the aims and objectives defined by the norms. Contradictions, which in the previous phase could be ignored, have now become obstacles and sources of conflict.

(2) Defined in this way, the decision establishes the link between the two time frameworks discussed earlier. That which is oriented from possibility to fulfilment (i.e., that in which the future is converted into the present and which can be compared to what has sometimes been referred to as *mythical* time) is dominant in the *purposes* phase. Causal, rational, and historical time is dominant in the *fulfilment* phase. The transition from one to the other is in fact a transition from principle to practice, from noncontradiction to contradiction and conflict.

(3) The three controls represent another phase. Their simplified

graphic representation as a *loop* is not meant to suggest a *feedback*, which is itself a very obscure concept at best when applied to social phenomena which have neither the structure nor the simplicity of machines and automatons.

The concept of *control* as used here means, in fact, merely a decisional phase in which differences between what was foreseen or desired and the final outcome are identified and explained. The concept is important in the systems analysis approach to decision-making studies as a link between knowledge and action. Modern theories of decisional programming give it a central role, though reducing it to a problem of social indicator technique and thus betraying their scientist bias.

Each control determines a process of decisional channelling. Validity control is part of a socio-cognitive process oriented towards the construction of the logical models already mentioned. Ideological control is predominantly linguistic; it is directed towards the perfecting of terminological systems insofar as these express motivations steadily giving rise to new needs and new aspirations, as well as new strategies for meeting them. It operates through conflict and rhetoric. *Routine* control is in practice confined to the practical phase of fulfilment. Its regulatory features (based on trial and error) are the nearest thing to a control mechanism relying on negative feedback. This type of control may also be thought of as that most heavily stressed, to the detriment of others, by the historico-positivist approach.

Some Problems of Systems Analysis as Applied to Decision-Making Studies

Let us now reconsider, in the light of the foregoing, some of the research problems of approach relevant to decision-making studies.

Programmed and Nonprogrammed Decision-Making

In *The New Science of Management Decision,* Herbert Simon establishes a basic distinction between two types of decision: programmed and nonprogrammed. [30] He defines the former by reference to elements of repetition and routine which permit the application of exact and stable procedures. As examples, he quotes the fixing of prices and salaries, and the management of inventories.

Nonprogrammed decisions are defined as new, nonstructured, and important. "There is no cut-and-dried method for handling the problem because it hasn't arisen before, or because its precise nature and structure are exclusive or complex, or because it is so important that it deserves a custom-tailored treatment. General Eisenhower's D-Day decision is a good example of a nonprogrammed decision".

Simon himself acknowledges that this distinction is not as clear as it seems. The mere fact that a system responds to a situation suggests that there must be something determining the response. What, then, is that *something* if not a programme? Simon's answer is as follows: "By nonprogrammed I mean a response where the system has no specific procedures to deal with situations like the one at hand, but must fall back on whatever *general* capacity it has for intelligent, adaptative, problem-oriented action". This distinction provides a basis for classifying decisions by type (i.e. programmed or nonprogrammed) and technique used (i.e. traditional or modern). Simon thus arrives at the following table:

TABLE 2

Decision-Making Techniques

Types of decision	Traditional	Modern
Programmed: Routine, Repetitive decisions	1. Habit 2. Clerical routine: Standard operating procedures 3. Organization structure: Common expectations, System of subgoals, Well defined information channels	1. Operation research: Mathematical analysis, Models Computer simulation 2. Electronic data processing
Nonprogrammed: One-shot, ill-structured novel, policy decisions Handled by general problem-solving process	1. Judgment, intuition, and creativity 2. Rules of thumb 3. Selection and training of executives	Heuristic problem-solving techniques applied to: (*a*) training human decision-makers, (*b*) constructing heuristic computer programs

Jacques Mélèse draws a similar distinction between programming and decision-making in systems analysis as applied to business administration. [31] Programming, as he sees it, entails "the application of explicit rules so that there is a 'response' to every situation; such actions can be carried out by men or machines". Decision-making, by contrast, is not based on a complete set of explicit rules and, therefore, entails a choice: "the information in this case is incomplete and affords no basis for a complete correlation between possible situations and responses".

This distinction enables him to postulate that in any organization there is an area of programmed decisions and one of nonprogrammed decisions, there being such a thing as an ideal balance between the two — which can of course be upset. This distinction, which is widely accepted today, suggests the following remarks:

(1) It grossly oversimplifies the problem by saying in effect that some decisions are repetitive while others are not, the former being amenable to mechanical or electronic treatment and the others not. The concept of programme is of course borrowed from the technology of computers, and any distinction so based is bound to reflect the limitations of the *technicist* terminology which inspired it.

Thus, the limitations of the terminological system used account in part for the ambiguous way in which nonprogrammed decisions are defined. What is there to prevent us from interpreting Simon's *general capacity* as referring possibly to a type of programme other than mechanistic? Mélèse suggests further possibilities when he defines programming by reference to *explicit rules*; for a programme (in the technical sense of the term) can be visualized as an extreme instance of a norm characterized not by *explicitness* but by the virtually absolute certainty of the expected outcome.

(2) Programmed decisions in this sense correspond to Thompson's concept of technical rationality, or *technical core* as found in any organization at that level where certainty is maximized. The diagramme of decisional channelling also suggests that the routine process is that which lends itself in some cases to mechanistic analysis. In neither of these two approaches, however, does the introduction of mechanical or electronic techniques seem to be a decisive element of decision-making. Use of these techniques is made possible by certain decisional situations but does not determine them.

The main problem remains that posed by other decisional situations, and here the technicist terminology is, I fear, not very helpful. The second line in Simon's table shows clearly that the differences between traditional and modern techniques are minimal and semantic rather than conceptual (the concept of *heuristic programme* not withstanding). This leads us to consider a very different form of programming, as accounted for by the concept of institutionalization.

Institutionalization

Two premises must be posited at the outset.

(1) Just as man is capable, as we have seen, of programming an outcome which is certain (routine, repetition), so he should be able to construct mechanisms which will enable him to "expect the unexpected" to use Thompson's expression, or again to deal with "turbulent field" decisional environments, as contemplated by Emery and Trist. These are the mechanisms to which the term *institutionalization* refers.

(2) The expression institutionalization (or institution) is one of the most disputed in the social sciences generally — one of the vaguest and most uncertain, whose scientific value is seriously open to question. This, to my mind, is not an obstacle but a problem. Mechanisms for dealing with the uncertain are bound to be many, ambiguous, and debatable. But their very ambiguity makes them a fit subject of research. For this purpose, confrontation with empirical-logical models is not good enough, and reference to socio-linguistic mechanisms and language (in the framework of channelling as defined by ideological control) a constant necessity.

Hitherto, theories of institutionalization have concentrated mainly on the means used for institutionalizing and the observed outcome, i.e. the duration of the institutionalized object. A common feature of such theories, whether expounded by legal scholars, political scientists, or sociologists, is the stress they lay on the regulatory factor and the legal or financial devices (in other words, the norms) by which a particular social activity is protected and its duration guaranteed, even at the price of rigid constraints. Merely shifting the emphasis from the evaluation of past results to a future-oriented outlook or, more precisely, to what a decision-

48

maker can do in the present to control the future (his time framework) gives us the definition of institutionalization as contemplated here; a form of control brought to bear on the environment, whereby an action or activity acquires a degree of autonomy in relation to the unpredictable fluctuations of the environment. Such autonomy, it must be stressed, is a source of constraint and rigidity for other actions or activities which, being less protected, will bear the full brunt of unforeseen environmental disturbances. This reflects the element of *privilege* in institutionalization.

The aspect of institutionalization just outlined is concerned mainly with the essentially normative form of the process, whose content or substance, resides in a principle very much akin to that described by Robert Merton as "displacement of goals" in bureaucratic organizations. It is, in effect, the process by which "an instrumental value becomes a terminal value". [32] Viewed in terms of the socio-linguistic mechanisms which it implies, this process acquires the status of a general principle typifying many situations in which absolute uncertainty attends decision-making and which can be formulated as follows:

(1) Uncertainty leads not to a formulation of objectives, but to the shaping of institutions (organizations and procedures) for the continuous formulation of successive or simultaneous objectives in response to unforeseen environmental change.

(2) Such uncertain and fluctuating objectives cannot constitute criteria for evaluating outcomes (validity control). Their external, formal validity stems from the agent which formulates them and the procedure by which they are formulated.

(3) Such validity is assessed by reference to the legitimacy of the implied institutions (organizations and procedures). The concept of legitimacy varies from one society to another. It is based on magic, religion, divine grace, the democratic principle, etc. Stress is commonly laid on the irrational or mythical aspect of these legitimizing principles, in contrast to rational behaviour, and on a resulting dualism in human behaviour, with all that it connotes — rational versus irrational, good versus bad, civilization versus barbarity, etc. What has been written about Nazism affords many examples of this moralizing Manicheism. It seems, however, more appropriate to look for the answer at the level of language —

its potentialities, and the use made of it in different socio-linguistic contexts.

I have already made this point in discussing open systems. To conclude, I shall give an illustration drawn from anthropology.

In his book on the Trobriand Island fishermen, B. Malinowski reports that they engage at great length in a wide variety of magic practices before setting out on perilous fishing expeditions on the high seas (but not when they fish in the lagoon) in the hope of controlling the outcome of their enterprises.

These magic appeals to the supernatural are more pressing as the uncertainty is greater and dependence on the environment more strongly felt. This type of behaviour can, of course, be interpreted in psychological or psycho-sociological terms — e.g. as designed to reduce anxiety or express solidarity — but the fact remains that language plays a decisive part in these rituals by expressing deep-rooted social motivations. [33]

Other anthropologists have sought to apply the games theory in identical situations involving dangerous fishing in primitive communities. The optimal strategies arrived at through this rational method were remarkably similar to those followed in practice. [34] It seems probable that a similar enquiry concerning Malinowski's Trobriand Islanders would have yielded the same findings. This being accepted, it becomes very difficult to define magic merely as the opposite of rationality; the two concepts simply do not belong on the same level. At the same time, it can be said that magic has succeeded in institutionalizing methods which have in practice lessened risk (probably by trial and error), which modern methods of calculation make it possible to calculate but not to assume. Thus institutionalization in this case was socially useful: dangerous fishing expeditions were profitable in certain conditions, and it was sound policy to protect them.

Conclusion

I have tried, first of all, to show that the decisional approach in political science is most frequently defined in terms of constraints arising out of its application to a particular academic discipline — that it is defined, in other words, as a method peculiar to political science — and that this approach has its theoretical shortcomings. This led me to consider the problem of decision-making from an epistemological and methodological point of view, divorced from any disciplinary context. This, in turn, disclosed the existence of two models, each with its own logic, defined by its own conventions, whether explicit or implicit. These two fundamental and mutually incompatible models — any mixing of which can only breed confusion and ambiguity — are the historic and the systems models. Logic, time, the environment — all of these concepts constitute as many criteria for differentiating between them.

In the second place, I have sought to evaluate the potentialities of systems analysis when applied to decision-making in general and political decisions in particular, while drawing attention to the many gaps still existing in this field, both in the concepts and in the theory as a whole. The work of theorists such as Thompson and Meehan provides a useful starting point for political scientists, not to mention the importance of language and the socio-linguistic mechanisms — though it is doubtless commonplace to observe that any decision is, first and foremost, a process of communication using signs and symbols. The next step is to develop hypotheses and methods, and hence classifications and typologies, adequate to the true complexity of the problem. The formulation of decisional channelling patterns is an attempt in this direction, though surely neither the last nor the most complete.

NOTES

[1] Dusan Sidjanski, "Un aspect du processus de décision: décisions closes et décisions ouvertes", (*11 Politico,* XXIX, 1964, 4; XXX, 1965, 1), pp. 865–867.

[2] Richard Snyder, "A Decision-Making Approach to the Study of Political Phenomena", in *Approaches to the Study of Politics,* Roland Yound, Ed. (Northwestern University Press, 1958), p. 15.

[3] Ibid., p. 10.

[4] Ibid., p. 22.

[5] David Easton, *A Systems Analysis of Political Life* (New York: Wiley, 1965), p. 26.

6 J.L. Bodiguel and B. Gournay, "L'étude des décisions et de l'action politiques" (Paris: Fondation Nationale des Sciences Politiques, April 1965, Mimeographed).

7 See in particular Herbert A. Simon, "A Behavioral Model of Rational Choice", *The Quarterly Journal of Economics* (LXIX, 1955); James G. March, "Some Recent Substantive and Methodological Developments in the Theory of Organizational Decision-Making, in *Essays on the Behavioral Study of Politics,* A. Ranney, Ed. (Urbana: University of Illinois Press, 1962).

8 It takes something as unexpected and accidental as the recent publication of the *Pentagon Papers* (as published by the *New York Times,* New York: Bantam Books, 1971) to show just how fragile and incomplete is the information upon which the most serious and apparently best documented interpretations are based. One of the editors of these papers rightly remarks: "The internal functioning of machinery of the post-World War II Executive Branch has been much theorized about, but only intermittently perceived in authentic detail. Usually these perceptions have come in the personal memoirs of the policy-makers, whose version of history has been understandably selective", (p. XII).

9 Snyder, in *Approaches to Study of Politics,* pp. 16—17.

10 Martin Meyerson and Edward C. Banfield, *Politics, Planning and the Public Interest, The Case of Public Housing in Chicago* (The Free Press of Glencoe, 1955). "Note on the Conceptual Scheme" by Banfield, pp. 303—329.

11 Robert A. Dahl, *Who Governs? Democracy and Power in an American City* (New Haven: Yale University Press, 1961). On the discussion and the use of the empirical argument, see: Nelson Polsby, *Community Power and Political Theory* (New Haven: Yale University Press, 1963).

12 Sidjanski, "Aspect du processus de decision", p. 871.

13 Fernand Braudel, *Ecrits sur l'histoire* (Paris: Flammarion, Coll. Science de l'histoire, 1969), pp. 44ff.

14 Apart from the work of F. Braudel, the reader is referred to those of George Gurvich on the social times, in *La Vocation actuelle de la sociologie,* volume 11 (Paris: P.U.F. 1963), and to the remarks of Louis Althusser in *Lire le Capital* (Paris: Maspéro, 1968), volume 1, pp. 112 ff.

15 Haroun Jamous, "Eléments pour une théorie sociologique des décisions politiques", *Revue Française de Sociologie* (IX, 1968).

16 See particularly the writings of S.F. Nadel, "Social Control and Self-Regulation"; Leslie T. Wilkins, "A Behavioral Theory of Drug Taking"; Magoroh Maruyama, "The Second Cybernetics: Deviation-Amplifying

Mutual Causal Processes": reproduced in *Modern Systems Research for Behavioral Scientists,* Walter Buckley, Ed. (Chicago: Aldine, 1968).

[17] James D. Thompson and Arthur Tuden, "Strategies, Structures and Processes of Organizational Decision", in *Comparative Studies in Administration,* James D. Thompson, Ed. (The University of Pittsburgh Press, 1959).

[18] See Charles Roig, *Analyse de système et sciences sociales, perspectives de développement théorique* (Association Française de Science Politique, Journée d'étude sur l'analyse systémique, Paris, April 1970).

[19] F.E. Emery and E.L. Trist, "The Causal Texture of Organizational Environment", *Human Relations* (18, 1965), reproduced in *Systems Thinking,* F.E. Emery, Ed. (Penguin Books, 1969).

[20] James D. Thompson, *Organizations in Action, Social Science Bases of Administrative Theory* (New York: McGraw-Hill, 1967), p. 159.

[21] Emery and Trist, "Causal Texture of Organizational Environment", p. 252.

[22] James Thompson, *Organizations in Action*, p. 19.

[23] Ibid., p. 10.

[24] Ibid., p. 143.

[25] Eugene J. Meehan, *Explanation in Social Science: A System Paradigm* (Homewood 111.: The Dorwey Press, 1968).

[26] Ibid., p. 31.

[27] The terminology and the linguistic model to which I refer in this note are borrowed from the works of Kenneth Burke, in particular: *A Grammar of Motives,* 1945 (Berkeley: University of California Press, 1969), and *A Rhetoric of Motives,* 1950 (Berkeley: University of California Press, 1969). See also: Ernst Cassirer, *Language and Myth* (New York: Dover Publications, 1953); *Readings in the Sociology of Language,* Joshua A. Fisherman, Ed. (Paris: Mouton, 1968); "Linguistique et Société", presented by J.B. Marcelles, *Langue Française* (9, February 1971). These works (and others) should be studied by all political scientists. In this note, I can do no more than mention them and emphasize their importance for political science.

[28] Jean Piaget, *Le structuralisme* (Paris: P.U.F., Q.S.J. no 1311, 4th edition, 1970), p. 27.

[29] Jean Piaget, "Problèmes généraux de la recherche interdisciplinaire mécanismes communs" in *Tendances principales de la recherche dans les sciences sociales et humaines,* 1st part: Sciences sociales, UNESCO (Paris: Mouton, 1970), pp. 578−581. The work of Piaget deserves more than a passing reference, but more detailed discussion of his thinking would upset the balance of this note.

[30] Herbert A. Simon, *The New Science of Management Decision* (New York: Harper & Row, 1960), pp. 5—8.

[31] Jacques Mélèse, *La gestion par les systèmes, Essai de praxéologie* (Paris: Hommes et Techniques, 1968).

[32] Robert K. Merton, "Bureaucratic Structure and Personality" in *Social Structure and Theory* (New York: The Free Press, 1957).

[33] Bronislaw Malinowski, *Magic, Science and Religion* (New York: Doubleday Anchor Books, 1954), and the commentary by Arthur L. Stinchcombe, *Constructing Social Theories* (New York: Harcourt, Brace & World, 1968), pp. 82—83.

[34] William Davenport, "Jamaican Fishing: A Game Theory Analysis", in *Papers on Caribbean Anthropology* (Yale University Publications, 1960); see also a criticism in *Game Theory in the Behavioral Sciences*, Ira R. Buchler and Hugo G. Nutini, Eds. (University of Pittsburgh Press, 1969), pp. 9—14, 117—125.

An Analytical Model of Hegemonical Tension Among Ghanaian Elites

SANJEEVA NAYAK*

Ghana is, strategically, an unimportant country. Yet, Kwame Nkrumah's political activism earned Ghana an unusual share of world publicity. Nkrumah always compelled attention. Because of this focus, the import of his endeavors to establish a one-party state has been the subject of intense scrutiny by scholars.[1] Nonetheless, there is no clear answer to these questions: Was Nkrumah attempting to bring stability to a political community in which instability was inevitable?[2] Was he the driver on the road he had freely chosen or was he driven by circumstances he could not escape? Was the one-party state a ploy or an inescapable necessity? This paper seeks to answer such questions by creating a new model which views Ghanaian politics as a hegemonical tension among the elites and the one-party state as a consequence of the contest for power among competing elites. The model, while drawing from writings of Mosca and Pareto, is anchored upon the *mandala* (concentric circles) theory of Kautilya as propounded in

* This is a revised version of the paper read at the VIII World Congress of the IPSA, Munich 1970. The author wishes to thank Southampton College Faculty Research Committee for financial assistance and Dr. Charles H. Sheldon and Dr. J.K. Phadke for their comments.

Arthashastra. [3] It accepts the basic premises of his speculative model: that the wise and sensitive statesman should make his seat of power the center of a series of concentric circles, that neighbors are natural enemies, and that all politics is primarily a struggle for power. This conceptual lens provides not only a better view of the blurred areas of Ghanaian politics but also identifies the decision-outcome nexus of Nkrumah's decision-making process. There is a discernible correlation, even a causal interrelationship, between the contest for power among various elite groups and the one-party system. Apart from its heuristic value, this conflict-coercion model has holistic implications that can encompass the entire Third World.

The Model

The political power in Ghana under Nkrumah, as in all political communities, was controlled by elites. [4] The elites could be further divided into governing, and nongoverning who aspire and attempt to replace the ruling elite. The political process involves a competition between these two elite groups to occupy the seat of power. [5] Pareto holds that there is a natural tendency among these elites to rotate positions. He presents a cyclical theory of social change under the rubric — circulation of elites.

Furthermore, Mosca envisages the possibility of the existence of "a plurality of elites functioning outside the governing class, each representing an important social force". The ruling elite, obviously, utilizes the differences among its opponents to its advantage. "One could explain", states Mosca, "the whole history of civilized mankind in terms of the conflict between the attempt of the rulers to monopolize and bequeath political power and the attempt of new forces to change relations of power". [6] Historians often narrate these contests as "a glorious war of liberty when what took place was a mere struggle between two elites competing for supremacy". [7]

The Ghanaian political process, in observable social reality, involved a competition for power within the elites. [8] In them the diverse forces of society were represented and their shape and action reflected the diversity of the social structure of Ghana.

There was no single, closed, master caste, nor one elite group to dominate Ghana. All elite groups lacked the liberal tradition and as a political class were pluralistic. The governing elite acted in the name of the masses with *double legitimacy* as heirs to the British and as custodians of the general will. Though initially the Convention People's Party (CPP) organized the masses, during the crucial struggle before independence it ignored them and adopted an elitist approach to resolve the problem of federalism. The opposition too nurtured similar ideas. After meeting J.B. Danquah, the opposition leader, Richard Wright averred: "One did not speak *for* the the masses; one told them what to do". [9] Apter also discovered that all concerned members of the legislative assembly felt that *the people* did not understand their problems. [10] Thus the reality behind the battle between political parties over the constitutional form before independence was a conflict between competing elites.

In this contest for power, Nkrumah realized that to remain in power he must intercept the process of circulation of elites. [11] Politics being a zero-sum game, his primary concern was to remain in power in a stable Ghana. His strategy resembled Kautilya's *mandala*, which was designed to serve as a speculative model to an ambitious and aggressive prince. Such a prince was advised to act on the premise that power is the taproot of politics. The prince, therefore, is required to manipulate his relations with neighboring princes to his advantage. He should make an isomorphic model by placing his kingdom in the center of a series of concentric circles and should develop a strategy based on the hypothesis that neighbors are natural enemies. This enmity may be actual or potential. But there is an element of "locational determinism". [12] The prince is surrounded by realms hostile to him. The kingdoms beyond the neighboring realms, being opponents of neighbors, are patently his friends. Those realms in the fourth circle are allies of his neighbor and, therefore, represent a more remote danger. Thus the checkerboard pattern alternates between friends and enemies.

In developing this strategy, the prince should realize that every ring has subdivisions, which betray natural and inherent animosities, and he should exploit those differences. He should also be aware that there is a rival *mandala*. Whenever possible, he should try to win over a strong adversary without war. His diplomatic technique should include conciliation, concession, use of force, and *divide et impera* in that order. In short, "a statesman operates, perforce, in an exceedingly complicated act of stresses and cross-stresses, always assuming that neighbor to be unfriendly, jealous, aggressive, and always watching for his own time of surprise and treacherous attack". [13] This isomorphic model, designed as a guide to international relations, is conceived in territorial space. For our purpose, we shall recast it in social space.

In remolding Kautilya's model, we have grouped the elites according to their special interests, which are also their constitutive interests. The elites operate in groups. [14] These include traditional rulers, entrepreneurs, intellectuals, religious groups, the civil servants, the police, the judiciary, the military, the trade unions, the farm leaders, and the United Party with its factions based mostly on ethnic loyalties. Each group had internal diversity of opinions, which as a coterie made these groups politically varied and at least partially contradictory. Often they were motivated by the will not to submit to the ruling elite. Besides, there was no free exchange of views among elite groups, all of them lacked a commitment to liberal tradition, and as a political class they were pluralistic. [15] The encounter of these groups resulted not in coalition, but in competition.

It is now necessary to arrange these groups, with Nkrumah as the center of gravity of concentric circles. The principle that governs this classification is the proximity of each elite group to the commanding heights of the polity. The colleagues of Nkrumah, his nearest rivals, whom he initially employed to suppress the opposition, remained with him in the central circle. The United Party, being the immediate competitor in the sense that the fall of CPP government would have brought it into power, occupies the second ring. The governing elite, therefore, creates auxiliaries like the Trade Union Congress (TUC), the National African Socialist Student Organization (NASSO), the Party Vanguard Activists (PVA), the United Ghana Farmers Council (UGFC), the Council of Ghana Women (CGW), the Workers Brigade (WB), and the Young Pioneers (YP), and places them in the third circle to crush the common enemy in the middle — the United Party. The CPP also enlists apolitical groups like the civil servants, the police, the judiciary, and the military by offering them quick material rewards. All elite

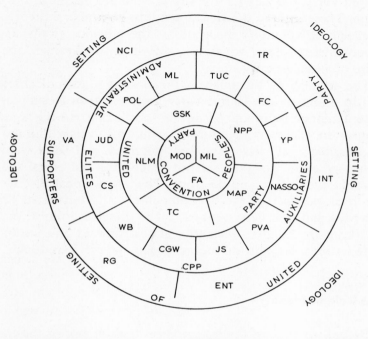

Central Circle	Second Circle	Third Circle	Fourth Circle
CPP	*United Party*	*(a) CPP Auxiliaries*	*Supporters of UP*
MOD-Moderates	NPP – Northern	TUC – Trade Union	TR – Traditional
MIL –Militants	People's	Congress	Rulers
FA – Faithfuls	Party	FC – Farmers Council	INT – Intellectuals
	MAP-Muslim	YP – Young Pioneers	ENT- Entrepreneurs
	Association	NASSO-National African	RG – Religious
	Party	Socialist Students	Groups
	TC – Togoland	Organization	VA – Voluntary
	Congress	PVA– Party Vanguard	Association
	NLM-National	Activists	NCI – Neocolonial
	Liberation	JS – Journalists	Influences
	Movement	CGW- Council of	
	GSK –Ga Shifimo	Ghana Women	
	Kpee	WB – Workers Brigade	
		(b) Administrative Elites	
		CS – Civil Service	
		JUD – Judiciary	
		POL –Police	
		ML –Military	

Fig. 1. The Circles of Elites.

groups in the third circle are ministrants to the ruling elite. The United Party too has its supporters, who are placed in the outer circle. These include the traditional rulers (chiefs), entrepreneurs, intellectuals, voluntary associations, the religious groups and the neocolonialist forces, which are, according to Nkrumah, the root cause of all his troubles.

The strategy of Nkrumah in the ensuing hegemonical tension, was to eliminate the United Party first; and then to suppress the distant supporters of the UP in the fourth ring. Having liquidated opposition, Nkrumah then turned against his rivals within the CPP. All possible rivals were disgraced, detained, and some went into voluntary exile. He then set out to control and corral the civil servants, the police, and the army. The last two coalesced to form the rival *mandala* or the "counter-elite", and outwitted him by "surprise and treacherous attack". The inverted political pyramid of Nkrumah collapsed instantly, almost unwept and unsung, despite its apparent political success during the previous decade.

The Role of Ideology

Before we analyze the hegemonical tension among the elites, it is imperative to assay the role of ideology in Ghanaian politics. Nkrumah is generally believed to be an ideologue. But his ideology was a mere montage to disguise, rationalize, and legitimize the contest for power. [16] Political decisions were based not on advertised ideological foundations of the political kingdom but on realities of power equations. Ideology was no more than a "political formula", to wheedle the masses, to raise their sense of importance, and to justify Nkrumah's "actual exercise of power by resting it on some universal moral principle".

Almost all facets of Nkrumah's ideology fall within the ambit of Mosca's theory of "political formula", or Sorelian myth. As a legitimizing banner that can be dangled before the expectant masses, ideology has its utility. [17] It enables the rulers to convert their might into right, obedience into duty, and acts as a lever "for obtaining political mobilization and for maximizing the possibilities of mass manipulation".[18] Moreover, recognizing that the masses readily defer to abstract universal principles, Nkrumah exploited ideology to his advantage.

Ideology in Ghana had not become dogma, because Nkrumah-ism was continually refined and its oscillations reflected the political realities of the system. Nkrumah, for example, had no difficulty in accepting the Lenin Peace Prize and signing a military training agreement with Britain in the same month. He could even play down the role of "ideology" when it was convenient and necessary. For all his explanation, Nkrumah did not have a single solid structure of a philosophy of life. [19] Thoughts he had many, explicit and implicit, but thought he had none.

The Setting

It is necessary that we evaluate the setting in which Ghana gained her freedom before we describe the structure of this model. The organized violence in the early days of independence compelled the governing elite to put a premium on stability. [20] Almost every action of the state was subject to a test to determine its effects on security. This concern for order pushed Nkrumah slowly, though not necessarily reluctantly, in the direction of a one-party state, which was largely a consequence of historical circumstances that surrounded the birth of Ghana.

The Elite Groups

It is now essential to formulate and arrange various elite groups of the model. First, our analysis will begin with our evaluation of the role of Nkrumah, the nature of the CPP and its auxiliaries, along with administrative elites in the third circle. This will be followed by a study of the structure of the United Party and its supporters in the outer circle.

The Governing Elites

The governing elites include Nkrumah and the CPP with its three main factions. The moderates led by Komla Gbedemah and Kojo Botsio; the militants led by Ako Adjei and Tawia Adamafio; and Kofi Baako led the faithfuls, who basked in the reflected glory of Nkrumah. The governing elite was insulated by the CPP auxiliaries and administrative elites.

Nkrumah and the CPP

In Ghana, as elsewhere, personality rather than principles played a prominent role. As the hero of the freedom struggle, Nkrumah was the most tangible, visible and successful symbol available. He generally created and conducted opinion, for association with him provided the required aura of legitimacy. Nkrumah saw power in personal terms and associated it with his political survival, which was linked, he persuaded himself, with the continued existence of Ghana. Consequently, he was able to describe the struggle in ethical terms to justify the harshness of his means. He was determined to monopolize power, for to share it, he thought, was to surrender it.

Initially, he pushed the CPP in the direction of his choice slowly, bearing in mind his ultimate goal. He prolonged his policy of accommodation within the party. The political violence that accompanied new Ghana, and fear of the opposition displacing the ruling elite, made Nkrumah's associates his willing accomplices. He played his cards well. Conscious of the heterogeneity of the CPP, he often acted as a party manager holding the splintering groups — moderates, militants and the faithfuls — together. Later when the latent struggle within the party came into the open, Nkrumah found himself its unintended beneficiary. It enabled him to remain at the apex of the political structure by manipulating the factional fights to his advantage.

The CPP Auxiliaries

To augment his power within the Party and also to fight the opposition, Nkrumah created a number of auxiliaries. They were to act as counterpoise to local branches of the party and also to serve his political needs. The constituent interests of these groups and the political power they enjoyed as satellites of the ruling elite made them antagonistic to the opposition. These included the trade unions, women, youth and the farmers.

Trade Unions. The CPP and the trade union movement were, from the beginning, political allies. But the trade union movement

62

was weak. There were as many as 130 local unions and only five national unions in 1957. These small and overlapping unions were to be merged into a single Trade Union. Nkrumah, therefore, offered the Trade Union Congress (TUC) a better financial base, and expressed the hope that "the TUC would become the 'Industrial Parliament' of Ghana, prepared at all times to advise the Government on labor questions". The national executive of the CPP exhorted the workers to join the TUC. In December 1958, the Industrial Relations Act was passed and this made the TUC a protective shield over the entire trade union movement. Its financial base was further strengthened in 1960, when all wage earners with an income up to $1900 a year were required to join the union after continuous employment of one month. The number of authorized unions was reduced to sixteen to strengthen the TUC leadership. Finally, in April 1961, the TUC was appropriately declared an integral part of the CPP. The elite group within the trade union movement, naturally, stood behind the ruling elite.

Farmers' Council. The United Ghana Farmers' Council (UGFC) was created in July 1953. In September 1957, the UGFC received statutory recognition as the sole representative of the farmers. Before long the UGFC was declared an integral wing of the party and, in 1961, was given the exclusive right to buy cocoa from the farmers — eliminating all middlemen and cooperatives — for the Cocoa Marketing Board. The political power of the UGFC was thus linked with the CPP.

Young Pioneers. Nkrumah had, in his bid for power, relied on the youth. It was his Committee on Youth Organization that permitted him to challenge the leadership of the UGCC. The Ghana Young Pioneers (YP) was founded in June 1960. The Kwame Nkrumah Youth Training School recruited and trained young people, who on graduation occupied key positions among the YP. In November 1960, Nkrumah ordered the expansion of the program to cover all regions in Ghana. By May 1961, more than 20,000 young people were participating in the movement. [21] All participants were required to pledge loyalty to Nkrumah, who exploited them to serve his political aims.

NASSO. In 1953, the CPP founded the National African Socialist Student Organization (NASSO) purportedly to work on ideological education. In 1959, it was officially declared to be the "ideological" wing of the CPP.

A number of militants and political opportunists had joined the NASSO to gravitate to the center of power. It enjoyed considerable political leverage. The editors of influential papers were its members. From this vantage point the NASSO later initiated the struggle within the CPP.

Party Vanguard Activists. Nkrumah, however, fearful of NASSO's expanding influence created another elite group called the Party Vanguard Activists (PVA). It was expected to be in perpetual preparedness to serve the party; maintain, propagate and defend its aims; and finally to act as a vigilante group within the CPP. Nkrumah structured PVA as a counterpoise to the NASSO. [22] Significantly, the PVA gained more prominence when the NASSO fell from his grace.

Journalists. From the beginning, Nkrumah was aware of the power of the press. It was an instrument of indoctrination, not information. [23] Nkrumah's political career rose and fell with *The Evening News,* the propaganda arm of the CPP. Gradually Nkrumah made entire media an auxiliary of the party. The pattern of takeover was, again, familiar. Bankole Timothy, the respected editor of the *Daily Graphic,* was deported for a critical editorial. The opposition paper — *The Ashanti Pioneer* — was placed under government censorship. *The Ghanaian Times* was bought and run by the Guinea Press, which was financed by the Industrial Development Corporation. Other organs of mass media — radio and television — were completely dominated by the governing elites.

Newspapers undeniably played a prominent role in the factional fights within the CPP. *The Spark,* with its radical elan, illustrates the nature and critical importance of journalism in Ghanaian politics. Kofi Batsa, the editor, and Samuel G. Ikoku, a contributor, were manipulated to attack Nkrumah's rivals. As co-opted colleagues, they did not have a popular base. Being completely dependent on him, they were controllable and formed a sort of reserve to keep Nkrumah's competitors in check.

Council of Ghana Women. The women in Ghana were well organized and played a prominent role in the economic life of the country. They controlled retail trade and the transport system. It is estimated that 83 percent of the 323,900 traders in 1966 were women. They constituted nearly one-eighth of the labor force and one out of twenty-two persons in Ghana was a trader. Initially the CPP formed a Women's League but did not give women a separate status. Later, they were organized under the Council of Ghana Women. In 1960, the membership of the National Assembly was raised to 114 by the addition of ten women members.

The Workers' Brigade. The Brigade was created primarily to relieve the problem of unemployment among school-leavers. [24] They were to be instructed in discipline, responsibility and citizenship. The Brigade had two divisions — agriculture and works. There was also a ceremonial branch drawn from both divisions. Its functions involved participation in parades on ceremonial occasions and at political rallies. Later the Brigade was utilized for political and security purposes.

The Administrative Elite

The CPP also succeeded in winning over the administrative elite, which was considered apolitical at the time of independence. This elite included four groups — the civil servants, the police, the judiciary, and the defense forces. All of them, in the initial stage, enjoyed considerable material benefit and power and therefore became willing partners of the ruling elite.

Civil Service. The rapid Africanization brought immediate gains to civil servants. Most of them got quick promotions. Senior officials benefited from the fact that expatriate officials could not represent Ghana abroad. Besides, Nkrumah did not disturb the colonial power structure. But there was suspicion on both sides. The civil servants generally had little respect for political carpet-baggers, and the CPP politicians were aware that some of the civil servants had been their active opponents in the colonial days. Nonetheless, the civil servants did exercise considerable influence on decision-making power.

Judiciary. The judiciary was initially treated with deference. In September 1957, Nkrumah underscored the independence of the judiciary by referring to the appointment of political opponents to the bench. The judges actively collaborated with Nkrumah. It was Chief Justice Sir Arku Korsah, who signed, as acting governor-general, the Preventive Detention Act. The Supreme Court later upheld its constitutionality and denied the writ of *habeas corpus*, to those detained under the Act. Significantly, in summer 1961, the chief justice was named a member of the three-man commission to govern Ghana during Nkrumah's long tour of Communist Bloc countries.

Police. The police too received generous attention. Police officers received a good salary, had good barracks, and an annual growth rate of 8.5 percent gave the police enormous patronage. [25] If Nkrumah suspected the senior officials, there was no public indication of this in the early years of independent Ghana.

Military Elite. Nkrumah expanded his army at a phenomenal rate. He did it to build influence and prestige in Africa and also to develop a stronger base for his government. Without financial consideration, Ghana created a defense force with three arms: the army, the navy and the air force. The growth rate of the army was better than that of the police. The rate of promotions of Ghanaian officers was astounding. From twenty-seven in 1957, their number had risen to nearly seven hundred at the time of the coup. Thus, the persuasiveness of material benefits enabled the army to collaborate with the ruling elite.

The Nongoverning Elite

The nongoverning elites consisted of two groups — the United Party in the second circle and its supporters in the fourth circle. Their main goal was to displace the ruling elite.

The United Party
In 1957, all opposition groups, except the Muslim Association Party (MAP), were organized on a tribal-territorial basis. The Northern People's Party (NPP), the National Liberation Movement

(NLM), and the Togoland Congress (TC) were regional parties which relied on ethnic loyalties and interests. The chiefs, who supported them, used national organizations of the tribe to mobilize support. Despite the fact that they lost the 1956 election in terms of their parliamentary strength, the opposition declined to accept that verdict. In independent Ghana, the TC initiated the struggle. As Ghanaians were hoisting their new flag, the TC mounted an insurrection to unify Ewe people. The government was able to restore law and order in the Volta region but only after a loss of five lives and a large number of arrests.

The political stability of Ghana was also threatened by a new tribal organization — Ga Shifimo Kpee (GSK), the Ga Steadfast Association. The GSK described itself as a nonpolitical association to "protect the interests of Ga people". It used "action squads" called "Tokyo Joes" as part of its direct action to achieve its objective, and organized cells and administered a secret oath. In the violence that followed, life in the capital became insecure. The government declared a state of emergency and used its powers to suppress the GSK.

Furthermore, the opposition used ethnic ties to entice the back benchers of the CPP. A member of the ruling party from Builsa resigned to join the NPP. Fearing more desertions, the CPP girded itself to fight for survival. [26] It attacked tribalism, parochialism and religious nationalism, which the CPP identified as the fount of its rivals' strength. First, the government deported the leaders of the MAP, and then passed the Avoidance of Discrimination Act to deny the various opposition parties their right to exist under tribal or regional banner. The opposition, consequently, joined together to form a secular national party — the United Party.

The formation of the UP did eliminate overt tribal politics, but failed to eradicate tribalism. The ruling elite averred that to survive politically, it had to liquidate the "violent, waspish and malignant" opposition. The zero-sum game of politics had its roots in this struggle.

Supporters of the United Party

There were a number of elite groups which, while not being in the forefront, provided material and moral support to the UP. Their support, however, did not form a substantive component.

Being subliminal, Nkrumah relegated them to the outer circle signifying their relative unimportance. These included most of the chiefs, intellectuals, entrepreneurs, religious groups, and the neocolonial forces that directed opposition from abroad.

The Traditional Rulers. The traditional rulers (or chiefs) who enjoyed social status by ascription found it uncomfortable to be among those who emphasized achievement. The role of charisma, emphasis on democratic system, and glorification of popular sovereignty by the CPP unnerved the chiefs, who rightly feared the eventual loss of their political power base. They had everything to gain by continuation as the local wheels of the system. But the chiefs and their supporters were realistic enough to present their case as a part of their demand for local autonomy. The CPP, for its part, attacked chieftaincy stating that lineage could not be a criteria for political office in a democracy.

The traditional rulers, therefore, cast their lot with the opposition. The NLM was financed and actively supported by the *Asantehene* and his council. The NPP was openly linked with the chieftaincy. Its election *Manifesto* called for the preservation of the rights, privileges and status of the chiefs and exhorted them to join the political struggle. The MAP affirmed "the traditional alliance between the Muslims and the Chiefs" and promised to restore the chiefs to their ancient dignity. The TC too had manifest support of the chiefs. When these parties merged to form the UP, they changed the pew but not the church.

Intellectuals. Education in Ghana is the pathway to success and social status. The CPP understood its role and made access to education open to all. A large number of schools, colleges, and a few universities were opened, and admission was largely on merit. The intellectuals had enough opportunity for advancement in the growing academic community. As the rate of expansion slowed down, there was discontent on the campuses. The faculty wanted the right to comment on political issues without party constraints. The educated felt that the CPP was indifferent, if not hostile, to them. These factors juxtaposed with the increasing fear of the ruling elite — which seemed to suspect everyone not enthusiastically supporting its policies — created a milieu where struggle was unavoidable.

68

The Entrepreneurs. The entrepreneurs were hurt by some of the CPP's policies. The ruling elite openly courted the workers. The enactment of laws favorable to the workers, both in restructuring their unions and in terms of establishing a minimum wage, further alienated the commercial groups. Moreover, the CPP, in its "Work and Happiness" program reserved only small-scale enterprises for Ghanaian entrepreneurs. The entrepreneurial group, naturally, publicly acquiesced but privately resisted the CPP. Recognizing the realities of the situation, their support to the UP was covert.

Religious Groups. The CPP was a secular party, but it did not ignore the cultural ethos of Ghana. It tried to accommodate the Christians, the largest religious group in Ghana. While claiming to be a Marxist-Socialist, Nkrumah insisted he was a Christian. The ruling elite initially left the missionaries alone, but this policy of noninterference did not last long.

The second largest religious group in Ghana consisted of followers of traditional religion, which founded the "new shrines". [27] The priests in these "shrines" advised and helped people to resolve their problems. The investigations in connection with the first bomb incident against Nkrumah revealed the role of the "shrines". Geoffrey Bing has pointed out that the CPP coined adulatory slogans like "Nkrumah will never die" to counteract the activities and influences of "shrines".

References have already been made to the third largest religious group in Ghana — the Muslims. The religious groups in general were not considered friendly by the CPP. While manipulating them to its advantage, the CPP did not hesitate to act against them during the crisis.

Voluntary Associations. In order to balance the forces in the intraparty and interparty struggle, Nkrumah created party auxiliaries. They were also supposed to supplant gradually various voluntary organizations — church groups, Boy Scouts, the Y.M.C.A., the Federation of Ghana Women, the Cooperative Societies. Nkrumah organized the CPP auxiliaries to compete with them. In 1957, in Accra alone there were more than three hundred voluntary organizations. By 1966, their number, however, had sharply declined. The pliant auxiliaries of the party were aspiring and attempting to fill the void.

Neocolonial Influences. Nkrumah feared the intense pressure of neocolonial forces generated by international capitalism on Africa in general and Ghana in particular. Within Ghana many elite groups in the second, fourth, and even the central circle were vulnerable. These groups, by their life styles and consumption patterns, acted as if they were extensions of an international community of elites. Such apparent similarity helped Nkrumah to brand them as clients of neocolonialism. By repeatedly invoking the enemy-at-the-gate principle, he sought to consolidate his power. Ghanaians were constantly reminded that eternal vigilance, attained through strong and stable government under the aegis of the CPP, was the only alternative open to them to crush this subversive force.

There was an obvious contradiction in Nkrumah's attack on neocolonialism. Apart from his earlier coalition with the colonial administration, he actively solicited economic aid and private investment to accelerate economic development. Given these limitations Nkrumah could not, and did not, place neocolonialism in the second circle as his unflagging attacks would have us believe. It served his immediate political purpose to relegate it to subordinate status in the fourth circle.

The Hegemonical Tension

Having identified the various primary and secondary elite groups in the political edifice, it is pertinent to analyze the pattern of hegemonical tension among the various components of the *mandala.* The armed revolt that accompanied the birth of Ghana and subsequent rise of the GSK persuaded Nkrumah that it was impossible for him to co-exist with the opposition. He was not combating the conduct of the opposition but its existence; convinced that its existence and its hostility were identical. Then, as was his wont, Nkrumah pursued his enemies with single-mindedness. Strategy followed the general pattern prescribed by Kautilya. Adversaries were sometimes lulled into passivity through patronage, but assaulted when he could not entice them to join the CPP. The spectrum of the struggle had "divide and rule" and "destroy and rule" as its terminals.

The fear of being swept away by the opposition enabled the CPP to forge its internal unity. The UP, on the other hand, was a divided house. The astute leadership of the CPP did not fail to grasp its significance and exploited those differences to its own advantage. After suppressing the armed revolt organized by the TC and violent activities of the GSK, the ruling elite turned against the MAP, the weakest link of the opposition. The attack commenced with the Deportation Act of 1957 under which two prominent leaders, who were aliens and hence whose "presence was considered not conducive to public good", were deported.

The CPP then concentrated on other political parties. Realizing that the strength of opposing groups was based on their appeal to primordial ties — ethnic, regional and religious — the government enacted the Avoidance of Discrimination Act. Under its provisions ethnic, regional and religious parties were not allowed to function. The opposition, to circumvent this law, formed the United Party, which was nominally national as well as secular.

The ruling elite followed a two-pronged policy. It used both the carrot and the stick. To the wavering members of the UP, it offered a share in the patronage, provided they join its ranks. Before long it was able to entice a substantial number of UP members to its side in the parliament. But it was the stick that enabled the CPP to regulate the velocity of its attack. With the Preventive Detention Act as an instrument, it was now possible for the ruling elite to detain any member of the UP without having to prove his guilt. The decline of UP membership in the parliament was swift. By 1960, Nkrumah correctly surmised that the emasculated opposition was no longer a threat and he even abolished the post of Leader of the Opposition. He reorganized his strategy to deal with the groups in the outer circle.

The most prominent and powerful group in the outer circle was that of the chiefs. The CPP had in the beginning, "destooled" the chiefs antagonistic to it, but "enstooled" those that were friendly. Some of them were even given positions of power. Nkrumah had twin motives: a belief in a reformed chieftaincy and social necessity. The rulers were aware of the hold of the chieftaincy and Nkrumah adopted the traditional title *Osagyefo* to pacify those groups that respected and revered tradition. Besides, it established political legitimacy.

In 1961, the government tightened its control and downgraded the role of traditional rulers. The Chieftaincy Act denied the chiefs political tools to fight the CPP. They were earlier excluded from participation in the central government in 1954, and under the new act the chiefs were barred from local government. Some of their functions, outside their traditional duties, were transferred to the local councils. The chiefs were classified into four grades, and the powers of each rank were clearly defined within traditional limits. The government reserved the right to withdraw recognition, regularize customary "destoolment" and even prohibit such a person from residing in a specified area. A House of Chiefs was set up in each region but its functions were confined to advising the regional government on issues connected with the customary law.

The first major attack on the intellectuals came in 1959 when the opposition had lost its power. Nkrumah in an important address warned the universities to reform themselves. "If the reform does not come from within", he insisted, "we are going to impose it from outside. . ." This demand was a consequence of the government's unhappiness about the direction in which the universities were moving. Both faculty and students were critical of the government, encouraged, it was believed, by the expatriate staff. Nkrumah was also laying the foundation to isolate intellectuals from the community. In 1961, he became the Chancellor of the universities and this allowed him to appoint his supporters to Legon's University Council. In the same year the terms of six faculty members were terminated without much ado. Nkrumah came to believe that he had silenced the intellectuals effectively.

The assault on entrepreneurs began in 1960. The government announced that it would give no further financial aid to Ghanaian entrepreneurs. They were urged to be self-reliant. The following year, the UGFC was given complete monopoly over cocoa purchasing for the Cocoa Marketing Board. The Timber Marketing Board was declared the legal purchaser of all timber exports in logs. Nearly twenty-five foreign firms were compelled to withdraw from the timber business. This prevented them — as they had been doing in the past — from extending short-term credit to wealthy farmers hostile to the CPP. Besides, the CPP controlled businessmen through an import licensing system, which was one of the causes of perpetuation of that omnipresent social evil — corruption. The licensing system also permitted the government to give preferential treatment to public sector establishments at the expense of Ghanaian entrepreneurs. Finally, the government established a new trading company, Ghana National Trading Corporation (GNTC), in December 1961. [28] Its ultimate goal was to have "People's Shops" all over the country, and these would have supplanted the private traders. The Ghana Commercial Bank, the State Insurance Corporation, the Ghana Hotel and Tourist Corporation, the Ghana Fishing Corporation, the Ghana Distilleries Corporation, the State Furniture Joinery Corporation, and so on, completed the circle of controls around the entrepreneurs.

In mining, the State Mining Corporation took over five of the seven gold mines, which were unable to operate on a commercial basis. In the diamond industry, the government established a Diamond Marketing Board in 1962 to replace the Government Diamond Market. The board bought all diamonds won and produced in Ghana and sold them to its agents operating on the market. In manufacturing, the government built a number of factories managed by state-private companies, which were given priority in the distribution of imported materials.

In the agricultural sector, the entrepreneurial group was, once again, circumscribed by state enterprises. The UGFC established cooperative farms, though their number declined toward the end of Nkrumah's rule. [29] In 1962, the State Farms were established with Israeli technical assistance, overseen by the Ministry of Agriculture. Through these organizations, the ruling elite made inroads into the power structure woven around wealthy farmers and chiefs, while the small farmers were deflected by public assurances that the State Farms Corporation was neither intended to cripple nor displace them.

Nkrumah's attitude towards neocolonialism has been examined earlier. Nkrumah believed that political emancipation was not accompanied by economic independence. The fall of cocoa prices was interpreted as a deliberate, though covert, effort by the neocolonial forces to subjugate Ghana and convert it into a client-state. Nkrumah also used it as a ploy to condemn his opponents as stooges of faceless neocolonialism. It was, however, relegated to the outer circle because it did not challenge the ruling elite openly, but only through its proxy.

The religious groups hostile to the CPP were mainly controlled through deportation of their leaders. We have already discussed the fate of the MAP leaders. The government was able to secure the appointment of Mallam Mutawalimu as the *Zerikin Zongo* to succeed the deported leader. The CPP also founded a Muslim Council, a wing of the party, to give the muslims a medium for political expression. The missionaries were suspect because they were a part of the colonial triptych — gold, glory and god. The government reacted, or rather overreacted, at the slightest sign of political interference. When the Bishop of Accra objected to the indoctrination of the Young Pioneers, he was asked to leave the country. After the Kulungugu incident, the Anglican Archbishop of West Africa was deported from Ghana. The "new shrines" were countered largely through propaganda. The CPP, thus, refused to countenance religious interference in politics.

Intraparty struggle followed interparty rivalry. By 1959, Nkrumah realized that he had subdued the opposition. In his tenth anniversary address to the party, he talked of the second revolution, the need to regroup the CPP and plan a strategy for the future. The submerged factionalism within the CPP came to the fore. The groups vied with one another to gravitate to the center of power, but they found that the slope of power was steep near its apex. By July 1960, Nkrumah felt that he could no longer rely on his colleagues. He rightly perceived that the main threat was from the moderates. Komla Gbedemah, the man who brought him to power, was his immediate rival. Nkrumah covertly encouraged a camarilla of militants, led by Adamafio, to attack the moderates. He also enlisted the civil service to his cause. [30] The struggle gained momentum in early 1961. [31]

The strategy was clear, and its objective was to dismiss Gbedemah from the cabinet. On 13 February 1961, the world learned of the death of Lumumba. Irate Nkrumah blamed the West and deliberately courted the Soviet Union. He hurriedly invited President Brezhnev, who was then in Guinea, to visit Ghana. The Soviet president accepted the invitation and arrived in Accra on 16 February. Two days later Nkrumah laid the foundation stone of the Ideological Institute at Winneba. The rival fractions manoeuvered for supremacy. The militants pressed for the expansion of the public sector through Soviet aid. Gbedemah questioned the feasibility and propriety of such a move. This debate took place while Nkrumah was attending the Commonwealth Prime Ministers' Conference in London.

On his return, Nkrumah intensified the pressure on the moderates. Early in March, Nkrumah demoted Gbedemah by changing his portfolio. On April 6, he told the Teachers' Association that the aim of his government was to create a socialist system. Two days later, he brought the simmering crisis within the party into the open. The "Dawn Broadcast", inspired by Adamafio, attacked that ubiquitous social evil — corruption — but its real intent was to hurt the moderates. To strengthen his base, he also declared the party auxiliaries to be integral wings of the party. On April 22, Nkrumah called a meeting of a study group on "building a socialist state". His action granting the UGFC a monopoly over purchase of cocoa was designed to hurt the middlemen, who supported the moderates.

The struggle continued unabated. On May 1, Nkrumah took over the office of the secretary general of the CPP, in addition to being its life chairman and secretary of the Central Committee. "In centralizing control of the government he assumed direction of the armed forces, the police, the budget bureau, and the African Affairs Secretariat; by June 3, 1961, Nkrumah was directly responsible for thirty-eight subjects and departments in the government". [32]

The following month Nkrumah left on an extended tour of the Soviet Union and other Communist Bloc countries. In his absence Ghana was left to the care of a presidential commission, which included both Gbedemah and Botsio. Nkrumah felt this necessary to soothe Gbedemah because he did not want a political crisis before or during his tour. It is also likely that "at this time Nkrumah's sounder instincts warned him to consolidate his own position before offering an open challenge to Gbedemah, whose power he never underestimated". [33] This may be partly due to his appreciation that Gbedemah's "wings had been sufficiently clipped". Nkrumah decided to challenge the moderates after completion of his tour and assurance of Soviet support if the fight were to turn into an international crisis.

Events, however, did not move according to his preconceived plan. The strike in Sekondi-Takoradi had almost shaken the foundations of Ghanaian polity. The UP and the minor unions, who ignored the TUC leadership, joined hands to paralyze the country. They were supported by some *market-women* and the presidential commission, dominated by Gbedemah, was suspected of complicity. Nkrumah's militant supporters, who were with him during the tour, pressured him to dismiss prominent members of the moderate faction. The pressure was overwhelming and Nkrumah utilized the situation to rid himself of his rivals.

Naturally, Nkrumah acted swiftly to re-establish his power. First, he took a soft line to end the strike. When this failed to evoke the anticipated response, he threatened to use force. The strikers relented and returned to work. To protect himself from the army, with whom Gbedemah was reportedly plotting, he dismissed General Alexander. A week later he demanded the resignation of six ministers, including Gbedemah and Botsio. Gbedemah, after denouncing the government in Parliament, fled the country. Nkrumah had apparently no rivals.

The militants were jubilant. But Nkrumah was not. Though he outwardly kept his militant posture, Nkrumah stealthily moved to thwart the ambition of his new rivals. He did not like his reliance on the militant faction or its movements in the corridors of power.

Nkrumah sought to balance the groups within the CPP, not so much to achieve equilibrium, but to protect his flanks. In March 1962, he announced his willingness to admit former UP members into the CPP. In May, he declared a general amnesty to all former adversaries. Exiles were encouraged to return home and toil for the "Work and Happiness" program. The following month he released over 150 detainees, and the CPP press again appealed to former opposition leaders, including those just released, to join the CPP. The response was poor.

Nkrumah viewed Ako Adjei, the widely traveled leader of the militants, as his next rival. He reduced Adjei's effectiveness as minister of foreign affairs by slowly reducing his powers. Gradually Adjei lost influence, and even ambassadorial postings no longer came within his purview. When the Ghanaian ambassador to China ignored his directives, Adjei sought powers to discipline the ambassador. Nkrumah ignored him.

In August 1962, an attempt was made to assassinate Nkrumah at Kulungugu. He used it as a pretext to weaken the militants. The failure of his earlier appeals to entice the moderates, and continued terrorism, compelled Nkrumah to rehabilitate old stalwarts like Krobo Edusei, Botsio and N.A. Welback. Simultaneously, he used the columns of *The Spark* to keep them in line.

There was a third group, deferential and pliant — the faithfuls. It was led by Kofi Baako. He was one of the few who survived throughout Nkrumah's rule. Since this faction relied on Nkrumah for its survival, it distrusted other factions, which considered Nkrumah expendable. It never challenged Nkrumah's position nor did it attempt openly to subvert him. Nonetheless, towards the end of his rule, Nkrumah came to rely on members of his own ethnic group — the Nzimas.

Nkrumah began his assault on the administrative elite after assuring himself that the CPP was well within manageable limits. His initial distrust of the civil servants peaked in 1959, but then he conceived the police as their rivals. He found it, however, prudent to draft the civil servants in his fight against his rivals within the CPP. In 1960, he set up a presidential system with civil servants as its pillars. But he kept his options open by cleverly managing the senior officials by a judicial use of political appointees.

Once the civil servants had served his purpose, he turned against them. He compelled the officials to undergo ideological training, allowed the party activists, who were clamoring for rewards, to infiltrate the civil service, and introduced measures that affected the security and tenure of public servants. [34] The civil servants, who failed to cooperate with the CPP, were arbitrarily transferred to hardship posts.

The civil servants, for their part, did not fully cooperate with their political masters. They did not feel the need to compromise with the CPP because they "found it easy to get a job with one of the international agencies, or the United Nations itself". A demanding and self-recruiting elite group, that desired the continuation of the existing power structure, it scuttled the administrative orders unacceptable to it.

The judiciary, alone among the elite groups, enjoyed a long span of noninterference. But in December 1963, when the court acquitted the alleged "conspirators" of the Kulungugu plot, and that too without informing the president, Nkrumah struck back. Geoffrey Bing has argued that being a political trial, as in the colonial days, the government should have been informed "as to how it was progressing and given the opportunity to discontinue the prosecution if an acquittal seemed likely". The failure of the chief justice to forewarn Nkrumah was interpreted as a challenge to his position. He therefore dismissed the chief justice. The judiciary never recovered from the blow until after his fall.

The police too joined the fray. An attack by a policeman on duty at the Flagstaff House, in January 1964, was perceived as another challenge to Nkrumah's leadership. He dismissed the commissioner of police and nine senior officals. [35] The security arrangements were handed over to the army. But the new commissioner, a critic of his predecessor, could not have missed the consequences of such an act. His tenure of office was dependent on Nkrumah's pleasure, and he, therefore, had no hesitation in joining the organizers of the coup d'etat.

In 1965, Nkrumah set out finally to tame the military. His relations with it were always tenuous. He expanded the defense forces and insisted on their having all the branches — army, navy and air force. The interservices rivalry, he thought, would be to his advantage. During the Congo crisis, Nkrumah realized that his army officers were not pliant tools. [36]

Unlike some other elite groups, the army was always enmeshed in the political struggle. In 1961, Nkrumah dismissed General Alexander and eighty British officers before acting against the moderates. General Otu, the new chief-of-staff, was not an admirer of his predecessor. The president thought that this personal factor would help him. Simultaneously, to divide the ranks of the officer corps, Nkrumah sent a group of cadets to the Soviet Union for training. Naturally, this was intensely resented by the military elite.

The army had a number of grievances against the CPP. [37] It did not like the efforts of the party to politicize the army. It resisted efforts to induce army officers to attend classes at the Ideological Institute. The ethnic composition of the army officers, with Fantis dominating, betrayed a trend that was not reassuring. Nkrumah, despite his public opposition to tribalism, was not averse to exploitation of latent ethnic rivalry. The army could not tolerate the pretorian guard — the President's Own Guard Regiment — organized by Nkrumah with Soviet assistance. Afrifa, a leader of the coup, later wrote: "... the relationship between the President's

Own Guard Regiment and the Regular Army was far from cordial. Nkrumah was beginning to manipulate certain officers for the purpose of undermining the authority of the Military Command. The policy of divide and rule was actively pursued among all ranks of armed forces. It had become difficult to trust one's officer colleagues". [38]

The military elite was fighting for its life. [39] It feared the military intelligence headed by Colonel Hassan. His appointment "meant the introduction of informants into the army linked with the National Security Service system. The Officer Corps were made conscious that they were under surveillance. Each man became careful to guard his remarks in front of strangers". [40]

Then in summer 1965, Nkrumah dismissed General Otu and Ankrah, who later headed the National Liberation Council after the coup. According to Nkrumah, Ankrah was "lazy, incompetent and unreliable". Besides, both generals confessed to him that they had been asked anonymously to subvert his government. Nkrumah therefore felt that they should not continue their commands. The dismissal was, however, admittedly one of the immediate causes of the coup d'etat of February 1966.

The army also suspected that the change in the status of the Workers' Brigade was an attempt to create a "storm trooper organization". The brigade officers were sent to Ghana Military Academy and the Police College. As the brigaders came increasingly under the influence of the army, they even took to soldier's uniform. This unnerved the military. It averred that it had to fight for its survival and surprised Nkrumah by deposing him to protect its "corporate interests". [41]

Conclusion

The model has four concentric circles, alternating between governing and nongoverning elites and their supporters. Nkrumah occupied the center of the circle, the seat of political power. The governing elite, with all the advantages accruing from control of governmental machinery, sought to protect itself, while the nongoverning elite tried to displace it. The ensuing political struggle followed the exigencies of this conflict-coercion model. The pattern of "friends and enemies", alternating in the concentric circle of the elite described in the model, is substantiated by Nkrumah's domestic policies. [42] These were not unsystematic, fickle, unexplainable, or incomprehensible. [43] The conflict-coercion model presented above does enable us to descry a pattern in the Ghanaian polity. It must be conceded, at once, that the struggle among elite groups does not always meet the requirements of the model chronologically. Nor do the elite groups conform strictly to the pattern we have developed for analytical purpose. Consequently, the strategies adopted by Nkrumah to achieve various objectives did sometimes overlap. But there are unmistakable signs that the overall decision-making process had a *mandala* syndrome. [44] For example, during the first two years, Nkrumah destroyed the UP, and the next two years saw a swift drop in the powers of chiefs, entrepreneurs, voluntary organizations, religious groups, and the bastion of the intellectuals, the university. Between fall 1961 and 1963, Nkrumah subdued his rivals in the party, the civil service, NASSO, and the judiciary. The following year he reorganized the police, and in 1965, with a change in army command, Nkrumah came to believe that his control was complete and comprehensive. He expressed surprise when he was told of the coup.

Nkrumah was fascinated by political power. It was, as elsewhere, "surrounded by ideologies of legitimacy which adduce tradition, divine grace, or law in order to support the establishment at the top". The dramaturgical prominence of ideology only masked the reality of political struggle, unless one argued that "political incantation" has a role. Power, rather than ideology, is the key to the Ghanaian political process. Nkrumah used Marxism, according to Kojo Botsio, "largely as a directive — as a pretext — for increasing his power". "Comprehensive ideologies", argued Jack Goody, "systematic structures of belief, these are social artifacts of strictly limited distribution, both within and across societies". [45]

It is appropriate that we answer the questions we raised at the beginning. The relevance of political stability in the development of the model is obvious. Apart from the violence that accompanied independence, there were at least seven attempts on Nkrumah's life. Most of his political rivals considered Nkrumah a political parvenu. Since his rise to power was sudden and meteoric, they thought that he did not have deep political roots and therefore could be uprooted by the first adverse wind. Nkrumah in applying his struggle theory to ingroup-outgroup relationships displayed considerable dexterity. He saw that the choice before new Ghana was not between a single-party or multiparty state, but between a "one-party state and either anarchy or military regimes or various combinations of the two". Nkrumah made the obvious choice and this helped him to prevent the circulation of elites.

The other two questions we posed were concerned with personal ambition and political necessity. The dividing line between the two is obviously thin. Most students of Ghanaian politics have viewed — not without reason — Nkrumah as a vain megalomaniac, who increasingly betrayed a neurotic tendency towards the end of his rule. He had come to believe his own propaganda. He perceived himself as a product of circumstances, a child of the "revolution". "I am only the instrument of history", he once remarked, "not its creator".

This conflict-coercion model, viewing a political process from a specific angle, provides unity to the plot of the political drama acted out by Nkrumah. The hegemonical tension among the elite groups was the cause, rather than consequence, of the one-party State. [46] The decision-making process followed the exigence of this analytical model. [47]

NOTES

[1] David E. Apter, *Ghana in Transition* (New York: Atheneum, 1963); Dennis Austin, *Politics in Ghana* (London: Oxford University Press, 1964); Geoffrey Bing, *Reap the Whirlwind* (London: MacGibbon and Kee, 1968); Henry Bretton, *The Rise and Fall of Kwame Nkrumah* (New York: Frederick A. Praeger, 1966); David J. Finlay, Ole R. Holsti and Richard R. Fagen, *Enemies in Politics* (Chicago: Rand McNally, 1967); Bob Fitch and Mary Oppenheimer, *Ghana: End of an Illusion* (New York: Monthly Review Press, 1966); Roger Genoud, *Nationalism and Economic Development in Ghana* (New York: Frederick A. Praeger, 1969); Jon Kraus, "Arms and Politics in Ghana", in Claude E. Welch, Jr. (Ed.), *Soldier and State in Africa* (Evanston, Ill: Northwestern University Press, 1970); Peter Omari, *Kwame Nkrumah, The Anatomy of an African Dictatorship* (Accra: Moxon paperbacks, 1970); and Aristide R. Zolberg, *Creating Political Order* (Chicago: Rand McNally, 1966).

[2] James O'Connell, "The Inevitability of Instability" (*Journal of Modern African Studies*, V. 2, 1967), pp. 181–191.

[3] Gaetano Mosca, *The Ruling Class* (New York: McGraw-Hill Book Co., 1939); Vilfredo Pareto, *The Mind and Society* (New York: Dover Publications, Inc., 1935); R. Sharma Shastry (tr.), *Kautilya's Arthashastra* (Mysore: Wesleyan University Press, 1923).

[4] "In all societies ... two classes of people appear — a class that rules and a class that is ruled. The first class, always less numerous, performs all political functions, monopolizes power and enjoys the advantage that power brings, whereas the second, the more numerous class, is directed and controlled by the first, in a manner that is now more or less legal, now more or less arbitrary and violent, and supplies the first, in appearance at least, with material means of subsistence and with the instrumentalities that are essential to vitality of the political organism". Mosca, *The Ruling Class*, p. 50.

[5] "... Mosca insists that the contest for control is not between the many and the few but between one elite and another". James H. Meisel (Ed.), *Pareto and Mosca* (Englewood Cliffs, N.J.: Prentice-Hall, 1965), p. 3.

[6] Quoted by Rolf Dahrendorf, *Class and Class Conflict in an Industrial Society* (Stanford: Stanford University Press, 1959), p. 198.

[7] Pareto quoted by Meisel, *Pareto and Mosca*, p. 13.

[8] In his latest book Nkrumah refers to both Mosca and Pareto and dismisses elitism as the ideology of the bourgeoisie and holds that it was "tailor-made to fit capitalism". The book, published after the author had written this paper, hardly challenges the empirical evidence. Nkrumah's rejection of elitism is in line with the weight of the burden of his past inconsistency. See Kwame Nkrumah, *Class Struggle in Africa* (New York: International Publishers, 1970), pp. 30–35.

[9] Richard Wright, *Black Power* (New York: Harper and Row, 1954), p. 221.

[10] Apter, *Ghana in Transition*, p. 287.

[11] For various interpretations of the concept of circulation elites, see "Politics and the Circulation of Elites", in T.B. Bottomore, *Elites and Society* (New York: Basic Books, Inc., 1964), pp. 42–61.

[12] "The 'locational determinism' implied in Kautilya's Circle may need to be qualified and was, in fact, qualified in the *Arthashastra*". George Modelski, "Kautilya: Foreign Policy and International System in the Ancient Hindu World" (*The American Political Science Review*, LVIII, 3, September 1964), p. 555.

[13] Adda Bozeman, *Politics and Culture in International History* (Princeton: Princeton University Press, 1960), p. 123.

82

[14] "... those who belong to the ruling class begin to acquire a group spirit". Mosca, *The Ruling Class*, p. 68; "But unless such an assortment of persons (a class in a mathematical or statistical sense) also possesses the characteristics of a group with internal cohesion and a consequent capacity for acting jointly, it is hardly justified to speak of them as a political elite". ... and "The reason for Pareto's failure to develop significant insights is due to his not recognizing the cohesive group character of political or governing elites". Carl J. Friedrich, *Man and His Government* (New York: McGraw-Hill Book Co., 1963), pp. 315 and 319; "The political class, therefore, is composed of groups which may be engaged in varying degrees of cooperation, competition or conflict with each other". Bottomore, *Elites and Society*, p. 9; Nkrumah later admitted the role of groups and conceded the principle that interests, not ideas, dominated political activity. He wrote: "Usually, this ruling party is made up of several *groups* each with its distinct economic and political *interests*" (emphasis added). Kwame Nkrumah, *Handbook of Revolutionary Warfare* (New York: International Publishers, 1969), p. 11.

[15] "Plurality is the principal political problem of most of the new states..." W.A. Lewis, *Politics in West Africa* (New York: Oxford University Press, 1965), p. 66; "Ghana is not merely a plural but a segmentary society". Donald G. MacRae, "Nkrumahism: past and future of an ideology" (*Government and Opposition*, I, 4, 1965—66), p. 544.

[16] "Ideology and ideologists were thin on the ground in the CPP". Ruth First, *Power in Africa* (New York: Pantheon Books, 1970), p. 182. The only exception seems to be pan-Africanism. Nkrumah has been a consistent supporter of African unity. But his methods to achieve that goal were hardly uniform. On the other hand, Mr. Alex Quaison-Sackey told this writer that Nkrumah had, despite his vacillations, a deep commitment to uplift the "underdog".

[17] "Pareto does not dispute the social utility of ideals; he points out that they are irrational constructions on irrational foundations". Charles Madge, *Society in the Mind* (New York: The Free Press of Glencoe, 1964), p. 93. Ideology also can serve as a tool "to segregate and consolidate competing groups around rival ideas". Ben Halpern, "Myth and Ideology in Modern Usage" (*History and Theory*, I, 1967), p. 136.

[18] Giovanni Sartori, "Politics, Ideology and Belief Systems" (*The American Political Science Review*, LXIII, 2, 1969), p. 411.

[19] "Nor can the fact that some particular ideology is not explicit on paper prevent it from being one. What is crucial is not the paper, but the thought". Kwame Nkrumah, *Consciencism* (New York: Monthly Review Press, 1964), p. 59; "... Nkrumah had a brilliant, intuitive mind, but one devoid of fundamental orientation. Intellectually, he struck one as being a muddle of undigested traditions". William P. Mahoney Jr., "Nkrumah in Retrospect" (*The Review of Politics*, XXX, 2, April 1968), p. 247; "His is

a failure of intellect, not of imagination". Ronald Segal, *African Profiles* (Harmondsworth: Penguin Books, 1962), p. 237.

[20] "The first duty of a government is to govern. Hence the preservation of our internal security is paramount. It is imperative". Nkrumah, *I Speak of Freedom* (New York: Frederick A. Praeger, 1961), p. 113.

[21] See the statement by Mr. A.J. Dowuona-Hammond, the minister of education and social welfare, in the Parliament on 9 May 1961. *Ghana Parliamentary Debates, Official Records, First Series,* Vol. 23, Cols. 443–46 (Hereafter referred to as *Debates*); By 1964, the movement had over 3000 district centers to cater to its million members. See Ghana Ministry of Information, *Nkrumah's Subversion of Africa* (Accra-Tema: The State Publishing Corporation, 1966), p. 52.

[22] C. Lloyd, *Africa in Social Change,* (Baltimore: Penguin Books, 1969), p. 284.

[23] Rosalynde Ainslie, *The Press in Africa* (New York: Walker and Co., 1967), p. 63. "... no news medium within the country provides a vehicle for objective presentation of facts and the critical discussion of issues of public concern". W.B. Harvey, *Law and Social Change in Ghana* (Princeton: Princeton University Press, 1966), p. 321.

[24] For an analysis of the Workers Brigade, see Peter Hodge, "The Ghana Workers Brigade: A Project for Unemployed Youth," (*British Journal of Sociology*, XV, 2, June 1964), pp. 113–128.

[25] J.M. Lee, *African Armies and Civil Order* (New York: Frederick A. Praeger, 1969), p. 105.

[26] Mr. Komla Gbedemah told this writer, in a personal interview in Accra in September 1970, that the opposition gave Nkrumah the opportunity to employ draconian methods, which once used lingered to become a habit, later a disease.

[27] A shrine is a place where the individuals could ostensibly contact the spiritual world, or where a spiritual being allegedly makes its existence felt by mortals.

[28] "The Corporation took over from Messrs. Commonwealth Trust Limited, LACO and A.G. Levantis and Company Limited a total of 24 wholesales, 12 central stores and 74 retail outlets ..." Statement of minister of finance in Parliament on 14 March 1963. *Debates,* Vol. 31, Col. 354; By 1965 the GNTC had 207 stores, 52 wholesale stores and its profit, up to September 1964, was placed at nearly five million dollars.

[29] "There were 992 cooperative farms in 1964, 870 in 1965, and 504 in 1966". Jean M. Due, "Agricultural Development in the Ivory Coast and Ghana" (*The Journal of Modern African Studies,* VII, 4, Dec. 1969), p. 646.

[30] In 1960 Nkrumah, by setting up a secretarial pattern, downgraded the politicians. The 1961 budget was "more administrative than political in its character". His colleagues saw that "the new staff of the President and its administrative emphasis was an ultimate threat to their security and power". Lionel Tiger, "Ghanaian Politics and Social Change" (*International Journal of Comparative Sociology*, VII, 1–2, March 1966), p. 249.

[31] The international situation reinforced Nkrumah's domestic policy. His helplessness in assisting Lumumba, the role of the Western powers, the conflict between his generals and his ambassador at Leopoldville, and finally the assassination of Lumumba that killed his dream of Ghana-Congo Union, coalesced to compel him to alter his political stance. His attack on the West became bitter, and he was determined to eliminate the faction that was, in his opinion, sympathetic to it.

[32] Finlay et al., *Enemies in Politics*, p. 157.

[33] Colin Legum, "Socialism in Ghana: A Political Interpretation", in William H. Friedland and Carl G. Rosberg Jr., *African Socialism* (Stanford: Stanford University Press, 1964), p. 148.

[34] J.S. Annan, "Ghana's Brain Drain Under Nkrumah" (*Venture*, London, XVIII, 5, June 1966), p. 10. Some of them suspected that the Winneba Ideological Institute "was in business to train cadres politically loyal to Nkrumah and Socialism, who would eventually replace established civil servants and key workers in every segment of the Ghana economy". Ghana Ministry of Information, *Nkrumah's Subversion of Africa*, p. 44.

[35] Mr. Eric Madjitey, the leader of opposition in 1970, told this writer that as the commissioner of police he did try to "slow down" Nkrumah and all officers involved were trained at Scotland Yard. Nkrumah, he implied, wanted to eliminate British influence.

[36] Kwame Nkrumah, *The Challenge of the Congo* (New York: International Publishers, 1967), pp. 48–55; Though suspicious of the army, Nkrumah "cultivated the officers corps with banquets and other signs of anxiety to maintain their loyalty ..." William Gutteridge, *The Military and African Politics* (London: Methuen and Co., Ltd., 1960), p. 99.

[37] For a description of the coup and the army's case against Nkrumah, see A.A. Afrifa, *The Ghana Coup* (London: Frank Cass, 1966); A.K. Ocran, *A Myth is Broken* (Harlow, Essex: Longman, Green, 1968); Peter Barker, *Operation Cold Chop The Coup that Toppled Nkrumah* (Accra: Ghana Publishing Corporation, 1969).

[38] Afrifa, *The Ghana Coup* p. 100.

[39] Afrifa told Colonel Kotoka, another leader of the coup, that he may be removed from his command. Ibid., p. 41.

[40] Lee, *African Armies and Civil Order,* p. 67.

[41] Dr. Eric Nordlinger's argument that "the military act to maintain or increase their wealth and prerogatives" is sustained in Ghana. Despite the "shattered" economy, the NLC increased the ratio of the defense budget from 8.3 percent in 1965 to 10.3 percent in 1968—69 of the total budget. The NLC said that this raise was necessary to overcome past neglect and to re-equip the entire army to make it justify its existence. For Nordlinger's analysis of "corporate interest" see "Soldiers in Mufti: The Impact of Military Rule Upon Economic and Social Change in the Non-Western States" (*The American Political Science Review,* LXIV, 4, Dec. 1970).

[42] This is also true of his foreign policy. Ghana's alliance with Guinea and Mali followed Kautilya's premise that a neighbor is a natural enemy. Those who believe that the Ghana-Guinea-Mali Union had ideological foundations will be disillusioned to know that Sekou Toure and Madibo Keita were upset when Nkrumah paid a state visit to Upper Volta in 1962. See W. Scott Thompson, *Ghana's Foreign Policy* (Princeton: Princeton University Press, 1969), pp. 206—7; and also, I. William Zartman, "Africa as a Subordinate State System" (*International Organization,* XXI, 3, summer 1967), p. 556; Claude E. Welch, Jr., *Dream of Unity* (Ithaca: Cornell University Press, 1966), pp. 326—335.

[43] See Jon Kraus, "A Marxist in Ghana" (*Problems of Communism,* XVI, 3, May—June 1967), p. 42; Finlay, et al., *Enemies in Politics* , p. 163; Legum, "Socialism in Ghana", in Friedland, *African Socialism* p. 132; Zolberg, *Creating Political Order,* p. 98.

[44] Even his political techniques followed guidelines presented by Kautilya. Nkrumah did try to negotiate with the opposition, he did make some concessions, and only when he thought he failed, he resorted to repression with a muted mixture of cruelty and clemency. Finally, he sought to destroy his political rivals within the party through a policy of divide and rule.

[45] Jack Goody, "Consensus and Dissent in Ghana" (*Political Science Quarterly,* LXXXIII, 3, Sept. 1968), p. 352.

[46] It is possible to impute, as Nkrumah's critics are prone to do, causal significance to the converse of this conclusion. Nkrumah may have had a premeditated design to rule not only Ghana but also the rest of Africa. There was an incipient tendency toward a secret society called "The Circle" based on personal loyalty. It is conceivable that his dormant and cloaked desire for personal power was resurrected to match obtaining political conditions. Even if one were to advance such a hypothesis, the struggle in Ghana would still conform to the content of this model. It is likely, however, that it is basically a product of muddling through, fear and faith, indolence and improvisation, rather than conscious conspiracy.

[47] The developments since the 1966 coup support the basic hypothesis of the

model. The Second Republic was controlled by the non-governing elite groups of the model. The Progress Pary was known as the United Party. Its supporters in the fourth circle enjoyed considerable power. The traditional rulers played a significant role. The entrepreneurs were awarded a large share of commerce and industry through the Ghana Business (Promotion) Act, which barred aliens from operating in Ghana if their annual turnover was less than $500,000. The small businessman was helped by the ban on petty trading by non-Ghanaians. Though the relationship between the Busia government and the TUC was initially cordial, it soon deteriorated. In 1971 the government imposed the Development levy on all workers earning over $1,000 and the new Industrial Relations Act was rushed, under a certificate of urgency, through parliament to break the power of the TUC. The Sallah case betrayed the underlying tension between the judicial and executive branches of the government. The Busia government's concern for compatability perhaps accounts for 568 civil servants dismissed in 1970. Some police and army officers were compelled to retire. The military, once again, stepped in and took over the reins of government on January 13, 1972. See Valerie Plave Bennett, "The 'non-politicians' take over," (*The Africa Report*, SVII, 4, 1972), pp. 19–22.

Interest Groups and the Canadian Parliament: Activities, Interaction, Legitimacy and Influence

ROBERT PRESTHUS *

The following analysis centers upon the activities, frequency of interaction, legitimacy and perceived influence of interest groups and their representatives in the Canadian national parliament. [1] The concepts and language of interaction theory will be used to order data gained from structured interviews with a random sample of M.P.'s (N—140) in Ottawa. [2] An essential formulation of interaction theory, which seems especially useful in explaining the structure of relationships between interest groups and M.P.'s, holds that individuals initiate and sustain interpersonal transactions that prove gratifying. The currency which mediates such exchanges, including those between members and lobbyists, covers a broad spectrum of values, ranging through affection, empathy, companionship, information, influence, and money. Such values, it should be noted, include both personal gratifications and instrumental services. Interactions, however, entail both costs and benefits, and actors probably attempt (in varying measure and degrees

* This is a revised version of a paper read at the International Political Science Association Meeting, Munich 1970. It comprises part of a larger study entitled *Elite Accommodation in Canadian Politics.* New York: Cambridge University Press, 1973.

of success) to achieve a rough cost-benefit equilibrium. Homans argues, quite specifically, that interaction will not continue unless both parties are making a profit. [3] Interactions that are sustained over time are assumed to be mutually rewarding to the actors. One consequence is the reinforcement of shared values and interpersonal solidarity. In the context of this analysis, it follows that the frequency and continuity of such transactions should provide a value index of the legitimacy imputed by M.P.'s to lobbyists.

The issue of legitimacy, defined simply as the transformation of power and influence into authority, is central to our analytical focus, since it is presumably the marginal normative status of interest groups that explains the pervasive ambivalence often exhibited toward them and their attending definition (by some segments of the public, at least) as a structural aberration in some western democratic political systems. Even when interest groups are accepted as necessary elements of a representational political apparatus, the obvious disparities in their resources sometimes prove disquieting to some M.P.'s. Since politicians tend to be eminently pragmatic men, they are usually able to accommodate any resultant tension. Yet, some ambivalence persists. A rather tenuous distinction is sometimes made between interest group executives who direct an organization and spend only a small proportion of their time attempting to influence legislators, and *lobbyists* who are available for hire by any interest and who work virtually full time on its behalf. Another reaction encountered occasionally during our research was that lobbying just did not exist in Canada.

The historical and philosophic bases of this appreciation may reflect what might be called the deferential style of Canadian politics. [4] According to this rationale, political leaders, including the higher bureaucracy, define and seek the public interest without much need for explanation of their actions or for participation by the general public. In this context, any patent recognition that interest groups actively share in decision-making would perhaps seem incongruous. This particularistic definition of reality may possibly reflect the normative gratification attending any conclusion that one's own political system is ethically superior to others. In effect, we have here a culturally-determined orientation, semantical rather than substantive, which attempts to sublimate a process that seems functionally essential in any political system.

Fortunately, the operational consequences of the going normative appreciation are not decisive, as our data on legitimacy will suggest. Despite occasional protestations of political innocence, interest groups and their representatives systematically attempt to influence Canadian M.P.'s using the usual methods. Such behavior seems to be an integral and generally accepted part of Canadian political life. Most M.P.'s, it seems, trust most lobbyist most of the time. When lobbyists are criticized, it is usually for excessive kinds of behavior, such as bringing undue pressure to bear on a member, entertaining him too fulsomely, or giving him slanted or inaccurate information. One gets the impression that any antipathy expressed by the Canadian M.P. toward interest groups or their agents is often a conditioned reflex, based in part upon his estimate of the expectations of his constituents who are thought to regard them as somehow inimical to democratic politics.

Such conditions underscore the utility of the concept of legitimacy in the context of group influence. Interaction theory assumes that processes and institutions that enjoy normative approbation tend to be more effective, in the sense of validating social roles, and to have more stabilizing consequences than those which are regarded with ambivalence. As I shall show, most M.P.'s have considerable trust in the interest group representatives with whom they interact.

In effect, in using these concepts, we are trying to explain the interest group—legislative interaction process, and to suggest the significance of interest group activities for the Canadian legislative system. Such activities, which always occur between individuals, even if symbolically, may be conceptualized at two discrete levels — in policy and in individual contexts. The policy context refers to such functions as providing information, legislative support, advice on legislative strategy, etc. Individual functions include such particularistic items as friendship, campaign support, and personal services. In either context, and again following interaction theory, any consequences which prove gratifying to M.P.'s will tend to reinforce the interest group representative's [5] role by encouraging future access and interactions, each of which provides him a dividend in the form of an opportunity to exert influence or to create an obligation against which a future demand may be made.

Political Functions of Interest Groups

We begin by analyzing some characteristic political functions of private interest groups [6] in terms of their frequency and effectiveness. To determine the extent of interaction between such groups and legislators, the frequency distribution of contacts between the two are presented, as experienced by M.P.'s and controlled for party affiliation.

These data indicate that interactions are indeed extensive among all parties but that these occur substantially more often among members of the ruling Liberal Party who make up over 50 percent of the Commons. When the entire sample (N−140) is combined, we find that 70 percent of M.P.'s see interest group representatives frequently (twice a week) or occasionally (twice a month). At the same time, it is clear from the data that interest groups are selective in their contacts with M.P.'s (no doubt, the opposite is true as well). Interaction, as noted, is significantly more likely to occur at the frequent level among Liberals, is virtually identical among Conservatives and NDP, while falling off sharply among the rural, right-wing *Creditistes*. While it may be incorrect to imply that lobbyists always assume the initiative in such interactions, they do usually seek out M.P.'s rather than vice versa. The latter can of course avoid such contacts, but this does not seem to be the usual case. Members, with the exception of ministers, will, in our judgment, talk to virtually anyone. As other men, they are often gratified by the knowledge that their help is

TABLE 1

"How often do you come in personal contact of any kind with interest group representatives during the legislative session?"

	Liberal (N = 74)	Conservative (N = 43)	NDP (N = 17)	SC (N = 5)
Frequently	47%	37%	35%	20%
Occasionally	25	28	41	60
Seldom	20	28	24	0
Rarely	7	7	0	20

χ^2 = not significant at 0.05. SC: Social Credit Party; NDP: New Democratic Party

being sought. Moreover, the limited role in policy played by the typical back-bencher in the parliamentary system often means that he has ample time for such interaction.

Looking again at the *frequently* level, one finds a linear regression across the parties. How does one explain this condition? One fairly obvious hypothesis is that the distribution reflects the realities of political power: in effect, interest group behavior provides us with a nice index of power in the sense that groups mainly seek access at that place in the Canadian legislative apparatus where the authority and power to make decisions reside — among members of the ruling party. At the same time, the distribution in Table 1, which shows Conservatives and NDP receiving equal attention, may indicate that beyond this initial commitment Canadian interest groups do not focus on parties entirely in terms of their numerical and power position in the national parliament. In sum, it seems that a highly selective pattern of interaction occurs, especially when compared with the United States, where, because the individual member has more influence due to the separation of powers apparatus, the locus of interest group activities is much less differentiated.

We turn next to the characteristic kinds of policy functions carried on by interest groups. Although activities other than those presented here no doubt occupy some of their time, I feel confident we have identified their major activities. Because time is a valued resource for interest groups they will tend to restrict themselves to those functions that seem to be effective; and such functions are probably limited in number. Beyond this, we have data from M.P.'s evaluating the frequency, utility, and effectiveness of selected interest group activities. These will be presented separately, beginning with four services often provided for members and ranked by them according to their utility. Given the critical need for technical information and constituent opinions by M.P.'s presumably hard pressed by a large volume of legislation, the distribution of these functions is somewhat unexpected. Since their informal comments reveal that M.P.'s depend heavily upon interest groups for information on pending legislation, it is not surprising that they should rank this function first. It is unexpected, however, to find that *only* 40 percent of them do so, particularly given the range and technical complexity of contemporary policy issues,

TABLE 2

Utility of Selected Interest Group Policy Functions

Function	Proportion of M.P.'s ranking very or fairly important (N = 136)
Providing information on pending legislation	40%
Helping me represent all community interests	39
Giving attitudes of my constituents	28
Building support for M.P.'s policies	25

and the inability of members, as generalists, to develop expertise in more than one or two substantive areas. It is also not unexpected to find the rather diffused function of *helping them represent all community interests* being almost equally highly valued as a service, since, as David Hoffman and Norman Ward have shown, the largest single category (36 percent) of members have a delegate style of representation; this requires a knowledge of constituency demands, which, in turn, often emanate from interest groups. [7]

The substantially lower ranking of the last two items seems less problematic, and explanations quickly suggest themselves. In the case of building support, such help would probably have to be exercised through the party caucus, to which interest group representatives are at times invited, or through interest group representations to the cabinet and to committees. This kind of individualized support apparently occurs rather infrequently. Regarding information involving the attitudes of constituents, we detected a competitive reaction to this item on the part of M.P.'s which may account for their marginal endorsement of this activity. The M.P., in effect, tends to be jealous of the belief that he knows best what his constituents are thinking about political issues. Since his very being in office is regarded as conclusive evidence of this condition, he tends, it seems, to reject the contention that interest groups can provide him valuable help in this sector.

We turn next to several rather different kinds of interest group functions. These comprise what might be called the groups' tactical weapons, including joint lobbying by several organizations having a common objective; formal submission of briefs to cabinet and committees; personal interactions with ministers and their executive assistants; personal contacts with M.P.'s and higher civil servants; testimony before committees; and a rather more generalized function which we have called mobilizing public opinion. Much stressed by both M.P.'s and senior civil servants, this latter function may be conceptualized at one level as the labor-saving role of interest groups, whereby they hammer out a consensus on a given issue among their members, and this is then presented full-blown and fully rationalized to the cabinet, parliament or bureaucracy. M.P.'s often expressed their appreciation of this function, saying in effect, "We can't deal with hundreds of uncoordinated demands".

The mobilization function also includes the efforts of groups to build public support for such positions once they have been rationalized. Such support, of course, provides both a demand and a resource upon which a member can draw to support any position he may decide to assume in caucus or in testimony before committees. Even in the parliamentary system, moreover, a back-bencher must be prepared to articulate and defend *his* (i.e., the cabinet's) policy in his own riding. It is mainly in these contexts that the interest group function of providing support for an M.P.'s policy becomes meaningful.

The following table presents the first three among such activities, ranked according to their effectiveness as experienced by M.P.'s. Effectiveness is viewed from the standpoint of achieving the interest groups' objectives.

Here, despite the presumed dictatorship of the cabinet in vital policy matters, we find a fairly broad consensus (compared with

TABLE 3

Selected Interest Group Policy Functions, Ranked by Effectiveness

Function	Proportion of M.P.'s ranking first, second or third (N = 134)
First: Mobilizing public opinion	56%
Second: Personal contact with cabinet	23
Third: Appearance before committees	20

their second and third choices) among M.P.'s that public opinion remains a major factor in policy determination, and that enlisting it in their own service is the most effective weapon possessed by interest groups. This finding is all the more impressive since, unlike the other functions, it was virtually unchallenged as their first choice. It is possible, however, that M.P.'s were somewhat influenced here by a subjective preference that public opinion *should* indeed play the central role in policy-making.

Further evidence regarding the relative salience of the *mobilizing public opinion* function among M.P.'s can be gained by analyzing the distribution by party affiliation. One would assume that the parties would differ somewhat here, perhaps with the majority parties, which by definition have a larger base of electoral support, stressing the role of public opinion more than their minor party opponents. The data indicate that this is indeed so, with 60 percent of Liberal M.P.'s (N−71); 56 percent of Conservatives (N−43); 47 percent of New Democrats (N−17); and *only* 40 percent of Social Creditistes (N−5) choosing *mobilizing public opinion* as the most effective interest group function.

Another aspect of interest group behavior concerns the types of communication used in their interaction with M.P.'s. Such media include informal group meetings, appointments, social affairs, telephone calls, letters, formal committee hearings, and chance meetings. We saw earlier how often many M.P.'s interact with interest group representatives. Here, however, we are interested in another aspect of interaction, the imputed *significance* of the various media.

Formal committees provide the arena in which M.P.'s receive the most substantial evidence and argument supporting a group's

TABLE 4

Media of Interaction, Ranked by Significance

		Proportion of M.P.'s ranking first, second *and* third
First:	Formal committee meetings	41%
Second:	Informal group meetings	33
Third:	Social affairs and telephone	20

position. This may seem unusual in view of the well-known fact that neither standing nor select committees have been very significant in the Canadian legislative process, [8] yet it may be that the recent strengthening of the committee system means that briefs presented before such committees by group representatives do indeed constitute their best opportunity to influence policy-making.

Informal group meetings were ranked second, and it is clear from other evidence that ad hoc strategy meetings among M.P.'s and lobbyists who share similar views on an issue provide a significant means of group access into the legislative process. Social affairs, however frequently they may occur, are usually not the occasion for interest groups to seek to promote their goals. The underlying objective instead is to nourish personal relations to the extent that subsequent official interactions can occur on a friendly, first-name basis. Using a social occasion to discuss legislation or political issues is generally regarded as gauche, and may even backfire on the lobbyist who attempts to do so. Here, it is interesting to note that the interpersonal styles of interest group representatives and M.P.'s are rather similar; this perhaps enables them to achieve rapport with more felicity than men in other occupational roles. Both, in effect, are essentially persuaders, a role which tends to evoke similar definitions of situations and similar behavior in them.

We now turn to an important *individual* interest group function, more directly related to the immediate survival concerns of the M.P., as contrasted with his larger policy interests. As Max Weber pointed out, a political vocation includes men who live both for and from politics. [9] One of the most pressing of such concerns would be retaining one's seat, and interest groups would seem to be vital here in providing campaign support, defined to include mainly the contribution of funds. Table 5 indicates the distribution of opinion as to the frequency of such help. It should be noted that we did not ask members to respond in terms of support for their *own* party, but regarding interest group contributions to parties generally. The values *very common, fairly common,* etc. are subjective perceptions of the M.P.'s. The data are presented according to party affiliation.

Although the combined sample reveals that almost two-thirds of M.P.'s believe that interest groups provide campaign support only

TABLE 5

Frequency of Campaign Support by Interest Groups

	Party			
	Liberal (N = 74)	Conservative (N = 42)	NDP (N = 16)	SC (N = 5)
Very common	8%	7%	53%	0%
Fairly common	22	26	24	40
Infrequent	36	45	12	40
Rare	34	21	12	20

χ^2 = significant at 0.001.

infrequently or rarely, striking differences exist among members of the various parties. Liberals, Conservatives, and *Creditistes* generally agree with the above generalization, but a significantly larger proportion of NDP members maintain precisely the opposite, with over half insisting that such support is very common. Given other disinterested evidence, it seems that both perspectives may be correct. [10] For the major parties, campaign funds come mainly from industrial or commercial firms and individual businessmen. Strictly speaking, these are not interest groups, although they may belong to such groups. NDP candidates, on the other hand, are more likely to receive contributions from collectivities such as labor unions. Apparently, only the *Creditistes* have had much success with rank-and-file contributions. With the possible exception of the *Creditistes* the overall distribution suggests that members tended to respond to this item in terms of their own party's experience.

We next present data which specify other characteristic kinds of interest group functions, again in terms of their relative frequency as experienced by M.P.'s.

As the data show, the most commonly perceived activity is the tendency of lobbyists to work through sympathetic M.P.'s in order to broaden their base of support for a given policy or legislative measure. Although expressed mainly through caucus in the Canadian system, this tactic is a common political stratagem, especially since persuasion is the primary legislative style, and interest groups

TABLE 6

Selected Interest Group Functions Ranked by Frequency

	Ranking by M.P.'s (N = 127)
Persuading fellow members*	73%
Providing valuable policy support to M.P.'s	65
Providing indispensable information	63
Drafting bills	49

* The complete item reads: The tactical basis of lobbyists and the groups they represent is to assist legislators already on their side to do the job of persuading fellow legislators.

who seek to influence policy are, in some sense, outsiders. Penetration is thus sought through the efforts of sympathetic insiders. The process entails the co-optation of established organized resources, including access and legitimacy, in the service of one's goals. Thus the lobbyist's use of members in this role is merely one example of a generalized process, common to most self-conscious groups and individuals. Indeed, members themselves are skillful practitioners of this art, as seen in their cultivation of organized groups during campaigns.

The extent of interest group participation in the legislative process is suggested by the fact that virtually two-thirds of the M.P.'s indicate that providing indispensable information about and drafting proposed legislation are among the most common functions of such groups.

Interaction, Legitimacy, and Influence

As noted earlier, the theoretical framework of interaction theory, following George Homans, assumes a positive relationship among activities, interaction, and positive sentiments. The latter are conceptualized here as the normative equivalent of legitimacy. To Homans' well-known syndrome, we shall add another variable, influence. Legitimacy (i.e., positive sentiments that validate the exercise of power and authority) is conceptualized as a prerequisite of influence. We have documented the pervasive interaction existing between M.P.'s and lobbyists. The motives for such interaction include both self-interest and altruism. The resulting hypothesis is that such interaction encourages the exchange of values that inspire positive normative feelings (i.e., legitimacy) on the part of M.P.'s toward lobbyists; these feelings, in turn, tend to provide the basis for further interaction and increased influence among the latter. The essence of the process is apparent in Homans' proposition, "the greater the interaction between two persons, the greater, in general, the sentiments of affection they feel for each other". [11] To this one must add another well-established psychological principle: that all else being equal, men tend to repeat interactions that are experienced as gratifying, while avoiding those that have proved unpleasant.

In this context, M.P.'s and lobbyists may be defined as mutually dependent parts of the legislative system. [12] For purposes of analysis, we can think of them as a small group, interacting in a larger environment comprising selected actors playing legislative roles within an institutionalized framework of norms, traditions and procedures, in which the behavior of the individual M.P. is clearly prescribed. This small group and the larger system are also mutually dependent. Any dependence of Canadian M.P.'s upon lobbyists, moreover, is probably reinforced by the amateur tradition and high turnover (about 40 percent in recent times) characterizing the Commons. The extent to which lobbyists play a socialization role for new and inexperienced members is suggested by the high priority given by M.P.'s to such interest group functions as providing indispensable information (Table 6) and providing information on pending legislation (Table 2).

In order to determine the normative attitudes of Canadian M.P.'s toward lobbyists, and presumably, the interest groups that lobbyists represent, we begin with a single item measuring legitimacy.

These data, based upon responses to a single item regarding the extent of trust M.P.'s place in lobbyists, indicate that over two-thirds of Canadian members feel they can rely on lobbyists either all or most of the time. A sharp difference exists between the two major parties, however, with fully 80 percent of Conservative M.P.'s indicating a high degree of trust (i.e., all or most of the

TABLE 7

Legitimacy Ascribed to Lobbyists by M.P.'s

Legitimacy*	Ranking by M.P.'s (N = 133)
All of the time	19%
Most of the time	50
Some of the time	28
None of the time	3

* *Legitimacy* is defined here by responses to the following item: Some observers have concluded that relations between a legislator and a lobbyist are based essentially upon mutual trust. Regarding lobbyists you have known, how much would you say you could rely upon them?

time) in lobbyists, compared with only 57 percent of Liberals. NDP members fall between, at 70 percent. The explanation for this distribution is unclear at the moment, but it may be that the party in power (here, the Liberals) often finds interest groups a disruptive presence in a cabinet system which presumably insures them a decisive, virtually autonomous role in the determination of policy. Certainly, the fashion in which the government's tax reform policy (1970–71) has been sharply modified by systematic interest group opposition seems germane here. The generally high degree of trust across all parties may reflect a type of response-set whereby M.P.'s tend to think mainly of interest group representatives who share their own policy orientations, but this again is only speculation.

These findings raise serious questions about both the validity and the extent of the anti-lobbying attitude we sometimes encountered among governmental elites during the research. In order to probe this matter a bit further, it seems useful to examine the attitudes of M.P.'s on a number of single items regarding lobbyist and interest group activity.

These responses enable us to differentiate selected attitudes that characterize M.P.'s in their interactions with lobbyists and interest groups. In general, the valences are highly positive. Certainly, item 1 indicates an impressive consensus that both the role and tactics of lobbyists are generally acceptable. Items 2 and 3 suggest a

TABLE 8

Legitimacy Ascribed by M.P.'s to Selected Lobbyist and Interest Group
Activities

Activity	Proportion agreeing (N = 136)
1. Most legislators do not regard the activities of lobbyists as a form of improper pressure.	93%
2. Interest groups are necessary to make government aware of the needs of all the people.	85
3. The information and services provided by interest groups are a necessary part of governmental policy-making.	74
4. Lobbyists are competent professionals who know their business.	73
5. I can rely upon lobbyists all or most of the time. *	67
6. Lobbying as we know it today is healthy for democracy.	51

* Unlike the other five items, this is not verbatim.

widely-held appreciation of the functional role played by interest groups in Canadian politics. Presumably, this legitimation would have to accommodate the role of lobbyists as well, since they are typically the agents of interest groups. Only when we reach item 6, regarding the contribution lobbying makes to democracy, does the fairly consistent, although diminishing, scale of relative support decline sharply and only half the M.P.'s accept the generalization. At the same time, the invidious connotation of the term *lobbying* mentioned earlier is again challenged by the widespread endorsement of item 1. Perhaps the striking disparity between it and item 5 reflects the difference between the acceptance of a going norm (i.e., lobbying in its operational forms) and some ambivalence about its larger implications for equality of representation.

In the following table we test the assumed relationship between frequency of interaction and legitimacy, again using the item: Some observers conclude that relations between a legislator and a

TABLE 9

Association Between Personal Interaction and Legitimacy, by M.P.'s

Interaction	Ascribed legitimacy			
	High	Medium	Low	
Frequently	26%	44%	30%	(N = 57)
Occasionally	13	50	37	(N = 39)
Seldom-Rarely	11	57	32	(N = 37)

χ^2 = not significant at 0.05.

lobbyist are based essentially upon mutual trust. Regarding lobbyists you have known, how much would you say you could rely upon them?

Although the evidence is mixed, the data generally fail to support the hypothesis that interaction and legitimation are positively associated. The association is indeed strongest in the High column, with a substantially larger proportion (26 percent) of these who interact frequently also ranking highest on ascribed legitimacy, compared with the other two interaction categories. Overall, however, the data fail to reveal the expected linear regression in trust as one moves across the legitimacy scale. Using these data, at least, Homans' proposition that frequency of interaction inspires an increase in positive sentiments does not hold.

The final step in the analysis is to determine the relationship among interaction, legitimacy, and influence. We have found that interaction and legitimacy are not positively related, but it could still be that legitimacy and perceived influence are so related. It is important here not to leap to the conclusion that of course they are, since a moment's reflection will indicate that the association can be inverse, as in France and the United States among some sectors of the public. Again following Homans, we predict that a positive relation will be found between legitimacy and the influence imputed to interest groups by Canadian M.P.'s. The following data, based upon a legitimacy scale and the responses of M.P.'s to a single item measuring influence, provide some supporting evidence.

Here the expected linear relationship appears, with a strongly

TABLE 10

Association Between Legitimacy and Perceived Influence of Interest Groups, by M.P.'s

Legitimacy*	Perceived Influence**		
	High	Low	
High	84%	15%	(N = 33)
Medium	62	38	(N = 65)
Low	45	55	(N = 31)

χ^2 = significant at 0.01. Gamma = 0.44.

* This scale is composed of responses to the following items: Interest groups provide indispensable information for legislators; The information and services provided by interest groups are a necessary part of governmental policy-making; In a complex society like ours, interest groups are necessary to make government aware of the needs of all the people; and The activities of interest groups tend to increase political knowledge and participation among their members. The coefficient of reproducibility of this scale is 0.88, and minimal marginal reproducibility is 0.62.

** Influence is defined by the following item: Generally speaking, how influential would you say interest groups are in shaping public policy in this country? Response categories were: Very influential; quite influential (high); not very influential; they have little or no influence (low).

positive Gamma correlation of 0.44. We find a significantly greater tendency among members who rank interest groups High on legitimacy, compared with those who rank them Low, to perceive them as being High on influence; those who impute the lowest measure of legitimacy to such groups rank them lowest in influ-

TABLE 11

Association Between Legitimacy and Perceived Influence of Interest Groups, by M.P.'s

Legitimacy	Perceived influence*		
	High	Low	
High	82%	18%	(N = 35)
Medium	62	38	(N = 69)
Low	53	47	(N = 30)

χ^2 = significant at 0.02. Gamma = 0.40.

* Influence is defined by the following item: Members get valuable help in drafting bills and amendments from interest groups or their agents.

ence. However, our use of only a single item to measure influence makes it advisable, at the very minimum, to test further the relationship using an alternative indicator. This is done in the preceding table, using the same legitimacy scale.

Here again, the hypothesized positive relationship between legitimacy and influence persists, and the relationship is linear, significant and strongly positive (Gamma = 0.40). Nevertheless, both here and in the following table, striking differences appear when the parties are analyzed separately. Conservatives, for example, fully 80 percent of whom ranked high on legitimacy, rank lowest in perceived influence. Similar differences are evident in Table 12, which presents the relationships for all parties.

TABLE 12

Perceived Influence of Interest Groups, by Party

Party	Perceived influence			
	High	Medium	Low	
Liberal	63%	30%	7%	(N = 75)
Conservative	53	39	8	(N = 43)
NDP	86	13	1	(N = 17)
Social Creditiste	60	20	20	(N = 5)

Clearly, the perceptions of members regarding group influence differ dramatically across the parties, with a much greater proportion of NDP members ascribing a high level of influence to them, while most members of the major parties rank considerably lower. In effect, the expected positive, linear association among interaction-legitimacy-influence never appears. (It is interesting that the data show the expected positive association among the three variables for senior bureaucrats.) Conservatives rank lowest on interaction, highest on legitimacy, and lowest on perceived influence. Liberals, significantly highest on interaction, rank lowest on legitimacy, and midway on influence. NDP, narrowly lowest on interaction, is medium on legitimacy, but significantly highest on imputed influence.

Explanations suggest themselves: As the party in power, Liberals tend to be the main target of lobbyists; hence they tend to rank them quite high on influence, but low on legitimacy. The highly positive normative valence of Conservatives may reflect the Canadian organic, corporatist conception of society, in which interest group penetration of government is fully legitimated. Finally, the frustrations of minor party status and ideological heresy may evoke the NDP consensus regarding the powerful role of interest groups in the legislative process.

In sum, the expected relationships posited by interaction theory are only partly supported by these data. Only when the entire sample is combined do we find (Tables 10 and 11) a fragment of the assumed syndrome between legitimacy and influence. The inconclusive association between interaction and legitimacy is particularly unexpected, since this is a well-documented proposition. However, we are not only concerned with replicating such relationships; our major aim has been to present several empirically-based generalizations about interest group behavior in Canadian legislative politics.

Conclusions

Perhaps most significant among such generalizations is the apparent hiatus between the assumed marginal role and normative status of interest groups and lobbyists in the Canadian political apparatus, and the ongoing reality. Contrary to conventional appreciations, most legislators tend to regard interest groups and their agents as functionally necessary and normatively legitimate elements in the political process. Legitimation, however, varies dramatically with party: although two-thirds of all members trust lobbyists all or most of the time, Conservatives are significantly more likely to trust them than members of the NDP, who in turn have a significantly higher positive valence toward them than Liberals.

Although the frequency of interaction between members and lobbyists varies substantially between the ruling Liberals and the opposition, among all parties the intensity of interaction commonly ranges between the frequently and occasionally levels. Interaction, however, is highly selective, in that lobbyists focus mainly upon the ruling Liberal members, with interaction decreasing linearly (although minimally between the SC and NDP parties) across the Conservative, NDP, and SC parties. In this sense, the pattern of interest group access provides a useful index of power within the legislative system.

Interaction, moreover, is not positively related to members' perceptions of interest group influence; thus the ruling Liberals, who receive the major thrust of interest group attention, are actually less likely than the Conservatives and NDP to impute the greatest amount of influence to such groups. Similarly, interaction does not exhibit the expected positive association with legitimation. Further analysis would probably reveal that imputations of both influence and legitimacy vary according to type of interest group, but we have not considered this important question in the present analysis.

The most effective interest group stratagem, as experienced by members, is the mobilization of public support for a given issue. This activity provides a factual and strategic base upon which members can advocate a policy in caucus, in commons debate, or in their riding. Also highly ranked by M.P.'s is the interest group practice of persuading sympathetic members to intercede with fellow members on behalf of the group. In this way, a bloc of opposition to (or affirmation of) cabinet policy can be marshalled for expression in caucus. Interest group representatives may at times be brought into caucus for such purposes. Providing information on pending legislation is the interest group service most highly valued by members, and such information is most effectively transmitted by interest groups through testimony in committee hearings.

In sum, the evidence suggests that interest groups play a functionally essential and widely legitimated role in the Canadian political system, an appreciation that calls into question the conventional tendency to characterize them as both normatively and operationally marginal in the system.

NOTES

[1] This is a report of a segment of a cross-national analysis (1968—72) of

private interest group interactions with government in Canada and the United States, including some 2500 interviews with random samples of interest group executives, legislators, and high civil servants in three Canadian provinces (British Columbia, Ontario, and Quebec), three roughly analogous states (Michigan, Washington, and Louisiana), and in Ottawa and Washington, D.C. I am greatly indebted to the *Conseil des Arts du Canada* for funding this research, a full report of which appears in *Elite Accommodation in Canadian Politics* (New York: Cambridge University Press, 1973) and *Interest Groups in Politics* (forthcoming).

[2] For an early statement of interaction theory, see George C. Homans, *The Human Group* (New York: Harcourt, Brace and World, 1950), especially chap. 4; refinements appear in Homans, *Social Behavior: Its Elementary Forms* (New York: Harcourt, Brace and World, 1961), particularly chap. 4, and Peter Blau, *Exchange and Power in Social Life* (New York: John Wiley, 1964). For a test of Homans' major propositions, see Ronald Maris, "The Logical Adequacy of Homans' Social Theory" (35 *American Sociological Review*, December 1970), pp. 1069–81. In Europe, interaction theory was central in the work of Georg Simmel, *Sociology* (Leipzig: Duncker and Humblot, 1908), and *The Sociology of Georg Simmel* (Glencoe: Free Press, 1950).

[3] Homans, *Social Behavior: Its Elementary Forms,* p. 61.

[4] Although on the whole it seems to be less characteristic, such deference appears in the United States as well. For evidence at the community level, see Robert Presthus, *Men at the Top: A Study in Community Power* (New York: Oxford University Press, 1964). There, the community which was most homogeneous in socio-economic and ethnic composition tended to exhibit more deferential patterns of political attitudes and interaction, compared with a second community which was highly differentiated along these lines. The explanation seems to be that homogeneity provides a *Gemeinschaft* basis for mass trust in leaders and attending delegation of decision-making to them. In the past, the hegemony of British cultural norms may have accounted for the deferential style of Canadian politics.

[5] In deference to some ambivalent responses to the terms *lobbyist* and *lobbying* revealed in the Canadian pretesting of our interview schedules, we occasionally substituted the euphemism *interest group representative* for the term *lobbyist.* As the research proceeded, however, we found that both the terminology and the activity commonly known as lobbying were operationally relevant in the Canadian milieu. The study also raised a question as to the relationship between the roles of the executive director of an interest group and a lobbyist. Our research indicates that there is no uniform practice, but that permanent interest group executives often spent part of their work time interacting with legislators and higher bureaucrats. Some refer to themselves as lobbyists, while others indicate that their organization employs a legislative representative who specializes in such a role.

[6] Interest groups are defined broadly to include any private, nonprofit group, with a permanent executive director, an office, and a telephone. Our Ottawa sample, for example, included the following types of groups, selected from a universe drawn randomly from current telephone directories:

Type of group:	Percent	Type of group:	Percent
Educational	18%	Professional	11%
Social-recreational	15	Fraternal	5
Labor	15	Agricultural	2
Welfare	14	Religious	1
Business	13	Other	6
			(107)

[7] *Bilingualism and Biculturalism in the Canadian House of Commons* (Ottawa: Queen's Printer, 1970), pp. 66—69.

[8] R.M. Dawson and N. Ward, *The Government of Canada* (Toronto: University of Toronto Press, 1963), p. 380.

[9] "Politics as a Vocation" in H. Gerth and C. Mills, *From Max Weber: Essays in Sociology* (New York: Oxford University Press, 1946) pp. 86—88. Such a generalization must, however, be qualified in the Canadian milieu where politics (and perhaps administration) retain substantial residues of amateurism. As Allan Kornberg found, turnover in the Canada federal lower house in 1962 was about 40 percent, *Canadian Legislative Behavior* (New York: Holt, Rinehart and Winston, 1967), p. 38. Cf. John Porter, *The Vertical Mosaic* (Toronto: University of Toronto Press, 1965), who speaks of "the practice of avocational politics, where a stint in politics is an interstitial stage in a career devoted to something else", p. 402; pp. 398—415. On the other hand, Hoffman and Ward found (1965) that almost all the M.P.'s in their sample planned to run again, mainly because they "liked the job" (42 percent), "wanted to finish the job" (29 percent), or "wanted to continue serving the public" (25 percent), *op. cit.* p. 123. Although my own research (1969) did not include this item, among back-benchers at least, a certain amount of disenchantment became evident in our interviews, which would seem to support the high turnover interpretation.

[10] *Report,* Canada. Committee on Election Expenses, *Studies in Canadian Party Finance* (Ottawa, 1966), see especially pp. 232—78.

[11] *Ibid.,* p. 43. Homans recognizes that interaction can also inspire *negative* affects.

[12] My data indicate that precisely one-third of all Canadian groups have at one time or another employed lobbyists; the comparative proportion in the United States is almost 60 percent. Presthus, *Elite Accommodation in Canadian Politics.*

International Educational
Policy Outcomes

ALEXANDER J. GROTH and LARRY L. WADE

Introduction

This study concerns relationships among educational policy outcomes — as measured by school enrollment levels and teacher/student ratios — and two other variables: (1) types of political systems, and (2) levels of economic development.

The analysis proceeds as follows: some sixty-seven nation-states are examined along two dimensions of educational activity. One dimension is taken as a measure of the *quantity* of educational opportunities provided by different polities. Educational quantity is measured by five variables, each of which involves the proportion of various age and population groups enrolled in school.

The *quality* of education provided by different political systems, we presume, bears some relationship to student/teacher ratios. We assume that, other things being equal, low student/teacher ratios are associated with quality education. Four variables, each of which related to educational quality at different levels of education, are employed in the analysis.

Each group of nation-states developed for analysis has also been assigned an index number which represents its average per capita income as a proportion of per capita income in the United States.

This measure is referred to as the Index of Per Capita Income (IPI). [1] Our sample of nation-states has been grouped into the four political system types discussed below in order to permit preliminary testing of a variety of hypotheses concerning the relationship between and among economic development, political system type, and policy outcome. [2]

Our major assumption is that, while levels of economic development impose some, at least ultimate, constraints upon what particular societies might achieve in terms of educational outcomes, political regime types heavily influence the variance between the possible, minimal, and maximal outcomes. [3]

The classification of political system types (a) focuses on characteristics which could be reasonably expected to produce relatively coherent public policy outcome tendencies, all other things being equal, and (b) contains a reasonably large number of identifiable empirical specimens in order to facilitate significant comparisons. The four categories of political systems include two types of democratic polities. The first, Affluent Democracies, span a per capita income range from the United States to the Netherlands which has an IPI of 44. This group consists of fifteen national political systems. [4]

Our second category of democratic states, the Poorer Democracies, includes some much less affluent members of the world community, from Israel (IPI = 35) down to India (IPI = 2). This group is also composed of fifteen systems. [5]

Economically, these two groupings of states differ widely. Politically, however, they share some important characteristics. Both meet a criterion of "democratization" in two respects: (1) in the cross-sectional openness and competitiveness of their electoral processes, and (2) in the effective time-series parameter of that electoral openness and competitiveness. Thus, in both cases we have included only states in which free and competitive elections have involved substantially more than 50 percent of the male electorate, and where such processes have operated for at least a decade, so that one could speak here of "democracy" as being reasonably well-established. [6]

Regardless of the significant economic differences between these two groups of democratic systems, we expected that both would demonstrate a relative tendency to high educational out-

112

comes. We thus expected the disparity in the educational outcomes between these two groups to be generally narrower than
income differentials would suggest. Our assumption was that open
and pluralistic political systems would tend to register a high popular demand for educational "goods", notwithstanding economic
and cultural differences; and we assumed that this relatively high
and consistent demand would be reflected in the de facto allocative decisions of the respective systems. [7]

Nevertheless, we also assumed that educational outcomes would
be moderated in pluralistic systems by an interplay of effective
demands for other types of "goods" — public and private — such
as "equitable" taxation and sundry consumables. These considerations suggested to us that democratic educational outcomes, both
of rich and poor states, would be "high" but not necessarily "highest" in relation to economic development for all possible/conceiv-
able political systems. [8]

We also believed it likely that Communist political systems
would prove relatively still more "generous" in their educational
outcomes. Our category here consists of states whose regimes have
avowed themselves to be Marxist-Leninist. [9] In the case of these
states, our expectation of high outcomes is endorsed by a shared
ideological bias toward educational expansion. The Marxist-Leninist orientation would be predisposed to the creation of a "socialist
man", both for reasons of political security (insurance against
overthrow by reactionary bourgeois elements) as well as socio-
economic development (attainment of the higher phases of Socialism and Communism would require the training of new and larger
cadres). We expected not only that this ideological common de-
nominator would be evident among the Communist states, economic and cultural differences notwithstanding, but also that its
expression would be aided by the less pluralistic power structure
of societies ruled by Marxist-Leninist parties.

Our final category of political systems, the Autocracies, consists
of states which during the past two decades have not resorted to
open elections on the pattern of the democracies, a clear obverse
of the democratic states, but exclusive of Communist states. [10] In
a sense, this is the least exhaustive of our categories and also the
most varied. It includes oligarchical regimes which are innovative
and mobilizational such as Sukarno's Indonesia or Chiang Kai-

shek's Taiwan but also relatively traditional ones such as Ibn Saud's Saudi Arabia and Haile Selassie's Ethiopia. In this group, we expected to find the greatest variation in educational policy outcomes, partly because of the heterogeneity of political orientations subsumed, but partly also because of attendant distortions resulting from the "closeness" of these political systems. We presumed that given strongly oligarchical power relationships, dominant orientations, whether innovative-expansionist or traditional-quiescent, would be less likely to be compromised by effective opposition. With these general remarks in mind, we turn now to the system comparisons, [11] which are expressed in a series of summary statistics: [12]

1) The IPI average for each political system type.
2) $\overline{X}$, or the average proportion of age or population cohorts in school and average student/teacher ratios.
3) The standard deviations from the means of educational activity at various levels (s.d.).
4) The coefficient of variability (V), which expresses the size of the standard deviation *relative to the mean.*
5) The coefficient of income elasticity for educational enrollments, which expresses the relationship between differences in IPI and educational enrollments.
6) Spearman's rank-difference coefficient (r_s), which is used to measure associations between IPI and educational activity within political system types.

Educational Quantity

Enrollments

We turn first to the relationships between and among economic development, political system type, and quantity of education provided, and call attention to Table 1. For columns 3—6 of that table, which comprise different measures of educational quantity, the Affluent Democracies consistently produce more educational opportunities than do the Poorer Democracies, the Communist states, and the Autocracies. Among the Affluent Democracies, an average of 88.6 percent of children ages 15—19 are in secondary

TABLE 1

School Enrollment Comparisons for Four Types of Political Systems by Country Averages

	(1) IPI* (U.S. = 100)	(2) First level				(3) Second Level			
		$\overline{X}$**	s.d.	V†	r_s††	$\overline{X}$**	s.d.	V	r_s
Affluent Democracies	57.4	70.73	9.93	0.14	0.27	88.6	18.59	0.21	−0.18
Poorer Democracies	16.8	63.13	12.31	0.19	0.57	47.73	22.86	0.48	0.46
Communist States	15.5	78.00	7.88	0.10	0.61	37.10	11.41	0.31	0.47
Autocratic	10.1	40.86	18.73	0.46	0.60	24.43	18.74	0.77	0.70

	(4) First and Second Levels Combined				(5) First and Second Levels Adjusted for Duration of Schooling				(6) Third Level, per 100,000 Inhabitants			
	$\overline{X}$	s.d.	V	r_s	$\overline{X}$	s.d.	V	r_s	$\overline{X}$	s.d.	V	r_s
Affluent Democracies	76.87	8.56	0.11	0.10	88.00	10.39	0.12	−0.01	1065	663	0.62	0.24
Poorer Democracies	59.20	11.77	0.20	0.73	74.73	14.18	0.19	0.46	629	413	0.66	0.46
Communist States	69.00	8.59	0.12	0.80	83.27	10.56	0.13	0.48	931	165	0.18	0.44
Autocratic	36.14	16.79	0.46	0.75	45.95	22.16	0.48	0.74	201	162	0.81	0.63

* IPI = Index of per capita income.
** $\overline{X}$ = for first level, proportion of children ages 5–14 enrolled.
$\overline{X}$ = for second level, proportion of children ages 15–19 enrolled.
† V (coefficient of variability) = $s.d.X/X$
†† r_s = Spearman's rank-difference coefficients for per capita income and enrollments.

schools; 76.87 percent of children ages 5—19 at both first and second school levels combined; and 88 percent of age cohorts when adjustments are made for the duration of schooling. This performance is achieved with an average IPI of 57.4. It is interesting to note that in spite of a far lower IPI, the Communist states, with some 78 percent of age cohorts enrolled at the primary (or first) level provide somewhat more schooling at that level than do the Affluent Democracies. Nor are the Communist states far below the Affluent Democracies in adjusted enrollments, which take into account the actual length of schooling provided at the first and second levels. The index figures here are 83.27 percent and 88 percent, respectively. This comparison suggests, then, that the Communist states, with much lower levels of economic development, (1) outproduce the Affluent Democracies in the sheer quantity of primary schooling provided, and (2) do nearly as well, in spite of much lower *unadjusted* enrollments at the second level, in retaining school enrollees for the duration of the school program at both first and second levels. Indeed, although the data are not clear on this point, it may well be that the Communist retention rate is *much higher* than in the Affluent Democracies, a possibility suggested by the relatively low Communist enrollments at the unadjusted second level (37.1 percent) but the relatively high adjusted ratio for both levels of 83.27 percent.

Also noteworthy is the fact that, although the IPI's for the Communist states and the Poorer Democracies are approximately the same (15.5 and 16.8 respectively), the Communist nations enroll a greater percentage of relevant age cohorts on all measures, excluding secondary enrollments. The difference is particularly marked in higher education, where the Poorer Democracies enroll, proportionately, only about two-thirds of the average enrollment in the Communist states. The Autocracies, with an average IPI of 10.1, rank last in enrollments at all levels.

The association between and among the quantity of educational goods furnished in various political system types, then, is not a completely unambiguous one. The Affluent Democracies do outrank the economically less-developed systems on most measures, although not, as we noted, at the presumably important primary school level. And in spite of a somewhat inferior or, if one prefers, roughly equal, level of economic development, the Communist states consistently outproduce the Poorer Democracies in educational opportunities.

Variability

Perhaps of greater theoretical interest than average enrollment rates in various political system types are the coefficients of variability in enrollment averages, which are also shown in Table 1. [13] The table reveals that variability is lowest at the primary and third levels of education in the Communist states. The coefficient of variability is one measure of the consistency or inconsistency of the pattern of public choice settled upon in different types of political systems. The relatively small variability in the Communist states at the first and third levels suggests a greater consistency among political decision-makers with respect to those areas of educational policy than is true for either the Affluent or Poorer Democracies or, perhaps understandably, for the Autocracies. An anomaly in this pattern intrudes, however, at the second level of education where the coefficient of variability in the Communist states is 0.31 whereas it is only 0.21 in the Affluent Democracies. When enrollments are adjusted for duration of schooling, the Communist states and Affluent Democracies maintain roughly the same degree of variability. When we recall that the average adjusted enrollment rates for the Communist states and the Affluent Democracies were not greatly different (83.27 and 88 percent respectively), the similarity of the variability coefficients takes on heightened significance. What might be suggested is this: when school enrollments are adjusted, the *overall* provision of combined first and second level schooling in both the Communist states and the Affluent Democracies is not greatly different. But also, as it turns out, despite the variability of decision-making at the first and second levels of education *within* the nation-states which populate these radically different political groupings, *aggregate* enrollments do not vary more in the one type than in the other. In spite of different resource constraints and political systems, Communist states and Affluent Democracies produce strikingly similar average adjusted enrollments at the first and second levels of education and do so with about the same degree of variability within their memberships.

Consistency in the Communist states in the provision of higher educational opportunities is particularly apparent: $V = 0.18$ for the Communist states, whereas the next least variable systems, the Affluent Democracies, maintain a much higher variability of 0.62. In one sense, this finding is as expected. The Marxist-Leninist ideological emphasis upon skill, achievement, "rationalism", social, cultural and economic development, universalism and egalitarianism might be expected to lead not only to an emphasis upon educational activity — a fact reflected in school enrollments at all except the second level — but to relatively similar patterns of public choice in different Communist systems. This appears to be the case with a good deal of educational policy and, we suspect, may be true of other policy areas as well. Ideology may function as a tacit coordinating instrument which produces rather similar allocative decisions in Moscow, Belgrade, Prague, and other centers of Communist decision-making.

The relatively low enrollments in secondary education in the Communist states compared to the Affluent and Poorer Democracies suggest, along with the data shown in Table 4, that more restricted, rationed access to secondary education characterizes those states. This rationing process is more variable than in the Affluent Democracies, although considerably less so than in the other two systems. Taken in conjunction with the levels and variability of third level enrollments, it strongly appears that resource allocation to secondary education is very closely linked in the Communist states to the training of third level students. Thus, as shown in Table 4, the ratio of second to third level enrollments is approximately 4 to 1 in the Communist states, while it is 5 to 1 in the Affluent Democracies, more than 9 to 1 in the Poorer Democracies, and more than 11 to 1 in the Autocracies.

The Autocracies, as shown in Table 1, are characterized by the greatest variability relative to the means at all levels of education and for adjusted enrollments as well. Moreover, the variability is very substantial along all measures, a fact most readily explainable, it would seem, by political and cultural, rather than economic, differences. Historical, material, and cultural heterogeneity is great among these systems, and attitudes towards, as well as efforts in, educational policy might proceed with considerable variation. Such differences, then, apparently produce greater variability in

118

school enrollments than in the other types of political systems, which are politically more similar.

A likely explanation for the higher coefficients of variability — relative to the Communist states — at the second level of education for the Autocracies and Poorer Democracies is that there is greater diversity of political types, hence less unity of performance.

At the first level, enrollments vary less radically than at other levels among all systems, perhaps because of the well-nigh universal acceptance of *some* primary education in virtually all political systems. For all system types but the Affluent Democracies, however, universal education at the second level has not been even approximately provided. A widely varied pattern of choice is apparent in the Poorer Democracies, for example, which is not highly related to resources. Ceylon, with an IPI of only 4, nonetheless enrolls 78 percent of eligible age cohorts in second level education, while at the same time Colombia enrolls 23 percent, Jamaica only 22 percent, and Mexico only 21 percent. The Communist pattern, as we noted, is to provide relatively low levels of secondary education but to be more consistent in establishing similar patterns than all but the Affluent Democracies.

At the primary school level, the distributions of nation-states within the Affluent Democracies, Poorer Democracies, and Communist states tend to cluster in somewhat common ways around their enrollment mean. Autocracies remain more scattered. At the secondary school level, however, the political and social forces which work toward a common variability of provision at the first level are no longer operative except in the Affluent Democracies and Communist states. Demands, expectations, traditions, and other forces unique to the particular political systems within the typologies assert themselves.

For all system types, third level variability coefficients are in the predicted direction. The coefficients are very low for the Communist states, suggesting a remarkably similar pattern of decision-making and allocations toward higher education in those fifteen societies. The coefficients for the Affluent and Poorer Democracies are in the middle range and quite similar, which again suggest a pattern of policy responses which may reflect certain political similarities. The heterogeneity of the Autocracies is reflected in their high variability coefficient.

In addition to sheer quantitative achievent in school enrollments and the oscillation of regime types with respect to those
achievements, we are interested also in the provision of educational goods relative to economic development.

Democratic theorists have not only traditionally placed a high
value on education but have tended to believe that democratic
political systems are in some sense more responsive to the shape of
the social and economic universe than other kinds of political
systems. There is, it is suggested, a relatively close association in
democracies between economic development (a measure of what a
society is able to do), political demands (a measure of what citizens want to do), and those public policies settled upon by democratic policy-makers.

Autocracies, on the other hand, are often viewed as less responsive to the environment and more dependent in their choices upon
ideology, tradition, caprice, and arbitrary power. As a consequence, environmental factors should not, it is suggested, be as
closely related to policy outcomes as in democracies.[14]

In this connection, an examination of the evidence as it applies
to the four types of political systems surveyed here is most revealing. For what we have found is that with respect to the quantitative variables (and, as we later show, the qualitative variables as
well), such hypotheses do not seem to hold. At the first level of
education, for example, Spearman's rank-difference coefficient reveals a low association (0.27) between IPI and average enrollments
in the Affluent Democracies. [15] This correlation can be compared
to the associations at the same level of 0.57, 0.61, and 0.60 in the
Poorer Democracies, Communist nations, and Autocracies, respectively. At the second level, the correlations extend in the same
direction and range from −0.18 in the Affluent Democracies, to
0.46 in the Poorer Democracies; to 0.47 in the Communist states;
and to a very high 0.70 in the Autocracies. For the same groups of
nations, combined enrollments correlate with average IPI at the
0.10, 0.73, 0.80, and 0.75 levels; while adjusted enrollments are
associated at levels of −0.01, 0.46, 0.48, and 0.74. Higher education enrollments run in much the same direction: r_s is 0.24 in the
Affluent Democracies, 0.46 in the Poorer Democracies, 0.44 in the

Communist states, and 0.63 in the Autocracies. These patterns are both revealing and suggestive.

They indicate, first, that to the extent that economic development is associated with educational enrollments, the associations are closer in the *poorer* nations, regardless of political system type. Thus, in the poorest group of nations — the Autocracies (average IPI = 10.1) — educational policy outcomes and economic development are strongly associated at every level of education. Enrollments in the Poorer Democracies (IPI = 16.8) and Communist nations (IPI = 15.5) are moderately (strongly, in combined first and second level enrollments) associated with per capita national income. Second, associations between economic development and enrollments in the Affluent Democracies are weak to slightly negative at all levels of enrollment. Thus, environment and educational opportunity and policy are most closely associated in the Autocracies. It is also instructive to compare the Poorer Democracies with the Communist states. The Poorer Democracies consistently, if marginally (we would say insignificantly, if the pattern were not so uniform), maintain a lower relationship of economic development to educational enrollments for five of the six measures of enrollment. A possible paradoxical conclusion, in view of the conventional hypotheses concerning relationships among economic development, democratic polities, and policy is that not only may the hypothesis be quite wrong but that precisely the opposite may be true.

One objection to this finding is that measures of enrollment impose automatic ceilings on the relationship between economic development and policy. If most eligible age cohorts are in school in most or all of the wealthy democracies (or other systems, for that matter), increasing levels of wealth will necessarily produce lower resources to policy correlations. In part, this objection is quite correct. Yet, we should recall (1) that the wealthy democracies by no means produce universal educational opportunities, and (2) that no such automatic ceiling exists for higher education. Moreover, additional confirmation of these tendencies will be developed in our discussion of qualitative educational effort.

Income Elasticity

The coefficients of income elasticity for school enrollments shown in Table 2 express relationships between differences in average per capita income and enrollment rates as they exist in different political system types. [16] If we compare the coefficients at all educational levels for the Autocracies and the Affluent Democracies, for example, we find coefficients of 0.16 at the first level of education; 0.61 at the second level; 0.21 at both levels combined and adjusted for duration of schooling; and 0.92 at the third level. All of these coefficients are positive, indicating that greater enrollments are associated with greater incomes at all levels. However, the size of the coefficients varies substantially. At the first level, the coefficient of 0.16 suggests that enrollment differences are *not* highly related to differences in income between these two

TABLE 2

Coefficients of Income Elasticity for School Enrollments Among Four Political System Types, by Country Averages *

	First Level	*Second Level*	*First and Second Level Adjusted For Duration of Schooling*	*Third Level*
Autocracies/ Affluent Democracies	0.16	0.61	0.21	0.92
Autocracies/ Poorer Democracies	0.82	1.44	0.94	3.21
Autocracies/Communist	1.70	0.97	1.52	6.78
Communist/ Affluent Democracies	−0.03	0.51	0.02	0.05
Communist/ Poorer Democracies	−2.27	3.42	−1.22	−3.87
Poorer Democracies/ Affluent Democracies	0.05	0.35	0.07	0.29

$$\frac{\dfrac{\Delta R \text{ (difference to next level)}}{R \text{ (lowest enrollment level)}}}{\dfrac{\Delta Y \text{ (difference to next level)}}{Y \text{ (lowest income level)}}} = \text{coefficient of income elasticity for school enrollments}$$

types of political systems. The second and third level enrollments, however, *are* moderately to highly related to income differences.

More specifically, the coefficient of 0.92 indicates that, given a positive difference in per capita income of 1 percent, higher education enrollments differ at nearly the same rate, or 0.92 percent. The 0.16 coefficient at the first level, however, indicates that a 1 percent positive difference in per capita income is associated with only a 0.16 percent positive difference in enrollments. Similarly at the second level a 1 percent positive difference in per capita income is associated with a 0.61 percent positive difference in enrollments.

When we compare the Autocracies with the Poorer Democracies, we discover that the coefficients are again all positive but are consistently much higher than between Autocracies and Affluent Democracies. This suggests that relatively smaller differences in per capita income (from 10.1 in the Autocracies to 16.8 in the Poorer Democracies) are associated with much higher levels of enrollments than in the previous case. There is further evidence, then, in addition to the low rank-difference correlations *within* Affluent Democracies between per capita income and enrollments, that the Affluent Democracies have either saturated their populations with educational opportunities (at least at some levels), and/ or have decided that further investments in education must yield to demands for other public and/or private goods. Very great relative differences in wealth in the Affluent Democracies are associated with relatively small differences in enrollments, not only in this comparison but in others as well (as shown below).

Differences in enrollments relative to differences in income in the Communist states vis-a-vis the Autocracies are once again uniformly positive and highly elastic. The coefficient for the third level (6.78) is extremely high and points up the great commitment of the Communist states to higher education. In other words, a 1 percent positive difference in per capita income is associated with a 6.78 percent positive difference in higher educational enrollments! The coefficient at the second level (0.97) approaches unity and thus shows considerable elasticity in the supply of educational opportunities when these two systems are compared; the coefficient, however, is less than at other levels of education, pointing up once again the *relative* neglect of second level education in the

Communist states compared to their quite exceptional performance at other levels.

One of the more interesting comparisons consists of the income
elasticities for enrollments for the Communist nations and the
Affluent Democracies. If greater wealth in the Affluent Democracies is associated with greater educational opportunities relative
to the Communist states, that fact should be reflected in the ratio-
income-elasticities for the various levels of enrollment. Such, however, is not the case. At the first level the coefficient is actually
negative (-0.03) and is virtually nonexistent for the combined and
adjusted (0.02) index and for higher education (0.05). Only at the
second level are differences in per capita income associated with
substantially higher enrollments, where income elasticity equals
0.51. The influence of political, rather than economic, differences
seems to be overwhelming.

We may also consider the coefficients of income elasticity for
enrollments developed for the Communist/Poorer Democracies
comparison for the first level (-2.27), the combined and adjusted
index (-1.22), and the third level (-3.87). These indices point up
the fact that the somewhat higher average per capita income in the
Poorer Democracies is *strongly* and *negatively* associated with
their enrollments vis-a-vis the Communist systems. At the second
level, however, the situation is reversed − here per capita income
differences are *strongly* and *positively* associated with enrollment
differences. In other words, a difference of 1 percent per capita
income is associated with a 2.27 percent difference in first level
enrollments in favor of the Communist states. At the third level, a
1 percent difference in income correlates with a 3.87 percent difference in enrollments, again in favor of the Communist countries.
Yet, at the second level, positive differences in income are associated with dramatic and positive differences in enrollments. A 1
percent difference in income is associated with a difference of
3.42 percent in enrollments.

These very high coefficients at all levels − negative or positive,
depending on the educational level under review − indicate that
radically different developmental strategies in educational effort
have been chosen by the Communist states and the Poorer Democracies. These comparisons suggest once again that the resource
constraint is not always the controlling element in public policy
development.

If we compare the Affluent Democracies to the Poorer Democracies along the same dimensions, further evidence is adduced for the hypothesis that differences in income in the Affluent Democracies relative to the other systems have rather low enrollment elasticities, although they do remain positive at all levels. Again, this is in part a function of the already considerable effort made in this policy area by the Affluent Democracies, with the result that a move toward 100 percent enrollment levels is associated with a declining income effect. Very great increases in income are apparently necessary to produce small upward shifts in enrollments, a relationship which provides empirical justification for the enhanced importance of the substitution effect which we have presumed to influence wealthy democracies, particularly as their provision of public goods reaches high levels. Given other needs where the presumed social dividends from public and/or private investment or consumption may be considerably higher, marginal improvements in educational enrollments may not appear to be worth the cost. Even at the third level where enrollments need not be related to age groups, ratio-income-elesticity is only 0.29 between these two types of democracies. The substitution effect may be operative here also to some degree, although we would not suggest that the "market" for higher education is at all saturated, even in the Affluent Democracies.

Educational Quality

We turn now from a focus upon the provision of quantities of educational goods to a discussion of economic development, political system type, and educational quality, the latter measured by student/teacher ratios.

Student/Teacher Ratios

Although data for the pre-primary level of education are somewhat fragmentary (as shown in Table 3) and must be used with even more than normal caution, they do show that the Communist states, in spite of an average IPI much below the Affluent Democracies, provide approximately 1 teacher for every 22 children

TABLE 3

Student/Teacher Comparisons for Four Types of Political Systems by Country Averages

	(1) IPI (U.S. = 100)	(2) Pre-primary				(3) First Level			
		$\bar{X}$	s.d.	V	r_s	$\bar{X}$	s.d.	V	r_s
Affluent Democracies	57.4	37.25[1]	12.64	0.34	−0.38	25.38	4.6	0.18	0.32
Poorer Democracies	16.8	32.53[2]	8.85	0.27	0.40	31.21	9.75	0.31	0.35
Communist States	15.5	21.68	6.10	0.28	0.80	26.56	3.64	0.14	0.54
Autocracies	10.1	39.61[3]	18.84	0.48	0.31	37.40	9.75	0.26	0.44

	(4) Second Level				(5) Third Level			
	$\bar{X}$	s.d.	V	r_s	$\bar{X}$	s.d.	V	r_s
Affluent Democracies	16.73	4.44	0.27	0.13	13.37	8.52	0.64	0.22
Poorer Democracies	17.41	6.17	0.35	0.54	12.78	5.13	0.40	0.45
Communist States	20.48	4.61	0.23	0.42	13.23	5.42	0.41	0.43
Autocracies	21.86	6.60	0.30	0.33	13.06	6.60	0.51	0.62

[1] Excludes U.S., Switzerland, Denmark, Australia, and West Germany.
[2] Excludes Ireland, Uruguay, Lebanon, and India.
[3] Excludes South Africa, Nicaragua, Saudi Arabia, Iran, Pakistan, South Vietnam, Nepal, Haiti, Burma, Afghanistan, and Ethiopia.
Note: See Table 1 for explanation of symbols.

enrolled, compared to a ratio of 1 to 37 in the Affluent Democracies. The structure of the Communists' economies, proportion of mothers in the labor force, the emphasis upon female emancipation from traditional roles, and the importance of the collective, all might be expected to lead to a qualitative emphasis upon pre-primary education. At this particular level, and even given the poor quality of the data, there seems to be a clear and important influence of political system characteristics upon the quality of educational goods.

The Poorer Democracies, however, also maintain a somewhat better qualitative performance (with a ratio of 1 teacher to 33 children) than do the Affluent Democracies, while the Autocracies (with a ratio of 1 teacher to 40 children) rank lowest.

At the first level of education, the Communist states again maintain relatively low student/teacher ratios, although at this point the Affluent Democracies appear to place a similar value upon educational quality. Since the Communist nations actually outperform the Affluent Democracies in first level enrollments in spite of a much lower average IPI, there seems little question that the Communist nations make a much greater relative effort, in both quantitative and qualitative terms, than do the rich democracies. The Poorer Democracies, although as developed economically as the Communist states, are below them in student/teacher ratios at the first level. The Autocracies remain relatively low in quality at this level, just as they were relatively low in enrollment rates. Still, with an average IPI of only 10.1, their 1 teacher to 37 children ratio suggests that even they are concerned to maintain a not inconsiderable level of educational quality.

When student/teacher ratios are examined at the second level, Table 3 shows that the Affluent and Poorer Democracies provide 1 teacher for every 17 students in spite of the much lower IPI for the latter group. And while the Autocracies again rank last among the four systems, they are only marginally below the Communist states. Important but apparently not great differences exist among the four types of systems in teacher/student ratios at the second level.

In the same vein, it will be recalled that enrollments at the second level in the Poorer Democracies exceed those of the Communist nations. Judging from enrollment ratios, secondary education in all but the wealthiest nations remains an elite activity. Luxembourg, for example, has the *lowest* rate for the Affluent Democracies with 65 percent of age cohorts enrolled, while Poland, with 62 percent enrolled, is *highest* among the Communist nations. Taiwan, with 58 percent of age cohorts enrolled, far outperforms all other Autocracies and, among the Poorer Democracies (and in spite of such deviant cases as Ceylon, where 78 percent of age cohorts are enrolled), the average enrollment rate is only 47.73 percent. Access to secondary education is not only relatively restricted in all but the wealthiest states, but, as we have said, quality as measured here is surprisingly uniform across the whole span of types of nation-states. *Mass* secondary education in the Affluent Democracies is associated with quality education as measured by student/teacher ratios. *Elite* secondary education in the other types of political systems has, in the Poorer Democracies, about the same degree of educational quality and, for the Communist states and Autocracies, a lesser — but not greatly so — level of quality as measured here.

Student/teacher ratios at the third, or advanced, level are both striking and unexpected, for there is no significant difference among *any* of the types of political systems; all provide 1 instructor for approximately 13 students. This similarity is conceivably an artifact of the nature of higher education; that is, the very character of advanced scholarship and training may impose such requirements, for reasons yet unclear, on all social systems no matter how varied they otherwise are. This possibility, however, is not persuasive to us. It is more likely, perhaps, that higher education remains a relatively elitist undertaking in *all* types of political systems and that qualitative provisions, again as measured here, reflect this fact.

Variability

This conclusion is bolstered by the coefficients of variability computed for student/teacher ratios for higher education in the various system types, also shown in Table 3. It is interesting that V is 0.51 in the Autocracies, while it is greater in the Affluent Democracies where V is 0.64 (which would be reduced considerably if the U.S. were excluded). The Poorer Democracies and the Communist states maintain still less variability. These measures of variability are not, however, dispersed very remarkably and suggest again that in higher education similar variability of choice exists concerning at least some important aspects of education, not only *within* types of political systems, but *among* those types as well.

The clusters about the means and the means themselves are not greatly different, regardless of political and economic differences.

Most interesting, perhaps, is that the coefficients of variability in Table 3 show that all four political system types perform more variably at succeeding stages of education, from the primary through the third level. Thus, a greater range of discretion exists within the national systems that populate each type at increased levels of education.

For all systems, variability is least in the Communist states at the first and second levels, pointing up once again the relatively similar structure of public choices in those states, a consistency which we can only impute to political and ideological similarities.

Variability is next lowest in the Affluent Democracies for those levels, as expected. An anomaly of some importance appears relative to the Poorer Democracies and the Autocracies; at both the first and second levels, variability is less in the Autocracies than in the Poorer Democracies in student/teacher ratios. Of the nine quantitative and qualitative variables, however, greater variability is found in the Autocracies than in the Poorer Democracies. The greater variability in first level education in the Poorer Democracies is explained in part by the relatively high student/teacher ratios in Mexico (47 students per teacher) and Jamaica (57 students per teacher). With IPI's of 15 and 13 respectively, these performances are not attributable to the resource constraint. Similar variations exist at the second level and are best explained in terms of particularistic political and social factors operating within the rough parameters of the Poorer Democracies as a regime type.

Economic Development

Table 3 shows the relationships of economic development to student/teacher ratios in the four political system types. If the rank-difference coefficients of association are examined, they show that, among the Affluent Democracies — which range from 44 to 100 in IPI — r_s is consistently low at all levels: -0.38 at the pre-primary level; 0.32 at the first level; 0.13 at the second level; and 0.22 for higher education. In other words, knowledge of economic development in a particular member of the Affluent Democracies would not allow one to predict with any measure of accuracy that country's ranking in providing faculty/student ratios at any level of education.

If we consider the Poorer Democracies, we find consistently higher degrees of association between resources and educational quality, even though the associations (established at the various educational levels at 0.40, 0.35, 0.54, 0.45) while important, are not strikingly close at any but perhaps the second level.

In the Communist states there is an impressive r_s of 0.80 at the pre-primary level — suggesting that Communist regimes respond rather predictably in improving pre-primary quality as resources become available. A moderately high association (0.54) exists among the same states in quality of primary schooling, and lesser associations, though no doubt meaningful, of 0.42 and 0.43 for the second and third levels, respectively.

Among the Autocracies, r_s reaches a quite high value of 0.62 for higher education. Associations are lower for the other levels: 0.44 at the first level and only 0.31 and 0.33 for the pre-primary and second levels, respectively.

If the coefficients of correlation for each level are summed and averaged for each political system type, a rough summary index relating resource constraints to educational quality is secured. The summary index of correlation for the Affluent Democracies is 0.08; for the Poorer Democracies, 0.43; for the Communist states, 0.55; and for the Autocracies, 0.42. Thus, while educational policy in the areas of teacher/student ratios is not highly associated with resource availability in any groups of states except in specific and limited cases, resources do have a discernible and moderate association with policy in all but the Affluent Democracies. The Communist nations, with a summary index of 0.55, perhaps surprisingly in view of some theories of democracy, are apparently influenced more in this policy area by economic development than any other system type. Again, and inconsistently with some democratic theory, the Autocracies, where environmental influences are supposedly less, generate educational policy in this area which is as much related to the environment as in the Poorer Democracies. From this perspective it appears that economic development is not closely, in some cases not even meaningfully, related to at least this policy outcome when gross controls are used for political system type.

For the Affluent Democracies, the substitution effect discussed earlier may well have come into play in this policy area. The nondemocratic polities in the Communist and Autocratic regime types, however, are as closely (or loosely) connected to economic development in this area as are the Poorer Democracies. The moderate relationships between economic development and student/teacher ratios suggest, then, that national political systems have considerable autonomy, over and above resource constraints, in providing one aspect of quality education. Public choices seem to be highly dependent upon political and other noneconomic factors.

Reporting by Populations

An alternative set of comparisons can be made by reporting income and educational data by the entire populations within each of the four types of political systems. Heretofore, of course, data were reported state-by-state and aggregated to arrive at summary indices for the political system types. How will these comparisons be affected, then, if national boundaries are analytically dissolved within the political system types and if we consider income, enrollment, and teacher/student data by entire combined populations within those types?

Table 4 reports per capita income as a percent of the United

TABLE 4

School Enrollments as Percent of Total Populations in Four Types of Political Systems

	IPI	Pre-primary	First level	Second Level	Third Level	Total population in School
fluent mocracies	72.01	1.49%	12.66%	7.63%	1.50%	23.3%
orer mocracies	8.98	1.82	9.88	4.08	0.42	16.2
mmunist tes	11.27	0.89	14.23	2.26	0.54	17.9
tocracies	5.22	0.32	8.61	1.89	0.17	11.0

States average and enrollment percentages by entire populations within the four groups of political systems.

The table shows (1) that for the Affluent Democracies, average per capita income increases to 72 percent of the U.S. level, compared to 57.4 for the state-by-state average. In large part, this is explained by the large population of the United States relative to the other nations within the grouping. (2) For the Poorer Democracies, average per capita income falls from 16.8 of the U.S. level to 8.98. This effect is due largely to the vast size of India's population (without India, average per capita income for the entire population of the Poorer Democracies is 21.32 of the U.S. average). (3) For the combined populations of the Communist states, average per capita income is 11.27, a decline from 15.5 in the state-by-state averages. This effect is due largely to the small per capita income of China (excluding China, per capita income is 25.6 of the U.S. level). (4) For the Autocracies, per capita income for the combined populations is 5.22 of the American figure, a fall from the state-by-state averages of 10.1. This effect is produced mainly by the large populations of Pakistan and Indonesia.

Considerable changes thus occur when population rather than country income averages are computed. Rank-order differences are also effected. The gap between the population in the Affluent Democracies and the other groups widens and, although they remain at roughly similar income levels, the Poorer Democracies are now somewhat below the level of the Communist population in average income.

The rank-order of the first level enrollments, however, is unchanged and the proportion of the combined Communist population in primary schools remains the highest of the political groupings. Nor do new ranks develop at the second level — the Affluent Democracies still lead in enrollments, followed by the Poorer Democracies, the Communist countries, and the Autocracies. The third level enrollment data are also in the same order as formerly.

These population comparisons, therefore, provide an additional vector from which to examine the income/enrollment patterns as developed through the state-by-state aggregations within political types. The main outlines of the state-by-state comparisons are similar to comparisons for entire combined populations. Most differences are not a function of any national differences that may

TABLE 5

Coefficients of Income Elasticity for School Enrollments for Combined Populations Among Four Types of Political Systems

	Pre-Primary	First Level	Second Level	Third Level	Percent of Total Population in School
Autocracies/Affluent Democracies	0.29	0.04	0.23	0.61	0.09%
Autocracies/Poorer Democracies	6.51	0.20	1.61	2.04	0.66
Autocracies/Communist	1.54	0.56	0.17	1.88	0.54
Communist/Affluent Democracies	0.13	−0.02	0.44	0.33	0.06
Poorer Democracies/Communist	−2.0	1.73	−1.75	1.12	0.42
Poorer Democracies/Affluent Democracies	2.03	0.40	0.12	0.37	0.06

exist within the political system types. This is not to say, however, that such shifts as there are within the pattern previously developed are unimportant. Indeed, some important changes do occur using this alternative reporting system. Consider, for example, the effect of the income shifts upon enrollments for entire political groupings.

Turning first to the total combined populations within Autocratic regimes and the populations of the Affluent Democracies, the coefficients of income elasticity for enrollments (Table 5) are 0.29 at the pre-primary level; 0.04 at the first level; 0.23 at the second level; and 0.61 at the third level of education. In terms of total proportion of populations in school, income elasticity reaches only 0.09. Thus, for every positive difference in per capita income of 1 percent, total school enrollments are characterized by only a 0.09 percent difference in the Affluent Democracies relative to the Autocracies.

133

Income elasticity for enrollments at the first level has declined relative to the coefficient of 0.16 for the country comparisons. The coefficient for the second level also declines, from 0.61 to 0.23. The coefficient for higher education falls from 0.92 to 0.61. In short, the population reporting system suggests that enrollments are associated somewhat less with income differences than they are when the state-by-state analysis is used.

Population comparisons between the Autocratic and Poorer Democratic systems show a very high income elasticity for enrollments of 6.51 at the pre-primary level (data for this level are fragmentary, as reported in Table 3); 0.20 at the first level; 1.61 at the second level; and 2.04 at the third level. There is then, using this system of comparison, a drop in income elasticity for enrollments at the first level, an increase at the second level, and a decrease at the third level, compared to the elasticities for the national averages. With the exception of first level enrollments the coefficients remain high, however. Overall, educational enrollments in Poorer Democracies considered by population totals are highly associated with differences in income relative to the Autocratic systems. For every 1 percent increase in income, there is a positive difference in school enrollments of 0.66 percent.

Turning to the population comparisons for the Autocratic and Communist systems, changes of an interesting sort occur relative to the national comparisons. First, it may be noted that income elasticity for enrollments at the pre-primary level is 1.54, which would seem high until compared to the Poorer Democracies' coefficient of 6.51 vis-a-vis the Autocracies. The coefficient at the first level falls from 1.7 to a still substantial but much smaller 0.56; at the second level, a decline from a coefficient of 0.97 to 0.17 occurs; and at the third level, the income elasticity coefficient falls from a very high 6.78 to a still high but relatively much smaller 1.88. Income elasticity for enrollments is quite high overall, although somewhat lower than for the Poorer Democracies.

Comparisons with respect to the Communist and Affluent Democracies return to the pattern revealed in the state-by-state comparisons. Only at the third level do the Affluent Democracies appear somewhat more responsive to income changes than was true for the country analysis: the coefficient increases from 0.05 to 0.33. Changes in total school enrollments in the Affluent

Democracies occur at the rate of 6 percent for every 100 percent difference in per capita income — the supply of total educational opportunities is apparently relatively inelastic, or resistant to changes in income levels.

In the case of the Poorer Democracies and the Communist systems, a large negative coefficient (-2.0) obtains at the first level, an unexpected finding that may be due to data gaps rather than real differences. Of greater importance, perhaps, is the fact that at all other levels of education, the signs of the coefficients developed in the country-based analysis are reversed. This is due in part to the fact that per capita income in the Communist populations somewhat exceeds the Poorer Democracies, while the opposite was true in the state-by-state comparisons. Nonetheless, the reversal in signs is both substantial and unexpected.

We have also computed, as shown in Table 6, the student/teacher ratios for entire populations within the four political groupings, computations that can be compared to the ratios developed by aggregating national averages.

By examining pre-primary student/teacher ratios developed for total populations, and comparing them with the country-based ratios, we find that, although the rank-order of performance remains the same, changes of some magnitude in specific values are found. In part, these changes may be attributed to the fragmentary character of the data, but to some extent the changes are real ones. In the Affluent Democracies, the ratio increases from 1 teacher to 37 students (country comparison) to 1 teacher to 43 students (population comparison). Increases are also registered in the Autocracies. Substantial decreases in the Communist systems occur, however (and here the data are quite complete). Declines of some importance also occur in the Poorer Democracies' student/teacher ratios.

The first level student/teacher ratios developed by populations relative to the national averages, differ only slightly in absolute value, although in the case of the Affluent Democracies the change is sufficient to alter the rank-order of political groupings. Using this approach, the Communist populations now outperform the Affluent Democracies qualitatively and, as we will recall, quantitatively as well, at this level.

For second level general education, the rank-order shifts some-

TABLE 6

Student/Teacher Ratios for Four Types of Political Systems by Population

	IPI (U.S. = 100)	Pre-Primary	First Level	Second Level			Third Level	All Categories Combined
				General	Voca-tional	Teacher Training		
Affluent Democracies	72.01	43.03	27.62	18.60	20.02	10.07	13.12	22.72
Poorer Democracies	8.98	28.14	29.83	17.49	15.10	11.90	12.89	25.28
Communist States	11.27	15.29	26.30	19.39	21.13	16.10	16.44	22.60
Autocracies	5.22	46.26	37.95	25.57	16.14	13.82	16.82	33.48

what from that found in the country comparisons although the absolute changes in magnitude are relatively small.

For second level general education, the rank-order shifts somewhat from that found in the country comparisons although the absolute changes in magnitude are relatively small.

Third level student/teacher ratios organized by populations rather than national averages change sufficiently to produce slight alterations in the rank-orders developed in the state-by-state comparisons. More impressive, however, is that, for all political system types, the ratios appear to remain reasonably small (testifying once again to the relatively uniform structure of higher education across the whole range of political systems and populations). Both the Communist states' and Autocracies' populations, however, are characterized by larger ratios than revealed in the state-by-state analysis. Viewed from this perspective, the performance of the Communist systems in higher education may be somewhat less spectacular, although still most impressive, in the over-view than indicated by some other measures.

Conclusion

Clearly, many other indices of educational quality and quantity need to be carefully examined before we can conclude that the relationships explored here describe accurately the relative impact of political and economic factors on educational outcomes around the world. There is also need for refinement of the political variables and for more complex measures of socio-economic "background" variables, and for longitudinal as well as cross-sectional analyses.

The findings advanced in this paper are suggestive, however, of needed changes and improvements in the state of empirical political theory. In particular, we have shown that, with respect to the policy area we have examined and the variables we have discussed:

1) Economic development is not more closely related to policy outcome in democratic than in nondemocratic political systems. In fact, the economically-advanced democracies produce policy outcomes that are only weakly or not at all associated with economic development, a conclusion that lends strong

evidence to the hypothesis of the substitution effect discussed in the body of this paper. Moreover, the Communist states and Autocracies reflect environmental differences as consistently as do the Poorer Democracies.

2) In all but a few isolated cases, relationships between economic development and educational policy are only moderate or less for *all* political system types. National decision-makers appear to have substantial latitude in which to shape policy and are not as tightly confined by resource constraints as sometimes suggested.

3) Differences in resource availability are not associated, as shown by the coefficients of income elasticity for enrollments, with similar differences in enrollments among all systems. In other words, small income differences (e.g., in the Communist states) may be associated with disproportionate differences in school enrollments, relative to the Autocracies. The reverse is true in other comparisons. The substantial variations in the coefficients are thus produced largely by noneconomic, presumably political, factors.

4) In six of our nine indices, the Autocracies maintained the greatest variability of policy outcomes among the four systems; in three cases, they ranked second. The combined variability scores in all nine categories were: Autocracies, 0.51; Poorer Democracies, 0.34; Affluent Democracies, 0.29; Communist states, 0.21.

5) The view that "Communism" as a "descriptive, analytical category ... has become useless" seems grossly premature to us if not clearly mistaken. [17] The consistency of patterns of public choice in education among the Communist states is observed for most of the variables examined here.

NOTES

[1] The per capita income figure used for the United States (IPI = 100) is $3303, the per capita net national income figure for 1967, the closest date for which comparable data are available. This index is lower than if per capita gross national product had been used, since net national income corrects for capital depreciation and indirect business taxes. Income data for the other national units are for 1967 and, except for the Communist

states, yield indices computed from raw data reported in the *1969 Yearbook of National Accounts Statistics* published by the United Nations. Income data for the Communist states present a problem in evaluation since national income accounting in those societies is based upon different assumptions than used elsewhere. For the Communist states, therefore, indices of per capita net national income are Western estimates taken from standard reference works and encyclopedias.

[2] Contrary to some other studies (see following note), we have not for several reasons selected educational expenditures as measures of educational outcomes. First, international expenditure comparisons do not successfully account for the radically different price structures which obtain in various countries. Second, we are concerned to observe a distinction between outputs (public decisions) and outcomes (substantive social consequences). On this point, see David Easton, *A Systems Analysis of Political Life* (New York: Wiley, 1965), pp. 351–352. Third, there may be considerable "slippage" between expenditure decisions and levels of service. See, for example, Ira Sharkansky, "Government Expenditures and Public Service in the American States" (*American Political Science Review,* LXI, December 1967), pp. 1066–77.

[3] The association between national per capita incomes and educational expenditures as percent of national income was moderately high ($r_s = 0.64$) in 1965 for 28 randomly selected countries, as computed from data reported in Friedrich Edding and Dieter Berstecher, *International Development of Educational Expenditure,* 1950–65 (Paris: UNESCO, 1969), p. 54. See also Friedrich Edding, "Expenditure and Education: Statistics and Comments", in E.A. Robinson and J.E. Vaizey, Eds., *The Economics of Education* (New York: St. Martin's Press, 1966), pp. 65–69. Friederich Harbison and Charles A. Myers, *Education, Manpower and Economic Growth* (New York: McGraw-Hill, 1964) showed a moderately strong relationship between GNP and enrollments, although GNP was only weakly related to enrollments in scientific and technical curricula. The relationship (puzzling, as it turns out) between spending on education and economic development is dealt with by Mary Jean Bowman and C. Arnold Anderson, "Concerning the Role of Education in Development", in Clifford Geertz, Ed., *Old Societies and New States* (New York: The Free Press, 1963); and Alexander L. Peasler, "Primary School Enrollments and Economic Growth" (*Comparative Education Review,* 11, February 1967), pp. 57–67. Frederic L. Pryor, in a model of social research, *Public Expenditures in Communist and Capitalist Nations* (London: George Allen and Unwin, 1968), p. 226, concludes that, for his limited sample of Communist and non-Communist states, "for total educational production and expenditure the most important determinants appear to be the level of economic development and the proportion of school-age children in the population. Other variables, such as those of economic system, do not seem to play any significant role in explaining educational expenditures".

139

We should point out here that our measures of educational development and income are not always consistent with these conclusions.

[4] United States, Sweden, Switzerland, Canada, Iceland, Denmark, Australia, France, New Zealand, Luxembourg, Belgium, United Kingdom, West Germany, Finland, and the Netherlands, in order of per capita national income. Data for specific countries in this and other categories will be provided upon request.

[5] Israel, Austria, Italy, Japan, Ireland, Uruguay, Malta, Mexico, Jamaica, Costa Rica, Lebanon, Colombia, Philippines, Ceylon, and India in order of per capita national income.

[6] Deane E. Neubauer, "Some Conditions of Democracy" (*American Political Science Review,* LXI, December 1967), pp. 1002−07, provides empirical justification for asserting that the two groupings of democracies used here are similar politically in openness and competitiveness. The wealthier countries as a group are not to be regarded necessarily as "more" democratic than the poorer ones. For Neubauer's set of democracies, ". . . there is simply no relationship between level of democratic performance and socio-economic development" (p. 1007).

[7] In a sense, we assume with Lucian W. Pye, *Aspects of Political Development* (Boston: Little, Brown, 1966), pp. 9−11, that demand for education has become an element of "world culture". To the extent that pluralism receives reinforcement from various strands of democratic, liberal ideologies, this, too, undoubtedly contributes to support of popular education.

[8] The emerging democratic theory of collective choice explains this expectation: social resources are limited and have alternative uses, and there is a limit to the satisfactions afforded by any one good. We would therefore predict that, at some point in economic development in democracies, ratio-income-elasticity in education should begin to decline. For an insightful treatment of these questions, see Joyce M. Mitchell and William C. Mitchell, *Political Analysis and Public Policy* (Chicago: Rand McNally, 1969), p. 15 and passim.

[9] East Germany, Czechoslovakia, USSR, Poland, Hungary, Rumania, Bulgaria, Yugoslavia, Cuba, Albania, and China in order of estimated per capita national income. Mongolia, North Korea, and North Vietnam are excluded because of the lack of comparable data.

[10] Kuwait, Spain, Portugal, South Africa, Nicaragua, Saudi Arabia, El Salvador, Iran, Peru, Jordan, Dominican Republic, Taiwan, Honduras, Paraguay, Bolivia, Liberia, Thailand, Indonesia, Pakistan, South Vietnam, Sudan, Nepal, Haiti, Burma, Afghanistan, and Ethiopia.

[11] Two caveats are in order at this point. Despite annual improvements in the quality and quantity of reporting, international statistical comparisons remain hazardous. Political scientists interested in questions of public pol-

icy face problems which vary greatly from one policy area to another, and which are not least serious in the area of education. Definitions of educational activity still vary somewhat among countries, although the Statistical Division of the UNESCO Social Science Department has had considerable success in standardization; we may consequently expect to see their data used with even more success and confidence than in the recent past. A further problem is that standard measures of educational activity omit all functional education, as carried out by the military, churches, trade unions, the mass media, and other "noneducational" institutions. Fritz Machlup, in *The Production and Distribution of Knowledge in the United States* (Princeton: Princeton University Press, 1962) has estimated the importance of this factor, plus opportunity costs, tax exemptions, and implicit rents for one country — the United States. For 1957–58, S20 billion was expended on public and private education; by computing the value of these additional factors, however, Machlup arrives at a figure of $136 billion for the same period! Unfortunately, we do not know how other countries might vary along these lines.

[12] Data on education are computed from the UNESCO *Statistical Yearbook, 1968*.

[13] The coefficient of variability allows one to compare groups in terms of their homogeneity in cases where the means of the groups differ considerably. Although standard deviations are presented in the relevant tables, it may be somewhat misleading to compare them directly. See Hubert M. Blalock, Jr., *Social Statistics* (New York: McGraw-Hill, 1960), pp. 73–74. The standard deviations and variability coefficients for higher education in Table 1 illustrate this question quite clearly.

[14] This argument is made explicitly by Charles F. Cnudde and Dean E. Neubauer, "New Trends in Democratic Theory", in Cnudde and Neubauer, Eds., *Empirical Democratic Theory* (Chicago: Markham, 1969), pp. 523–529.

[15] r_s may vary from -0.1 to $+1.0$. An absence of association is shown by 0.0. This nonparametric statistic is used rather than, for example, the Pearsonian product-moment coefficient of correlation, because of its ease of computation and because, appearances to the contrary, our income data are in fact arranged in ordinal and not interval categories. Comparisons based on conversions of national income concepts are not at all precise; they give a rough approximation for purposes of comparison, which is all we can claim for our data.

[16] For our purposes here, we have adapted the economist's coefficient of income elasticity, which is normally a dynamic concept used to measure the *responsiveness* of demand to price changes, to measure *differences* in educational activity and per capita income in different political system types. Our usage is strictly noncausal and descriptive, although further

141

research might impute some now unknown degree of dynamism to the relationships discussed below.

[17] John H. Kautsky, *Communism and the Politics of Development* (New York: Wiley, 1968), p. 216.

Decision-Making in International Organization:
A Report on a Joint Project[*]

ROBERT W. COX and HAROLD K. JACOBSON

Introduction

The growth of international organizations has been one of the significant changes in the modern international political system. This growth has been particularly marked in the period since the end of the Second World War and now there are more than 200 international organizations in existence. Despite their number, surprisingly little is known about international organizations, but more is known about what they do than about how decisions are made within them.

There is, of course, a certain literature on decision-making within international organizations. There have been excellent studies of particular decisions, [1] and of aspects of the process such as voting behavior, [2] but these have remained discrete endeavors. There has been no overarching theoretical framework that could link them.

Motivated by a desire to attempt to fill this gap, in 1967 we

---

[*] This paper constitutes a substantial part of Chapter 1 of Robert W. Cox and Harold K. Jacobson and others, *The Anatomy of Influence: Decision Making in International Organization* (New Haven: Yale University Press, 1973).

decided to embark on a joint project the aim of which is to analyze processes of decision-making in international organizations and particularly to show how influence is acquired and exercised. Our efforts have been supported by the Social Science Research Council. The notion of *decision* is interpreted broadly to include not only formal decisions by vote in assemblies, but also some decisions by bureaucratic authorities. It further includes *nondecisions,* that is failures to grasp opportunities, implicit decisions not to act, and failures to take decisions. Influence is used to mean the modification of one actor's behavior by the action of another.[3] This term is distinguished from power, which expresses capabilities or the aggregate of political resources available to an actor. Power may be converted into influence, but it is not necessarily so converted either at all or to its full extent. *Elites* are those who have the most influence. Who these elites are is to be determined empirically.

The study involves using a common framework in a comparative analysis of decision-making processes in eight international organizations. It has a time range from 1945 through 1970. The organizations covered and the scholars responsible for analyzing them are:

The Telecommunication Union (ITU), H.K. Jacobson;

The International Labor Organization (ILO), R.W. Cox;

The United Nations Educational, Scientific and Cultural Organization (UNESCO), J.P. Sewell;

The World Health Organization (WHO), H.K. Jacobson;

The International Atomic Energy Agency (IAEA), L. Scheinman;

The International Monetary Fund (IMF), S. Strange;

The General Agreement on Tariffs and Trade (GATT), G. and V. Curzon; and

The United Nations Conference on Trade and Development (UNCTAD), J.S. Nye.

These eight organizations have in common that they are in principle universal in terms of their membership and functional in terms of their coverage. At the same time they have some significant differences in the composition of their actual memberships and in their institutional structures; marked differences in the breadth, essentiality, and technicality of their functions; and important differences in the salience of the issues with which they deal for the central political authorities of member states.

144

Obviously, though, these eight organizations are only a small fraction of the total. They do not include regional organizations or other organizations with limited membership such as the Organization for Economic Cooperation and Development or the Council for Mutual Economic Assistance, nor do they include those with broad political mandates like the United Nations. For the generalizations developed through the project to be valid, they would have to be tested against a broader and more representative group of international organizations. Hopefully, the framework developed in the project will be applicable to other international organizations and will facilitate such a broader testing.

What follows is mainly a description of this framework with a few empirical findings interspersed.

Functions, Structure, and Evolution

Decision-making in international organizations occurs within a context shaped by the function, the institutional framework and basic procedures, and the historical development of the agency. As decision-making processes and distribution of influence are initially shaped by these factors, considering them is an essential first stage in any analysis.

International organizations have been set up to perform a variety of tasks: peacekeeping; promoting economic development; allocating the radio frequency spectrum; reducing obstacles to trade; insuring that technology is used only for peaceful purposes; and facilitating the maintenance of stable exchange rates, to name only a few. While a certain level of agreement necessarily must be reached at the time of the creation of an international organization about what it is to do, all parties to the agreement need not share the same conception of its meaning. On the contrary, there are often sharp differences, and these differences can provide essential clues to future dynamic developments in international organizations. Nor does the agreement reached about what an organization is to do necessarily represent all of the ambitions which the parties to the agreement might have concerning the functions of the organization. Many states may see international organizations principally as instruments for preserving their hegemony, or improving their relative status. Moreover, personal moti-

145

vations, for example to occupy top jobs, can be a factor alongside considerations of state interests in creating new international agencies. Such motivations as these, whether expressed or unexpressed, are also important in shaping subsequent developments in international organizations.

Whatever their specific tasks and fields of activity, international organizations can be divided into two broad categories according to the way in which they perform these tasks. Some organizations are established to provide a forum or framework for negotiations and decisions, others to provide specific services. This dichotomy establishes two ideal types: the *forum organization,* and the *service organization.* Organizations in the first category provide a framework for member states to carry on a variety of activities ranging from the exchange of views to the negotiation of legal instruments of a binding character. States also often use such frameworks for the *collective legitimization* of their policies or for propaganda. Organizations in the second category conduct activities themselves; they provide common and/or individual services. The delimiting principle involves who conducts the services; if they are carried out by states even though they may have been agreed to within the framework of an organization, they would not qualify that agency for inclusion in this category. The organization itself must conduct the services. An agency which collects, analyzes, and disseminates information would fit in this category unless the main use of the information were to falicitate discussions conducted within the framework of the organization, in which case it would be classified in the forum category.

In reality, of course, many international organizations fall in both categories. ILO, for example, has an extensive technical assistance program, but it also provides a framework for the negotiation of international labor conventions. Similarly, ITU, UNESCO, WHO, IAEA, and IMF conduct services in their own right and at the same time provide frameworks for discussions and negotiations among their member states.

The distinction nevertheless has meaning, and the distribution of an agency's activities between the two types of activity is significant, for each type has implications for patterns of decision-making and influence. On the most elementary level, the more an organization tends toward the service type, the larger its international bureaucracy and the greater the bureaucracy's potential role in certain types of decision-making. This scheme of categorization also provides helpful clues about how an organization can be studied, particularly about what bodies of theory developed in other contexts might be most germane. Organizational theory can have great relevance for understanding decision-making in service type organizations, and the more agencies tend in this direction, the more directly applicable this theory is. Conversely, theories about negotiation, such as game theory, can be extremely helpful in analyzing decision-making patterns in forum organizations.

This distinction between forum and service organizations relates to the way in which agencies perform their functions, not to the importance of these functions to member states or to the authority of the agencies. Whatever their mode of activity, the importance and authority of different organizations vary, and different states perceive them in different terms. An agency which is regarded as crucial by one state may be seen as trivial by another, and there is similar variance in the responsiveness of states to the decisions of international organizations. These differences too are important.

They are immediately apparent when one examines the structure of international organizations. The formal powers of the organization and its organs, the extent of regionalism, the forms of representation, the voting procedures, and the organization of the international bureaucracy, all tend to be prescribed at the time of the formation of an international agency. These initial understandings about how an international organization is to perform its functions inevitably represent compromises among conflicting points of view; all parties must be given some incentives to participate. If an organization is to have functions which might affect significant values, those in control of these values will generally demand structural and procedural devices to insure that they have special influence. How far they will press their demands and how successful they will be will depend upon the configuration of forces at the time. They might be dissuaded from pressing their claims too far by actual and potential counter claims in the same functional area or in another. In general, the broader the mandate of the organization, the more likely there will be such counter claims. Conscience or conceptions of long-run self-interest can also serve as moderating forces. Whatever the outcome, these initial understandings provide the basic "rules of the game" for subsequent decision-making.

In some instances, the parties to an agreement establishing an international organization will not only prescribe the structures and procedures for decision-making, but will also attempt to specify doctrines according to which decisions should be taken. Thus the constitutional documents of IMF and GATT contain detailed codes of conduct, and the charters of several other international agencies tend in this direction. The more they do, the more the organizations' activities are set in a particular mold and the harder it is to shift their direction.

Regardless of the rigidity of their charters, though, once established international organizations often evolve in ways which could not have been foreseen by their founders. To some extent this is because the interests and intentions of the member states change over time. These changes in turn may be the consequence of developments within states or in relations among states. Moreover, states may modify their interests and intentions with respect to international organizations as a consequence of participation in them. As in other contexts interaction among actors can result in changed views. In addition, international bureaucracies created to service international organizations may add new ambitions to those of states, ranging from pursuit of specific technical goals to the desire to play a role in making international relations more peaceful or in effecting redistribution of wealth between rich and poor countries. Thus, once established, organizations tend to take on a life of their own, to develop their own inner dynamics.

The major changes which take place in international organizations can be identified and measured in terms of their activities, their output. An organization may change in its functions, either as regards subject-matter — the addition of new areas of action or the abandonment of old ones — or as regards modes of action — for example, a switch from forum to service activities. Changes in functions can be traced in the program of international organizations. There may be changes in the scale of operations, significant increases or (less likely) decreases in the level of programs, for which budgets may provide an indicator. There may also be changes in the authority of an organization, either because members become more responsive to its decisions or because the organization begins to make enactments of a new kind placing more demands upon members. There is no necessary correlation between growth in budget and growth in authority; an organization's budget might grow at the same time that its importance for member states or its authority declines. Finally, there may be changes in the relative importance of an international organization within the issue-area or areas with which it is concerned. The extent to which the organization performs essential functions within the issue-area is relevant here. The existence or creation of another rival organization with overlapping jurisdiction would be indicative of significant change in this respect. Changes of the kinds suggested here may be explained by changing membership or changes in the top personnel of the organization's bureaucracy, by changes in the preoccupations of states, or the emergence of new currents of ideas.

Changes may be gradual, but it is important to be alive to the possibility of discontinuities in an organization's history, to significant changes in direction which could be termed *turning-points*. Such turning-points might relate to any of the dimensions of change in the outputs of organizations mentioned in the previous paragraph — functions, scale, authority, or importance in the issue-area. They may also relate to dramatic and important changes in inputs, for example in the intentions of major participants or significant changes in the membership of the organization. What makes a turning-point is the abruptness, the unpredictability of a significant change.

It has already been suggested that the environment of an organization — for example, the major preoccupations of governments, new currents of ideas, or significant changes in the international system such as the emergence of new nations — may affect its output. This relationship will be developed more fully below. Changes both in the environment and in the output of an organization may also be accompanied by an evolution in the *rules of the game* for decision-making within it. The interrelationships between internal processes on the one hand, and changes in the environment and in the organization's activities or output on the other, will have to be studied empirically. The importance of outlining the historical development of an international organization, particularly in terms of changing functions and structures, as a first phase in the study of decision-making, is to provide benchmarks for the deeper study of these relationships.

Decision-Making: A Taxonomical Analysis

Once the context provided by the functions, structure, and historical evolution of an agency is known, one can begin to consider patterns of decision-making and the distribution of influence. For this purpose, it is useful to be able to classify decisions by issue-areas. Issue-areas have proven to be important in studies of decision-making in local and national politics, [4] and it is reasonable to assume that issue-areas are also significant in differentiating patterns of influence in international organizations.

Testing this notion in a comparative study, however, poses problems, for the concept of issue-areas has most often been applied in a relatively concrete and specific manner. For example, studies of local political systems have shown important differences between patterns of influence in decision-making about educational and urban renewal issues. Attempts have been made to develop general typologies of issue-areas on the basis of the values at stake, [5] but these are difficult to apply empirically. A more manageable scheme for a comparative study of international organizations is to use a taxonomy of decisions based on the nature of the issues involved, a taxonomy which will also be comprehensive in the sense of covering all decisions of all the organizations studied.

This taxonomy divides decisions of international organizations into seven categories: representational, symbolic, boundary, programmatic, rule-creating, rule-supervisory, and operational.

Representational decisions affect membership in the organization and representation on its internal organs. They include decisions concerning: the admission and exclusion of members; the validation of credentials; determination of representation on executive organs and committees; and the manner in which the secretariat is composed, especially as regards its higher level posts.

Symbolic decisions are primarily tests of alignment of opinions from which no practical consequences for actions directly flow.

150

The intention in symbolic issues is to test the extent of acceptability of goals or ideologies held intensely by one group of actors, or the legitimacy of long-accepted norms of dominant elites. In some cases these goals or ideologies may relate to broad issues of international politics, in others, to matters specific to the organization involved. In an organization with a mandate in the economic field, decolonization might be an example of the former, improving the lot of developing countries, an example of the latter. Some decisions that might fall within the definition of other categories may be considered primarily symbolic, but as soon as the direct consequences of the decisions become appreciable, as for example in the controversies over the representation and participation of the Communist states in ILO, these decisions fall in another category, in this instance, representational. The criteria for classification as *symbolic* are thus, positively, symbolic intention on the part of the decision-makers, and negatively, the absence of significant practical consequences flowing directly from the decision. The absence of direct consequences does not mean that symbolic decisions are unimportant. On the contrary, in the long-run they may have profound consequences because of their effects on the milieu within which international relations are conducted.

This category of decisions can be singled out in order to test the hypothesis that symbolic issues tend to become acute during periods of adjustment within the organization to major changes in the environment that involve the possibility of shifts in the structure of influence and in the basic goals and policies of the organization. They may thus provide a particularly sensitive measure of changes in the internal distribution of influence.

Boundary decisions concern the organization's external relations with other international and regional structures as regards: (1) their respective scopes; (2) cooperation between and among organizations; and (3) initiatives taken in one organization to provoke activity through another. All eight organizations considered in this project have some relationships with the United Nations; and ITU, ILO, UNESCO, WHO, and IAEA receive substantial funds from the United Nations Development Program. A number of boundary issues arise in the context of these links. GATT and UNCTAD share overlapping jurisdictions, and to a lesser extent this situation also exists between and among other organizations. When this occurs, boundary problems inevitably arise.

Programmatic decisions concern the strategic allocation of the organization's resources amongst different types and fields of activity. (The principal types are forum or service activities; fields of activity tend to be specific to each individual agency.) Allocations usually result from negotiations among the actors concerning the main goals and program emphases of the organization. Budgets are often the framework within which programmatic decisions are taken.

Rule-creating decisions define rules or norms bearing upon matters within the substantive scope of the organization. The outcome of the decisions may, in some cases, be formal instruments such as conventions, agreements, or resolutions. Illustrations of decisions covered in this category include GATT's activity in the negotiation of agreements for tariff reductions, the establishment of Special Drawing Rights by the IMF, as well as the preparing of Labor and Health Conventions by ILO and WHO. It is also possible, in less formal ways, to define the normative content of organizational ideologies, for example, in speeches by the executive head or others which may never explicitly be the subject of votes but may nonetheless articulate widely shared norms or goals with which the organization is identified in the minds of many of its constituents. Such actions may in significant cases be considered as rule-creating decisions.

Some rule-creating decisions may seem to imply that certain priorities should be followed in making allocations; but decisions become programmatic only when they include a definition of priorities specifically for purposes of allocation or, more usually, make an actual allocation in terms of budget or personnel.

Rule-supervising decisions concern the application of approved rules by those subject to them. These decisions may involve various procedures ranging from those that are highly structured to those that are extremely subtle.

The process of rule-supervision passes through several stages, and organizations may develop distinct procedures for each of these stages. [6] The first stage is detection, or gathering information about the observance or nonobservance of rules. For example, are states complying with: the frequency allocations agreed to

152

within ITU; the standards set in International Labor Conventions; the safeguard provisions of IAFA; or the nondiscriminatory trading rules of GATT? The detection function may be performed by states acting unilaterally or jointly, by the international bureaucracy, by a private panel, or by some combination of these instrumentalities.

Verification of the observance or nonobservance of the rules is the second stage. Again, this function may be performed in various ways. Decisions could be entrusted to experts, to the international bureaucracy, or to representatives of member states, to list the most obvious alternatives. Proceedings could be public or private.

The final stage in rule-supervision involves the application of sanctions or punishments for violation of the rules or the award of privileges for compliance with them. As in the other stages, decisions about penalties and rewards can be made in several ways.

Operational decisions relate to the provision of services by the organization or the use of its resources in accordance with approved rules, policies or programs. They include, for example, decisions about specific technical assistance projects by UNESCO or other agencies, or the granting of loans by IMF. They are essentially tactical allocations of resources made within broad strategic (programmatic) allocations. Frequently such tactical, operational decisions are made largely between representatives of individual states and the international bureaucracy. In such decisions criteria referring to the pursuit of general goals may be diluted as a consequence of pressures for services and the need to retain client support.

Operational decisions may lead cumulatively to programmatic decisions. The inclusion of a program in an agency budget may be the culmination of a process in which the initiative came originally from an operational decision by the executive head or a segment of the international bureaucracy.

Patterns of interaction among actors within international organizations may be described for each of these decision-types and have been for the eight agencies included in the project. In these patterns of interaction, actors may perform four particularly significant roles. In each decision, some actor must take the initiative and hence becomes the *initiator*. The real initiators are not always the formal initiators; for example, secretariat officials sometimes prepare draft resolutions which are then submitted by members of national delegations. The identification of initiators consequently is more a problem of judgment and interpretation than of given fact. Some actors have the power, perhaps because of their strategic location in the line of communications, to block initiatives, and hence are *potential vetoers*. Others serve as go-betweens amongst the participants and as consensus-builders. They are *brokers*. Finally, there are some actors whose known or surmised views may have to be taken into account because of their control of resources, or formal authority, or some other reason. Their role is that of *controllers*.

Modes of interaction among actors may be divided into two broad categories, *analytical* and *bargaining*. When the first mode prevails, differences are settled by intellectual processes; facts are examined and rational arguments constructed. In the end, the more cogent argument is accepted. Usually this mode is employed when the parties involved share basic agreement about the values to be achieved. When this is not the case, rational arguments are much less likely to be persuasive. If agreement is to be reached, it will have to be on the basis of a compromise achieved more by barter than rational argument.

For each of the decision-types, organizations tend to develop regular patterns of interaction, thus, most decisions are routinized. Occasionally, however, because of the newness, or the importance of an issue, or for some other reason, these patterns are discarded and others substituted. Crisis decisions would be a subset of this category. This project seeks to describe both *routine* and *extraordinary* interaction patterns.

The salience of different decision-types varies in different organizations. Symbolic decisions are accorded considerable prominence in ILO and UNCTAD, but much less in the other agencies. Representational decisions also seem to be more salient in ILO than in the others. Programmatic decisions are a major focus of interest in UNESCO, WHO, and ILO, but are of less concern in ITU, IMF, and GATT. Rule-creating is relatively unimportant in UNESCO and UNCTAD, but quite important in the other agencies. Rule-supervision is important in IMF, GATT, ILO, and IAEA, but much less so in ITU, UNESCO and WHO. Boundary decisions are of some importance for all of the agencies, though seemingly least of all for IMF.

The relative salience of decision-types for each organization is important in shaping the general pattern of influence. Almost by definition, where operational decisions have the greatest salience, executive heads and bureaucracies tend to have the greatest influence, and where representational and symbolic decisions predominate, government representatives have the greatest influence.

The interaction patterns for the seven decision-types are conceived as what might be called the principal dependent variables of the project. In these terms the independent variables are the actors, or the actual participants in the decisions, and the broader environment within which the international organizations exist.

Actors and Their Sources of Influence

To consider international organizations as political systems raises certain conceptual difficulties. They are conglomerates, composed of bureaucracies and various conference structures. Nowadays the bureaucracies of international organizations tend to be recruited internationally, but except for this feature, as political organs, they are very much like national bureaucracies. The conference structures, however, have no direct analog in national political systems. In form they resemble legislative bodies, and many of the procedures are the same. The participants in the conference structures of international organizations in most instances, however, are representatives of states, who have more or less rigid instructions, and this makes these structures fundamentally different from national and local legislative bodies. Furthermore, only exceptionally do international organizations have actual authoritative control over substantial resources which might be needed to implement their decisions; generally such authoritative control is the prerogative of member states. Of the organizations treated in this project, only the International Monetary Fund has its own resources.

Because of their conglomerate nature, international organizations have been conceived in various ways. The term has been used to mean: (1) those appointed to act in the name of the organizations, usually the executive head and the international bureaucracy; (2) the direct participants in decisions, including the executive head, the international bureaucracy, and those who take part in the associated conference machinery (the assembly, the executive body, and other committees and commissions); and (3) a system of interaction including all of those who directly participate in decisions taken within the framework of the organization and in addition all officials and individuals who in various ways actively determine the positions of the direct participants.

Although the third conception conforms less to common usage than the first two, it is the most realistic basis for defining international organizations as political systems. It is important to conceive international organizations so as to include linkages with member states. Not to do so and to limit consideration of political processes to what happens in conferences eliminates some of the most important aspects of decision-making. As already noted, representatives of states tend to be instructed agents, and any conception which did not take this into account would be incomplete. Moreover, states are not monolithic. There may not be unanimity within a state about the policy it should pursue in an international organization, and interdepartmental differences or differences between an important interest group and a department of government can have extremely important consequences for decision-making in that organization. A final reason for favoring a conception that includes linkages with member states is that since the activity of international organizations is frequently dependent upon actions by member states, a narrower conception would indicate greater autonomy for international organizations than they actually possess.

The inclusion of national elements within the definition of an international organization as a political system raises a problem concerning the identity of the states which are members of these organizations. For example, the "United States" which is a member of the IMF is a subsystem composed of officials of the Treasury, the Federal Reserve, some other financial agencies, probably some Wall Street bankers, and a few individuals — theorists or practitioners — who influence financial policy. The "United States" which is a member of the ILO is another subsystem including some officials of the departments of Labor, State and Commerce, Mr. George Meany (President of the AFL-CIO) and his foreign policy advisors, Mr. Edward Neilan (the employer dele-

156

gate), and some officials of the US Chamber of Commerce. These two subsystems may have only the remotest and most tenuous relationship with one another, at least under normal circumstances, through the national political system. Although such country subsystems are composed of individuals, it is often convenient to refer to the components of the subsystems as limited collectivities such as a government department or an interest group or a segment of one of these, rather than to the individuals who compose it or act for it. Doing this implies that these limited collectivities achieve or enforce collective views. Country subsystems are subsystems both of the international organization to which they relate and of the national political system.

Other subsystems composed, for example, of those officials of major international institutional groups, such as the Roman Catholic Church, the International Chamber of Commerce, or even multi-national corporations which play a role in particular international organizations are similarly part of two overlapping political systems. In keeping with their formal functions, such subsystems generically may be referred to as representative subsystems. The most numerous and most important of these, of course, are country subsystems.

The direct participants in the decisions of an international organization may also be thought of as a subsystem, which can be called the participant subsystem. This subsystem is composed of those members of the representative subsystems who actually participate in the organization's decision-making processes, for example as delegates at international conferences, and of other individuals, such as the executive head of the organization, who also take part directly in these processes. Again, although individuals are always involved, there may be occasions when it is accurate to refer to limited collectivities, such as national delegations or segments of the international bureaucracy. In terms of the broad concept used here, as political systems international organizations include both the participant subsystem and the representative subsystems.

To conceive member states as country subsystems makes it easier to examine alliances between segments of these subsystems and segments of the participant subsystem, for example, an alliance between the international bureaucracy and certain functional

157

departments of governments based upon shared interests. Actors in the participant subsystem may be able to exploit cleavages within a country subsystem (or other representative subsystems) and to build up transnational alliances composed of segments from a number of representative subsystems as well as of actors in the participant subsystem. The possibility of such alliances is one of the most interesting aspects of the politics of international organizations. Some country subsystems will be more complex than others, and some are more open or penetrable by would-be alliance builders. Presumably there is some relationship between the degree of openness of a country generally and the openness of its country subsystem, but this and the whole subject need empirical examination.

The concept of a country subsystem must be related to the more commonly used juridical concept of a "member state", and an analogous problem arises for other collectivities, such as interest groups which participate in international organizations. The difference is essentially the distinction between those few individuals of the collectivity who shape and articulate policy in the international organization and the collectivity as a whole whose interest in the international organization in question may be only marginal.

In terms of the concepts used here states, or other major, relevant collectivities, are considered as parts of the environment of the international organization's political system (the environment is treated in detail in the next section). Country subsystems are the linkages between environmental forces and the participant subsystems of the international organization. *Representation* is the process of this linkage.

Each state has power, or the capability of exercising influence, with reference to international affairs broadly and also in terms of the specific field of the international organization in question. The country subsystem may mobilize these capabilities as resources for influence in the international organization. Such capabilities are always limited (even the most powerful country cannot effectively or credibly convert its power into influence simultaneously upon all the issues which might concern it), and there may be competing claims within the national political system for their use. For these and other reasons, a country subsystem may not be able to

158

command to the full the potential resources for influence of a state. The extent to which a state is prepared to convert its capabilities into influence within a particular international organization may often be determined by authority higher than and outside of the country subsystem, i.e. in the form of a decision by the high political authorities of the state either to limit their commitment or participation in an international organization or to press hard for certain goals through the international organization. The high political authorities' perception of the importance of an international organization for a state and the priority to be given to exercising influence in it in relation to other goals, is an environmental variable, an important aspect of the conditions within which the country subsystem operates.

The country subsystem can take part in the definition of national interests concerning the international organization, placing demands upon the national political system for resources to influence decisions in the international organization. Simultaneously it articulates interests (which may be national or sectional or both) on behalf of the national political system within the international organization, and in so doing it may interpret their meaning. Subsidiarily, the country subsystem also recruits new personnel into the political system of the international organization and socializes its members (individuals) to the norms of the political system. The country subsystem is thus a channel transmitting support and demands from the national political system (part of the environment) to the international organization, and also a channel for feedback of demands from the international organization on the national political system.

A political system conceived in this way, while it corresponds to the realities of politics in international organizations and permits an appreciation of the richness of relationships which develop, poses problems for comparative research because of its complexity. It is thus necessary to translate it into a more simplified set of working concepts which can be used in a comparative study.

Our comparative study focuses upon two levels of explanation: one is in terms of interactions in the participant subsystem, the other in terms of environmental variables. The extent to which the outcomes of interaction in the participant subsystem differ from what might have been predicted from an assessment of environ-

159

mental forces, measures the importance of processes within the political system of the organization in determining decisions. In regard to the participant subsystem, attention is especially focused on the sources of influence of the actors, factors affecting the orientation of actors, and the structuring of relationships among actors through interaction within the system — in short, on the dynamics of process and on the effects of process upon the system itself. The country or other representative subsystems have a less central place in this inquiry, although their usefulness, for explaining the resources and orientation of the actors in the decision-making subsystem should be underlined. Other studies might give a fuller place to this level of explanation.[7]

As conceived in this study, the actors are individuals who participate directly in the decisions of an international organization. They may be classified into the following categories:

1. Representatives of national governments (who may be appointed by various ministries to which functionalist theory accords great importance);
2. Representatives of national and international private associations (including interest groups and commercial enterprises);
3. The executive head of the organization;
4. High officials and other members of the bureaucracy of the organization;
5. Individuals who serve in their own capacity formally or informally as advisors;
6. Representatives of other international organizations;
7. Employees of the mass media.

Of course not all of these categories will be active in all organizations.

The power of actors — that is, their capacity to exercise influence — is derived both from their position and their personal characteristics. The representatives of some states or the occupants of some positions within international organizations will be important in certain decisions regardless of who they are. Even in these cases, though, the individuals can through their personal characteristics enhance or diminish the power that would normally accrue to someone in their role. For example, Ambassador Goldberg had considerable power in the UN because he was the United States representative (his position), but some of his power was also attributable to his qualities and skills as a negotiator and to his political connections (his personal characteristics).

Position includes as potentiality the resources of the collectivity represented by the individual and the priority given by the authorities of the collectivity to the use of these resources for influence in the organization. These resources can be of different orders: in the case of states, economic and military strength which may be deferred to in certain decisions; in the case of high international officials, information and recognized status which may give initiative in proposing action or the resolution of conflict. Position also includes its own history of previous actions which tend to predispose the behavior of the incumbent in certain directions, and the limitations in the form of binding instructions imposed by higher authorities in the collectivities represented.

Personal characteristics involve skill in the performance of position, including skill in mobilizing the resources of the collectivity represented for influence in the organization, skill in shaping the preparations of the instructions within which the position will be performed, and skill in influencing the behavior of other actors.

An actor's power or his capacity to exercise influence is thus compounded of his position and his personal attributes. For the sake of clarity the relationship can be expressed in symbolic form:

$$P \pm A = C.$$

Position or office (P) modified by personal attributes (A) (in this formula, plus or minus) equals the power or the capacity (C) of the individual actor. C is a function of P and also a function of A, but P and A vary independently. Although the form in which this symbolic statement is written assumes that A will add to or detract from P, in some circumstances the relationship may be multiplicative or more complex. This equation is not intended to create an illusion of precise mathematical treatment. Some of the concepts have not been, and at this stage probably cannot be represented in a numerical form that would lend itself to mathematical application.

Among the personal attributes which might enhance an individual's power in an international organization are his personal charisma, ideological legitimacy, administrative competence, expert knowledge, long association with an organization, negotiating ability, and ability to persist in intransigence. The personal status he has acquired outside the organization through such things as wealth, election to an important office, scientific achievements, and possession of significant influence in an important collectivity will also affect his power. The advantage of these personal attributes varies with organizations. For example, negotiating ability might be especially valuable in organizations like GATT where consensus must be achieved, while the ability to persist in intransigence might be a telling factor in UNCTAD if the outcome was to be a declaratory resolution.

An actor's power attributable to his position may be represented symbolically here as:

$$X_c\,(G \pm S) = P.$$

That is, the capability of the position of an actor (P) is a function of the priority (X_c) which the authorities of the collectivity attach to converting their capabilities in international affairs generally (G), as modified by their capabilities in the specific field of the organization in question (S) into influence in the organization. This anticipates somewhat the discussion of the components of the general and the specific capabilities of states to be presented in the next section, dealing with the environment, but it should be noted here that other kinds of power besides material power are included. Thus, this symbolic statement can be used for other collectivities as well as states.

Substituting the components of the actor's position for P, the symbolic statement for an actor's power is:

$$X_c\,(G \pm S) \pm A = C.$$

Like the authorities of the collectivities they represent, actors also exercise judgment about the conversion of their capabilities into influence. Here, we are referring to active influence in the sense discussed in the previous section. For both the individual actor and the authorities of the collectivity, the decision whether or not they should seek to use available resources to gain influence will depend upon several factors, including the intensity of their feelings about the issues at stake and their estimates of the probability and the costs of obtaining their goals. In estimating such probabilities actors make assumptions about the controller influence of others as well as about the likely extent of opposition and support. If they seek to exercise influence, the degree of their success will depend on how all the other influences within the organization are distributed on the issue at stake. For example, when faced with a united opposition, the representative of a powerful state might find it impossible to achieve an objective, whereas in other circumstances he would succeed easily.

Obviously, the influence that an individual actor actually exercises in the participant subsystem of an international organization may differ considerably from his capacity or power. Putting it in abbreviated fashion, the influence of an individual actor (I) is the result of his power (C) as modified by his decision to attempt to convert his power into influence (X_a) and by the distribution of all other influences within the organization on a particular issue (D). Symbolically, this can be expressed as:

$$X_a \cdot C \cdot D = I$$

The distribution of all other influences includes the pattern of alignments on a particular issue, as well as how other actors feel about it, the weight of their opinions, and their power. Thus, it concludes those who would support, oppose, or be indifferent. It also includes the deference accorded to the actor in question by other actors.

As the focal point of analysis shifts from the capacities of actors to their influence, attention must be given to their attitudes and perceptions and more broadly to process. Attitudes and perceptions are crucially important factors affecting actors' behavior; they have an effect, among other things, on whether or not the actors will seek to convert their capacities into influence. Process, the working out of strategies to obtain goals, the building of alliances, coalitions, and consensus, determine the configuration of forces within an organization.

The fundamental questions concerning attitudes and perceptions are how actors see the organization in question and how they understand its purposes and potentialities, particularly in terms of their own interests and objectives. The distribution and interplay between personal goals and public goals must be investigated in this connection. Personal goals involve such things as jobs, prestige, and tourism. There is every reason to suspect that such motives play as great a part in international as in national or local

163

politics. Public goals include those relating to both the substantive concerns of the organization and the interests of the collectivities which the actors represent. Concern for survival and growth of the organization as a whole or of subunits might be derived either from public or personal goals. Actors may have different points of view formed by their experience and professional training, as lawyers, economists, scientists, or engineers, for example, which mold their attitudes in certain directions. Actors may be grouped according to common perceptions of the organization and according to the intensity of their commitment to the organization and its goals.

A particularly significant case of regularities in perceptions and attitudes takes the form of organizational ideology. As defined here, an organizational ideology would contain:

1. An interpretation of the environment as it relates to action by the organization.
2. Specification of goals to be attained in the environment.
3. A strategy of action for attaining these goals.

Organizational ideologies might be narrow or broad. Functionalism is an ideology which is applicable to international organizations representing a variety of objectives. The precise nature of these objectives is largely irrelevant, but they must be specific. Marxist and populist ideologies compete with functionalism as other broad interpretations of the aims and strategies of international organizations. International organizations are seen in the Marxist view as expressing power relations between socialist and capitalist blocs; to the populist, they appear as a means of exerting pressure by the numerous poor upon the few rich. Along with these broad organizational ideologies are narrower and more task-orientated ideologies. Thus "education for development" is an ideology of UNESCO and to some extent of ILO, and nondiscrimination and the most favored nation are ideologies of GATT and IMF. It is of interest to ascertain whether such organizational ideologies exist, how they come into being, and how widely they are shared. Other important questions are whether they are especially linked with certain actors, whether they are publicized, and whether competing organizational ideologies exist.

Perceptions and attitudes are particularly important in identifying who pushes for what. No one assumes, however, that attitudes and perceptions impel actors in only one direction. On the contrary, actors may often be subject to cross-pressures, and one of the reasons why special attention is given to organizational ideologies is to see the extent to which these pressures act counter to other motivational forces. A particularly interesting question is whether dual loyalties emerge with some actors, leading them not only to represent the views of their collectivity in the organization but also to exert influence on their collectivity in line with the consensus reached by the organization, or in conformity with organizational ideology.

The formal structures and procedures of the organization are the institutional constraints within which the strategies of the actors are developed. But when attitudes are translated into strategies within these formal constraints, the actors create additional and often informal structures.

These structures created in the political process itself may be studied in various ways. In the first place, we look for persistent groupings of actors. [8] These may be such groupings as caucuses. There may also be informal networks involving an ingroup or "establishment" of actors who occupy key positions and who normally consult amongst each other about important decisions. Persistent groupings may enhance or decrease the possibility of an individual actor's exercising influence. An actor may find it easier to attain his objectives because of his membership in a coalition, or an opposing coalition may place obstructions in his path.

Such groupings determine, secondly, the configurations of influence within organizations, which may take forms approximating: (1) unanimity; (2) one dominant coalition, possibly led by a dominant actor; (3) polarization between two rival coalitions; (4) a larger number of alliances, none of which dominates; or (5) cross-cutting cleavages on different issues with no general pattern. The coalition policies of executive heads and members of international bureaucracies, as well as those of national representatives, are important factors determining these configurations.

Finally, there is the identification of elites made up of influential individual participants, elites which cut across groupings and configurations and thus show the stratification of influence in the organization. It is by knowing who are the most influential that we can infer which resources are the most significant determinants of influence.

No single measure of the influence of actors in international organizations is entirely satisfactory, but several methods in combination should make it possible to take into account the inadequacies of each. Analysis of voting has sometimes been thought of as one means of assessing relative influence. [9] However, in several of the organizations covered in this study votes are rarely taken, and in any case voting statistics are usually only useful to analyze the influence of states, not individual actors. Furthermore, analysis of voting cannot gauge influence exercised by those acting as brokers or controllers.

Other methods used in this study are similar to those in studies focusing on influence in other kinds of political systems. One of these methods is to note the formal structure of authority. Who holds the top offices in the hierarchy, including membership on executive bodies and the higher offices of the international bureaucracy? The limitations of this measurement are those which apply in any political system. Formal position in the hierarchy does not necessarily confer great influence. Some who are not influential will be included; and some who are influential may not appear.

Another device used in this study to measure influence has been to ask a panel of knowledgeable persons to list the individuals with the greatest general influence in each of the organizations. The weaknesses of the method lie in the variations in the judges' competency and the way they interpret general influence. Its advantage lies in the possibility that the answers may identify influential individuals who do not occupy positions of formal authority. It must be borne in mind that this is a measure of reputation for influence.

A measure of behavioral influence has also been attempted for some organizations, based on the scores actors achieve for success in initiating and obstructing proposals. This method ignores broker and controller influence and as a consequence could yield rather different results from the measurement of influence by reputation. Another problem in applying this approach is distinguishing the relative importance of the proposals which are the subject of initiatives and vetoes.

Finally, in some cases it has been possible to evaluate influence by closely studying the interactions involved in particular decisions. This method can yield greater insights into the processes of influence than other methods; but it is bound to be illustrative rather than comprehensive.

The other points of measurement of power and influence used in this study are to be viewed as rough approximations offered because they may help illustrate a model of decision-making which is too complex to allow for measurement of some of its more important variables and which directs special attention to process. The value of the study should rest on other grounds than the sophistication of its measurements.

The purpose of trying to measure influence goes beyond simply wishing to know which particular actors have the most influence at any particular time. Finding out more about the characteristics and sources of influence of each of the most influential actors, is one step toward inferring more generally the relative importance of different sources of influence in different international organizations. What other sources of influence compete most effectively with a position as representative of a powerful state? In which organizations does administrative competency or expert ability carry most weight? Which give preeminence to ideological legitimacy, i.e., the definition and articulation of an ideological position, whether in the form of an organizational ideology or of one of the major ideologies of world politics?

Analyzing the background of the most influential actors and the roads they have followed to gain influence should give some clues to the relative importance of various personal attributes and should help to single out the positions or offices which are most likely to be springboards to influence. In some organizations these may be membership on the executive board; in others, posts in the secretariat. Some study of persons without influence may also be revealing, particularly if they might have been expected to be influential because of their position.

Analysis of the political systems of international organizations on the above lines should show how the structures of influence within these systems arise and change. In part, this structure is determined by the capabilities and demands of the actors, that is, by inputs into the system from its environment. In part, it arises out of processes within the system itself. It would be particularly interesting to know how much is to be accounted for in terms of process alone; but this is very difficult to assess directly.

Environmental Impacts

The second level of explanation pursued in the project is, then, the terms of the environment. It will be evident that the separation between what is included in the international organization as a political system and in the environment is an analytical distinction: it concerns the aspect of the entity considered rather than the entity itself. States fall under both headings. Generally, characteristics of states that are relevant to the functions and activities of an international organization, but which do not involve active relationship with that organization, are elements of the environment. The machinery and personnel utilized for participation in an international organization are, on the other hand, considered part of the organization's political or decision-making system and have been given the label, country subsystem. Thus, a state's gross national product, exports, population, and type of policy are considered elements in the environment of GATT or UNCTAD; its ministry of commerce, office of the president, central bank, and other agencies, insofar as they are involved in briefing or participating in delegations to GATT or UNCTAD, are part of the political systems of those organizations.

The environment can be considered as composed of a number of relevant variables, some of which are general to all international organizations and some of which are specific to particular organizations. Drawing this distinction makes it possible to evaluate the relative importance of each in explaining decision-making processes and influence in international organizations.

The general environment is conceived here in terms of states, their characteristics, and broad policies. This is because states are the principal units in world politics. They are the dominant mode for organizing human and physical resources. They alone can become members of international organizations. This focus on states is, of course, a limitation. A case could well be made out for including some transnational societal phenomena as important elements in the environment of international organizations, for example, religious movements, multinational corporations, or the emergence of new forms of behavior and values. These are excluded from explicit consideration in respect to the general environment in order that the concept may be expressed as simply and clearly as possible; but societal factors may arise in connection with the specific environments of certain of the organizations studied.

The method proposed to describe the general environment is, first, to identify its key variables; then, to devise suitable indicators of change in these variables; and finally, to show the patterns made by changes in the variables, dividing the time-span of the study for this purpose into significant historical periods. This should make it possible to examine how changes in the general environment may help to explain changes in the structure of influence of international organizations.

Three major variables describe the general environment: the stratification of state power; the economic and political characteristics of states; and patterns of alignment and conflict of states. These three variables were selected in the light of assumptions about the relationship between certain preeminent characteristics of states and their behavior in international organizations.

In the first place, it was assumed that there is some relationship between the power of a state in international affairs generally and its power in international organizations. Since power is a primary factor in influence, there is likely to be a relationship between a state's relative power and its influence in international organizations generally. The point of considering the stratification of power is to explore this relationship. We would expect the United States and the Soviet Union, as powerful states, to have greater influence in any international organization, irrespective of its functional field, than would Canada, Sweden or India; and we would expect Canada, Sweden or India to have greater influence over decisions than Nicaragua, Gabon or Cambodia. In order to test the validity of this assumption and its limits, we have constructed a rank order of state power.

The second major variable in the description of the general environment is the distribution of states according to their economic and political characteristics. Here it was assumed that the level of economic development of a state is important in determining the demands that it will place on an international organization, especially in regard to such questions as the type and priority of services demanded, for example, whether it would prefer an organization to be a clearinghouse for information or an agency

169

for redistributing the world's wealth. Various questions merit exploration in this connection. Do the poorer countries tend to see in international organizations opportunities for pressure in favor of redistribution of the world's wealth? With this in mind, do they emphasize representational issues with the aim of enhancing their control over these organizations so as to be able to use them more effectively for redistribution? Do countries in the early stages of modernization (as distinct from the poorest undeveloped countries on the one hand and those which have achieved sustained growth on the other), because of their concern with the initial accumulation of capital and technical skills, place the heaviest demands upon international organizations for services in these areas? Is there a category of states which are concerned so much with internal problems of industrialization that they place fewer demands upon international organizations than poorer states in the earlier stages of modernization or than richer states? Do the richer states tend to demand technically sophisticated services of international organizations? And are they more likely than poor states to stress rule-creating and especially rule-supervisory decisions, perhaps as a means of protecting their own acquired positions?

It has also frequently been assumed that the nature of the internal polity of a state affects its behavior in international organizations in regard to such factors as the style of participation, its degree of commitment to international organizations and of responsiveness to their decisions. International organizations have sometimes been seen as the creation of democratic states in their own image. Their assemblies have been compared figuratively with the elected assemblies of democratic polities — as parliaments of mankind. The ideals of international organization have been seen as the logical extension of the ideals of democracy — universal respect for the rights of the individual and opportunities for his social fulfillment. But are there in practice any discernible differences in behavior in and towards international organizations between democratic and nondemocratic states?

To examine this assumption more closely it is necessary to be able to classify states according to a typology of political regimes. Classifying states according to levels of economic development is simple compared with the difficulties of conceiving and applying a typology of polities. Once again, we tread in an area where many issues have been raised and few resolved, and where terminology, as well as facts, are much in dispute. Nevertheless, it has been possible to build upon the work of others. [10]

Two dimensions of polities are particularly significant for the purposes of this study. In the first place, we want to know whether the polity is democratic in the sense that there is a regularly accepted and reasonably orderly competition for political power. Secondly, we want to know — in the case of countries which cannot be described as "democratic" in this sense — whether the state is in the hands of a revolutionary group seeking to use it to mobilize the population in order to transform society according to its ideology or of a more conservative group preserving in its broad outlines the existing structure of social power and wealth. These three types are called competitive, mobilizing and authoritarian. It should be stressed that the criteria distinguishing them relate to internal politics, not to external alignments. The purpose of the classification is to explore whether or not there are meaningful relationships between the internal character of the polity and its external behavior, particularly in international organization.

Another set of questions arises in this connection. It has often been thought characteristic of revolutionary governments that they use foreign policy issues as a means of mobilizing domestic support. Will it, then, be found that mobilizing regimes are most active in initiating and supporting symbolic decisions in international organizations? Will these regimes be more concerned than others that symbolic decisions and rule-creating or rule-supervision decisions conform with their ideology? Conversely, it may be assumed that authoritarian regimes care less whether the positions they take in international organizations reflect the characteristics of the regime. They can tolerate a hiatus between the principles they formally support in an international forum and their practices at home, precisely because their populations are not mobilized and articulate on the issues involved and the regimes are not seeking to mobilize them. Ideological consistency will thus be less important for authoritarian regimes than for mobilization polities. Will it then be found that the delegates of authoritarian regimes in international organizations are relatively more free and

171

less instructed than those of other types of regime, that their actions depend more on their personal or idiosyncratic characteristics, and that they have greater opportunities to act as brokers? It is often assumed that competitive polities are more penetrable, *open* societies, and that they are thus more likely to acquiesce in the authority of international organizations. There is more likely to exist within these societies groups which will protest nonobservance of international obligations. Will it then be found that competitive polities take rule-creating decisions more seriously than other polities and only agree to decisions with which they feel they can comply? Will it also be found that with competitive polities, changes of government and of policies at home are reflected in initiatives and support for rule-creating and programmatic decisions in international organizations? Finally, a number of countries have changed in type of regime during the time-span of this study. Have there been observable consequences in the international behavior of these countries, for example as regards joining or leaving international organizations, changing style of participation, or changing demands?

Patterns of conflicts and alignments on major world political and ideological issues constitute the third variable used to describe the general environment. It was assumed that these patterns would have some effect on decision-making in international organizations even where the subject matter of particular decisions may appear to be remote from the conflicts in which world political alignments originated. For example, many technical issues have turned out to be *politicized* by the East—West conflict. On the other hand, classical functionalist theory would have predicted that the more technical an issue, the more likely the chances of avoiding the complications of politics. Thus the exact effect of these patterns on particular types of decisions, at particular times, in particular organizations has to be considered.

Various writers on international relations have sought to describe the patterns of conflict and alignment among states in abstract terms. Usually, a dichotomy is created according to the writer's aesthetic and theoretical sensibilities between have and have-not, satisfied and dissatisfied, imperialist and status quo, or self-preservation and self-extensive states. Morton Kaplan has gone beyond this with his conceptualization of six political systems: the

172

"balance of power" system; the loose bipolar system; the tight bipolar system; the universal system; the hierarchical system; and the unit veto system. [11] He has developed patterns of interaction which pertain to each of these systems.

In the present project the patterns of alignment and conflict have been described in more concrete terms. The principal reason for this is that it was difficult to fit abstract schemes to the empirical facts. Indeed, many of the writers did not intend to provide descriptions of actual international political systems. For example, Kaplan viewed his systems primarily as heuristic models. [12] Also, perhaps because the time span involved in our investigation is relatively brief, the more abstract schemes provide categories which are too gross, which blur important distinctions. Even though states can be divided between the haves and the have-nots, or between those interested in self-preservation and in aggrandizement, the differences within the resulting groups are sometimes even greater than among them. And although it is possible to describe the international political system in the late forties and early fifties as a loose bi-polar system, this subordinates all other relationships to the Soviet—American, or communist—anti—communist clash. This clash was perhaps the most important conflict of that period, but not the only conflict and even less the only relationship. Instead, there were several overlapping patterns of relationships. The first of these involved the clash between the communist states and that group loosely termed the West. The second centered around the struggle to end colonialism. The third was the related but different controversy between the rich and the poor states of the world, and the fourth was the issue of regional integration, particularly in Western Europe. Each of these patterns has had its principle actors, but for various reasons, including the nature of contemporary communications, all have tended to involve in one way or another almost the entire world. Consequently, the patterns have been overlapping. The changing configuration of these patterns can be described in broad outline.

Since these patterns have not been congruent, it is impossible to create one wholly satisfactory scheme for classifying states according to their participation in them. Still, some scheme is necessary to facilitate comparison, and that which intuitively seems to have the most general applicability is the following three-fold division:

Western States: Australia, Austria, Belgium, Luxembourg, Canada, Denmark, Federal Republic of Germany, Finland, France, Greece, Iceland, Ireland, Israel, Italy, Japan, Netherlands, New Zealand, Norway, Portugal, South Africa, Spain, Sweden, Switzerland, Turkey, United Kingdom, United States.

Socialist States: Albania, Bulgaria, Byelorussian SSR, Peoples' Republic of China (after 1950), Cuba (after 1960), Czechoslovakia, German Democratic Republic, Hungary, Mongolia, North Korea, North Vietnam, Poland, Rumania, Ukranian SSR, USSR, Yugoslavia.

Other States: a residual category.

By contrast with the classification of states according to type of polity, this classification refers to foreign policy alignments rather than to the internal political system of a state. Since foreign policy alignments strengthen and weaken over time even if they do not shift, and since they may differ on different issues, a classification by alignments is bound to be conceptually unsatisfactory. In practice, however, such a classification may prove to be more relevant to the divisions within international organizations than will the one based on the nature of polities, since it is more directly related to the phenomena of behavior in international organizations. Its value may prove to lie less in conceptual clarity than in the extent to which it *fits* the facts.

The Western—Socialist—Others scheme of classification applies to both East—West and North—South cleavages. The Western group includes those countries which in the OEEC and NATO formed the core of the Western alliance from about 1949. It includes some other states which have been identified formally or informally with this alliance system, in particular, Australia, Israel, New Zealand, and Japan. In addition, the European neutrals (Austria, Finland, Sweden, and Switzerland) are included because it is assumed that these countries, though nonaligned in a military sense, are in close relationship with the Western group especially in economic matters. The Western group excludes some Asian countries which have been linked with the Western alliance system — such as Pakistan — since it is assumed that their primary identification in international organizations will be with the less developed countries, i.e. for them the North—South cleavage will be more salient than the East—West.

The Socialist group includes the members of COMECON and related countries. In the case of the less developed countries classified here, such as Cuba after 1960, it is assumed that the East—West cleavage is more salient for their foreign relations than the North—South. Yugoslavia is a doubtful case, but is included here on the grounds that it is more interesting to consider its behavior as a deviant from the Socialist group than as a member of either of the other two categories.

The "Others" classification, though technically residual, in fact corresponds roughly to the less developed countries, or in post-UNCTAD terms, to the 77. South Africa, which by the purely residual test might have been classified here, has instead been placed in Western category. In some instances it may be more meaningful to subdivide the Others category into regions: Asia, the Arab states of the Middle East, Africa and Latin America.

Using the three-fold "alignments" classification should help show the extent to which decisions of different kinds in international organizations reflect the major world political cleavages. This is, of course, only a first step towards explaining the degree of relevancy of these cleavages.

Movements in the three environmental variables can be traced through the time-span of this study, which can then be divided into significant historical periods, each characterized by a specific relationship of the key variables. This succession of historical phases provides points of reference for the evolution of each international organization, against which it is possible to test such hypotheses as the following:

Concerning the Stratification of Power:
1. The possibility of an international organization becoming aligned with the policies of one state, in the sense of the decisions of the organization following the orientation of that state, will increase as that state tends to dominate the environment.
2. The more technical the subject matter of the organization, the less likely it is to be affected by changes in the environment with respect to the type of polities of states. *Technical* is taken to mean dependent upon a generally recognized body of specialized knowledge. Used in this sense, the most technical subject

175

matter would be that related to the physical and biological sciences.

3. The more functionally specific the assigned functions of the organization, the less likely it is to be affected by changes in the environment with respect to the type of polities of states.

Concerning the Pattern of Alignments and Conflicts:

4. The greater the tendency toward biopolarity in the pattern of alignments and conflicts in the international arena, the greater the tendency for international organizations to become aligned with one or the other bloc, in the sense of the decisions of the organization following the orientation of the bloc.

5. The more diffuse the pattern of alignments and conflicts in the international arena, the greater the tendency of the international bureaucracy to play an arbitrative role, relying on the support of nonaligned actors.

6. The more diffuse the pattern of alignments and conflicts in the international arena, the greater the scope for coalition-building within international organizations.

7. The more diffuse the pattern of alignments and conflicts in the international arena, the greater the autonomy of the international bureaucracy.

8. The less salient the work of the organization to the central political authorities of states, the less likely it is that the patterns of alignments and conflicts in the international arena will affect the processes of decision-making within the organization.

9. The more essential the organization is to the conduct of minimal intercourse among states, the less likely it is to be affected by changes in the environment. In this context "essential" suggests a problem which requires international cooperation for its solution, such as the delivery of mail amongst countries.

10. The less the organization is oriented toward operational activities, the more it will be affected by changes in the environments.

There are no completely satisfactory ways in which the concepts involved in these hypotheses can be operationalized. However, there are various indicators which can be used as bench-

176

marks. These include: membership; composition of executive organs; composition of the bureaucratic leadership; defined aims of the organization; scope of the organization's functions; program emphases; and budgetary allocations and contributions. In addition, "turning points" in the sense used earlier can also serve as indicators.

Most international organizations also operate in the context of an environment specific to the organization. For example, decision-making in IMF is undoubtedly affected by the position of states in the international monetary system — which currencies are used as reserve currencies, the status of states' reserves, and the stability of currencies. The specific environment is conceived in quite broad terms to include such things as technological developments affecting communications in the case of ITU and articulated bodies of opinion like labor movements in that of ILO. Two concepts developed with regard to the general environment can be applied to the specific environment: the stratification of power (or capabilities) and the pattern of alignments and conflicts. Indices can be constructed for specific fields in which organizations operate, and states can be ranked according to these. The relationships among states can also be broadly characterized.

The organizationally specific environment of an international organization may be linked with or independent of the general environment. In most instances there is probably some relationship, but its strength will vary with different fields. The relationship between decision-making and the general and specific environments can be examined empirically. One or the other could be more important, and the specific environment could act as an intervening variable. The indicators cited above can also be used for examining these issues.

Just as each organization has a specific environment, so it may be argued has each issue-area, or even — at the limit — each decision. The concept of specific environment can be applied with some flexibility. If the most relevant capabilities of states differ for different issues arising in an international organization or for different types of decisions, it may be preferable to use several indicators of specific capabilities rather than a single composite indicator of organizationally specific capability. Similarly, certain

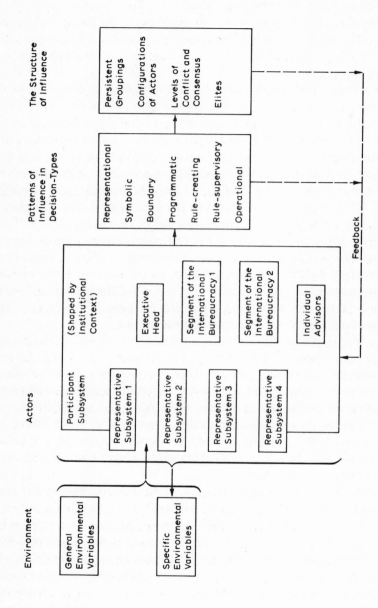

Fig. 1. Influence in international organizations.

178

cleavages in the specific environment of an organization may be more relevant to certain issues than to others.

Although it involves oversimplification, the basic concepts utilized in this study are summarized in Figure 1.

The Structure of Influence

The result of the analyses involved in this project should be a description and an explanation of the structure of influence in each of the organizations being considered. The questions to be addressed are several. Is there a single elite with dominant influence or is influence widely shared? In this context, what is the extent of the influence of the executive head or the organization and its bureaucracy? Is the structure of influence the same for all categories of decisions or does it vary? What are the typical patterns of interaction? Do they involve consensus or conflict? If there is conflict, how is it structured? Are alignments polarized or cross cutting? Do the alignments involve sides disparate in strength or evenly matched? How are all of these things to be explained? To what extent can they be explained in terms of the environment within which the organizations operate, and how important are the processes within the political system of each organization in explaining the generating and structuring of influence?

With answers to these questions, it should be possible to make some judgments about the likely outcomes of decision-making in the international organizations being considered, particularly with reference to whether they will tend to favor the status quo or redistribution. And given the time span of the project, and its concern with explaining how changes have taken place in the structure of influence, it should be possible to make some reasoned speculations about the future. The data acquired on all of these issues should provide the basis for empirically grounded generalizations. These should yield a sharper definition of the variables involved in decision-making in international organizations and a better understanding of the relationships among these variables, in other words, the rudiments of theory.

[1] For example, John G. Hadwen and Johan Kaufmann, *How United Nations Decisions Are Made* (Leyden: A.W. Sythoff, 1962).

[2] For example, Hayward R. Alker, Jr., and Bruce M. Russett, *World Politics in the General Assembly* (New Haven: Yale University Press, 1965).

[3] See Robert A. Dahl, *Modern Political Analysis* (Englewood Cliffs, N.J.: Prentice Hall, Inc., 1963), pp. 39—54. See also Dorwin Cartwright, "Influence, Leadership, Control", in James G. March, Ed., *Handbook of Organizations* (Chicago: Rand McNally, 1965), pp. 1—47.

[4] In addition to Robert A. Dahl, *Who Governs?* (New Haven: Yale University Press, 1961), see also Theodore J. Lowi, "American Business, Public Policy, Case-Studies, and Political Theory" (*World Politics,* Vol. XVI, No. 4, July 1964), pp. 677—715.

[5] See for example James N. Rosenau, "Pre-Theories and Theories of Foreign Policy", in R. Barry Farrell, Ed., *Approaches to Comparative and International Politics* (Evanston: Northwestern University Press, 1966), pp. 27—92.

[6] The stages outlined here were suggested by the work of Fred C. Ikle. See especially his *Alternative Approaches to the International Organization of Disarmament.* R — 391 — ARPA (Santa Monica, 1962).

[7] The studies of permanent missions are steps in this direction. The most detailed study published to date is Arnold Beichman, *The "Other" State Department* (New York: Basic Books, 1967). An ambitious comparative study of permanent missions is currently being conducted by the Carnegie Endowment for International Peace (1970).

[8] Various attempts have already been made to identify groupings. See especially Chadwick F. Alger, "Interaction in a Committee of the United Nations General Assembly", in J. David Singer, Ed., *Quantitative International Politics* (New York: The Free Press, 1968), pp. 51—84; Arend Lijphart, "The Analysis of Bloc Voting in the General Assembly" (*American Political Science Review,* Vol. 57, No. 4, December 1963), pp. 902—17; and Bruce M. Russett, "Discovering Voting Groups in the United Nations" (*American Political Science Review,* Vol. 60, No. 2, June 1966), pp. 327—39. However neither participant observation of interactions in a committee room nor the analysis of roll call votes, the two techniques involved in these attempts, fully measures what is involved in the concept of persistent groupings of actors used here. Among other things, neither gives adequate attention to actors who are not representatives of states.

[9] See in particular Hayward R. Alker, Jr., and Bruce M. Russett, *World Politics in the General Assembly* (New Haven: Yale University Press, 1965), chap. 9, "Who Initiates, with What Success?" pp. 167—90.

10 We are indebted especially to David Apter for some of the basic ideas underlying the typology devised here; Ernst B. Haas for his experiments in application of the Apter concepts; and Dankwart Rustow for his criticism of the initial results of our work.

11 See Morton A. Kaplan, *System and Process in International Politics* (New York: John Wiley and Sons, 1957).

12 Ibid., p. 21.

Decision-Making in National Defence in Switzerland: How a Fighter Plane is Chosen

PAOLO URIO

The extraordinary development of armaments since the end of the Second World War has confronted defence departments with problems of organization and techniques of analysis, resulting in profound reforms. These reforms go beyond the framework of defence departments and involve other sectors of state activity, even extending to the political system as a whole. This is especially true in the case of large countries, such as the U.S.A. and the U.S.S.R., but has also spread to small countries, such as Switzerland.

This report does not claim to be an exhaustive survey of the problems which face Switzerland in the choice of fighter planes. These problems have been dealt with elsewhere, and the reader may refer to various publications which have recently appeared. This report will confine itself to summarizing briefly the reforms adopted in this domain recently and to presenting the case of the choice — at the time of writing still in progress — of a fighter plane, which comes within the general framework of these reforms. In doing so, I hope to raise a certain number of problems and to show how their study can give the political scientist the opportunity of deepening his knowledge of the decision-making process in Switzerland at the federal level.

Introduction

We define *decision* as the act of choosing among several alternatives in a situation of incomplete information. Our starting point is linked to the notion of problem: every problem can be traced back to an objective (which corresponds to a need), the achievement of which depends upon a set of variables which can assume different values. The solution of the problem implies, therefore, knowledge of the variables and of their values, as well as a procedure which enables the variables to be linked together, so that every possible combination of them can be considered as a solution. If there is complete information and the procedure is known, the solution of the problem is automatic. Thus, for example, the formula πr^2 automatically enables one to find the circle of maximum area in a square of 3 × 3 cm. The goal having been set, the variables and the procedure (formula) known, the solution is automatic, and no decision is either possible or necessary. On the other hand, when the variables are not completely known (incomplete information) and/or when the procedure is unknown or allows only a part of the known variables to be dealt with, one is faced with a situation of risk or uncertainty, which implies a choice between two or more possible alternatives. In the political system, it is this second type of situation which is the most common, if not the only one, because the decision-makers are generally in a situation of incomplete information. The condition is further complicated in that a solution can be found in a situation of complete information at one stage of the decision-making process but not when later stages are reached.

Take for example the choice of a fighter plane between two possibilities, X_1 and X_2, manufactured by two foreign countries, P_1 and P_2, respectively. Let us suppose, greatly simplifying the question, that the aim is to acquire a plane which can fly at a speed of 2000 km/h and with maximum efficiency, measured in bombing load. The assessment of the two types of planes carried out by a team of competent officials leads to the conclusion that, the price being the same, the plane X_1 with 6 tons of bomb load is more efficient than plane X_2 which can only carry 3.5. At the level of this team of officials, no decision is necessary: the plane X_1 is the automatic choice. But a different conclusion may be reached by higher authorities, who have to take into account other aspects of the problem, such as the international one, the possibility of the choice between the two models having a bearing upon trade relations with the two producer countries. Now, at this stage, the situation is usually one of incomplete information. As a result, the first aim of every system is to reduce to the minimum the difference between situations of incomplete information and those of complete information. Secondly, the decisions taken at the lower levels of the administration having a strong influence on the decisions taken at the higher levels (administrative and political), it is important to be able to analyze side by side and conjointly all the factors relative to a given decision. [1]

The fact that it was unable to achieve these two objectives during the period 1958—1962 involved the Swiss Department of Defence (*Département Militaire Fédéral*) is one of the most serious failures of its history. In fact, at the time when a high performance plane was being chosen, neither the organization not the techniques for decision-making had been implemented which would have made it possible to gather and process all the necessary information (aim number one). [2] Furthermore, the study of some aspects of the problem (particularly economic, political and psychological), which corresponds to the second objective, was overlooked. This double failure led to considerable overexpenditure and a violent reaction from parliament and the public. [3] The consequences of this crisis were seen in the years 1962—68 and resulted in the reforms set out below.

The Strengthening of Parliamentary Control

As part of this reform, a parliamentary information service was set up. Furthermore, parliamentary commissions won the right to question civil servants, even against the government's will; parliamentary commissions of administration ("*gestion*") and those of finance gained the right to ask for useful information and to demand that all the official documents be produced; and parliament can set up commissions of inquiry. These commissions of inquiry can demand from the government the requisite staff or engage the staff themselves; interrogate witnesses and demand that documents be produced; call in experts and inspect sites; obtain all the official documents which the administration has relating to the case; gather written or oral testimony from legal authorities, civil servants, and individuals; and institute official hearings. [4] If civil servants are to be questioned by a parliamentary commission of inquiry about facts which are officially secret, the government must first be heard. If the government decides that this information should not be given, the commission of inquiry can override it. The other parliamentary commissions do not have this right.

The Reform of the Department of Defence [5]

This reform had two basic aims: One, the reduction of the number of subordinates directly responsible to one head, and two, the granting of an adequate place to the services which had to cope with the new decision-making techniques.[6] On the first point, the number of those subordinates to the head of the department (minister) has been reduced from sixteen to ten. These are, the director of the board of the military administration, the chief auditor, the four commanders of the army corps, the commander of the air force, and the heads of the three sections of the department (the general staff, the instruction section, and the armaments section). The idea of a reduction in the number of direct subordinates has also been carried out at the lower levels, in particular for the armaments section. The latter is, together with the section of the general staff, the most affected by the implementation of the second aim. Finally, it must be noted that this new organization strengthens the staff structure of the department: each of the three sections is given a staff, and the department itself a general staff of direction. This general staff is to coordinate at the highest level the tasks of the various services in training and equipping the army.[7] The new structure responds to the growing complexity of military problems by (1) a greater decentralization of direct authority to free the heads of the department from duties which are too numerous and too onerous and to give these over to specialized services, and (2) the creation of staffs to ensure coordination and control.

Decision-Making

The decree of 30 June 1969[8] subdivided the decision-making process on armaments into seven main phases: (1) definition of the conception of national defence, (2) general planning, (3) research, (4) definition of projects, (5) development and testing, (6) choice and acquisition of armaments, and (7) upkeep, technical modifications, standardization, improvement, inspection and liquidation.[9]

(1) The conception of national defence is defined by a section of the general staff in collaboration with the other sections and with the army and air force commanders, after an assessment of the potential threat and the general conditions of the environment. This examination should result in the necessary choices to ensure the defence of the country. It also evaluates the military potential of the country, and thus defines the existing conception of national defence. Later, the results of these two evaluations are compared, and this analysis leads to the modifications which must be made to the contemporary conception of national defence or to the military potential of the country. At the same time, the order of priorities is fixed. In terms of systems analysis, the objectives have been defined. The search for solutions (systems) enabling these objectives to be attained results in (2) general planning, which is the task of the head of the general staff, aided by the planning group.

Armament needs can give rise to (3) research, which is undertaken under the direction of the head of the armaments section. He decides what is needed in matters of research and inserts these needs into the long-term research plan, which is examined by the general staff of direction and approved by the head of the department. The research projects are mentioned afterwards in the annual programme of research, development, and testing. This programme serves as a basis for the preparation of the annual budget, which is presented to parliament together with the general budget.

It is only after the (4) definition of the projects that one comes to practical application, which must solidify the choices of the two first phases (conception of defence and general planning). The definition of a project comprises the preliminary examinations and definition of military and technical requirements. The head of the general staff directs the preliminary examinations and coordinates interested bodies (in particular the three sections and the board of military administration), which evaluate the various problems, according to their qualifications. Recourse can also be had to technical commissions or to bodies outside the department. When this work is finished, the head of the general staff presents a report which is submitted to the commission of military defence [10] and eventually to the general staff of direction. The head of the department decides on what is proposed. For particularly important projects, the heads of the three sections can propose to the defence minister that a projects center should be created. This procedure ensures an overall view, coordination, and control of costs.

If the preliminary examination shows that the anticipated project is necessary and can be carried out, the head of the general staff defines the military specifications, taking into account the opinions of the heads of instruction and armaments. With the military qualities defined by the military specifications in mind, the head of the armaments section in turn sets the technical specifications.

From then on, two possibilities are open: either, the equipment being available on the market, they proceed toward the choice and acquisition of the weapon system; or they decide to develop one or more weapon systems, and the choice is postponed until after the (5) development and the testing of the prototypes. In this case, the head of the armaments section draws up the long-term development plan on the basis of the military and technical specifications, in collaboration with the head of the general staff. This plan is later set up by the general staff of direction, subject to the advice of the commission of military defence. On the basis of the information thus gathered, the head of armaments draws up the definitive plan which must be approved by the minister. As in the case of the research projects, the new development projects are introduced into the annual programme of research, development, and testing and presented to parliament in the annual budget. It is, moreover, stipulated that for every project a credit must be voted by parliament, and the administration must indicate the purpose of the research, development and testing, as well as the financial limits set. As soon as it becomes apparent that this credit is not sufficient, a request for additional credit must be presented to parliament. When the latter approves the budget, the head of armaments orders the work to be begun and orders the technical tests. The results are laid before the general staff of direction. The appropriate services set up the projected programme of testing the weapon systems in the field and present the result to the head of the general staff for approval. He then orders tests to be carried out. A report on the results of these tests is presented through official channels to the head of the general staff.

The phase of (6) the choice of models and their acquisition begins with the preparation of criteria of appraisal in which, as a rule, all the sections and the appropriate services take part. The work is directed by the head of armaments, who can have recourse to the projects center if one has been created. Appeal also can be made, if necessary, to bodies outside the department. The head of armaments prepares in detail the scientific, technical, industrial, economic, and financial data and indicates what eventual modifications must be made to the weapon systems in question. He then designates the system which has been chosen, after consultation with the interested bodies, notably the head of the general staff. If, however, the choice is in the hands of a higher body, the head of armaments submits his proposal to the opinion of the general staff of direction and presents it to the minister for approval. It is then within parliament's competence to grant the necessary credits. These appear either in the annual defence budget or, for particularly important projects, in the "armaments messages" of the government. [11] In both cases, the chief of the general staff decides upon the needs of the sections and services from the military point of view, and the head of armaments examines the possibilities of the project from a technical and industrial viewpoint and considers any possible commercial repercussions. The projected annual budget is examined by the general staff of direction, set up by the head of armaments, and approved by the minister. The projected "armaments messages" are prepared under the guidance of the head of armaments, with the collaboration of the other sections, the board of military administration, the qualified services, and the general staff of direction, the Commission of Military Defence, and if need be, the projects centre. It is then set up by the board of military administration, submitted to the general staff of direction, and sent for approval to the minister. The latter presents it to the government, which makes the final decision.

Once parliament has agreed on the necessary credits, we come to the execution of the project under the direction and control of the head of armaments. He establishes both a six-monthly review of how the acquisition is going (which is submitted to the sections involved or to the air force commander), and an annual detailed account of each credit (which is presented to the department). If the credits are not sufficient, a demand for additional credits must be presented to parliament. Lastly, the head of armaments supervises the reception of the weapon system and delivers it to the appropriate services according to the instructions of the chief of the general staff. The latter, also, issues instructions about its use by the troops, in agreement with the head of instruction.

The weapon system thus delivered to the forces must be kept in condition according to the instructions of the head of the general staff. (7) The upkeep, technical modifications, standardization, revision, and liquidation are the province of the head of the general staff in matters concerning military needs and necessities, and of the head of armaments in technical matters.

These reforms, which have just been summarized, should result in the following goals:

1) More effective parliamentary control.

2) Better separation between the analysis of military aspects and the technical, scientific, and commercial aspects, as a result of the creation of the armaments section; simultaneous analysis of these aspects.

3) More time given to collaboration with scientific and economic bodies.

4) Greater importance given to the most advanced techniques of analysis in order to reduce uncertainty as far as possible.

5) Greater importance accorded to the coordination and control of the different duties of the department.

6) Better circulation of information within the department, and between it and others — government, parliament, public.

It is still too early to establish an objective and complete balance of the efficacy of these reforms. This balance can only be reached in about ten years' time, when enough case studies to make generalization possible have been completed. For the time being, it can be seen that (*a*) coordination and control could be improved by the setting up of a unified command in peacetime (in wartime the appointment of a general is foreseen), and of a general staff for planning attached to the minister (not to the chief of the general staff as at present). (*b*) The capacity for decision can be improved by a strengthening of the teams which work with advanced techniques of analysis (planning, operations research, etc.), and (*c*) the clearcut separation between development and acquisition could cause inconvenience in the case of particularly complex weapon systems, whose development necessitate considerable investment and a relatively long time. Too sharp a separation could, in fact, prolong the delay before delivery to the forces is made, as the decision to mass-produce can only be taken when the development phase is over.

On the practical plane, the only example of any importance which can illustrate the unfolding of the decision-making process after the adoption of the above-mentioned reforms is that of the choice of a new tactical support aircraft. During the study of this case, another difficulty emerged, in addition to the usual problems which spring from military secrets: the choice of the model being still in process, it is clearly not possible to present the whole of the process, nor to have recourse to information, which although today inaccessible, could be at the disposal of the researcher some time after the end of the decision-making process.

The Choice of a New Tactical Support Aircraft [12]

The conception of national defence adopted in 1966 distributed the following tasks to aviation: (1) defence of air space against enemy aircraft; (2) prevention of enemy air reconnaissance and air attacks against Swiss troops in specific areas; (3) attack against ground targets; (4) reconnaissance; and (5) transport of troops and equipment. [13] A comparison between these objectives and the means available showed that it was necessary to equip the Swiss air force with a new plane able to fulfill the third objective. [14] Once this necessity had been accepted, the National Defence Commission [15] specified in January 1967 the fundamental tasks which the new aircraft must be able to do: (1) to attack large ground targets which are strongly protected by anti-aircraft artillery; (2) to ensure its own protection; (3) to ensure, if need be and as far as possible, the protection of existing less powerful aircraft. [16] These requirements were sent to the chief of the general staff. Together with the long-term financial plan, they formed the basis for the selection of the aircraft under consideration. Within the framework of the financial plan, a sum of 1300 million francs was allowed for the acquisition of the new aircraft during the period 1970–74. Once the ends and the financial limits within which they were to be achieved had been defined, it was necessary to decide upon the best alternative to satisfy these objectives (search for the system with the optimal effectiveness for a given cost). We shall first examine the organization which was set up to deal with these problems and then pass on to the process and the techniques of decision which were used.

The Organization of Work

The supervision of the work was entrusted to an ad hoc body, the Projects Center for the Acquisition of Fighter Aircraft (*Centre des projets pour l'acquisition d'avions de combat* – CPAC), directed by Brigadier K. Bollinger and subordinate to the head of the planning section of the general staff. Composed of specialized officials, it ensured coordination between the military management of the project (responsible to the head of the air force), the technical and commercial side (responsible to the head of the armaments section), the other services involved, and collaborators outside the Department (notably the Zurich Institute for Operational Research). The head of the planning group keeps the head of the general staff informed of the progress of the work. The latter presides over another ad hoc body, the Committee for Coordination in which are included also the head of armaments and the commander of the air forces and anti-aircraft artillery. This committee deals with fundamental questions and issues basic directives. In turn, the chief of the general staff keeps the minister informed. The minister has at his disposal a consultative body, the Commission for Military Aircraft (*Commission pour les avions militaires* – CAM), which was set up in October 1966 and is composed of important persons from military, scientific and industrial circles, presided over by Professor E. Amstutz. This commission advises the minister or the head of the general staff who transmits the advice to the Committee for Coordination. The Commission for Military Aircraft is consulted about problems relating to planning, development, tests, evaluation, and acquisition of military aircraft. Lastly, the head of the air forces and anti-aircraft artillery has at his command a consultative commission, the Commission for the Military Requirements of Aeronautic Material (*Commission pour les exigences militaires du matériel aéronautique* — CEMMA) which, as its name indicates, deals with the military aspects of the systems of aeronautical armament. This commission is comprised of nonprofessional officers, to be precise, higher commanders of the air force units and commanders of professional air force units. Most of its members are engineers from the Federal Polytechnic School, who hold managerial posts in private industry. This organization, which enlists the help of collaborators and advisors from outside the department, should prevent military requirements from overriding the technical, economic, and financial aspects of the purchase.

Finally, after the reorganization of the department, it should be noted that the direction of the project passed from the head of the general staff to the head of armaments on September 1, 1969, that is at the end of the pre-evaluation. It is, nevertheless, quite clear that, even if the reorganization of the department had been carried out at the beginning of the work, the phase of pre-evaluation would still have been directed by the head of the general staff.

The Process and Techniques of Decision-Making

The Decision-Making Process and the Application of the Program Evaluation Review Technique (PERT) Method

This method has been used to organize the process of acquisition. This means that when describing it, we shall have the opportunity to follow along broad lines the process of decision-making. For the establishment of the PERT network, the Committee for Coordination defined the main events and activities, while the appropriate services fixed the intermediary stages and the components of the main stages. This network indicates the duties which must be carried out, as well as the time which will be needed. This enables an overall view of the whole operation to be taken. Also, the recording of the tasks which have been accomplished and the time taken makes possible permanent control and any necessary changes. The process is subdivided into three main phases: (1) pre-evaluation, (2) evaluation, and (3) the parliamentary phase. [17]

193

(1) *Pre-evaluation.* This phase was preceded in 1966 by a prospecting of the market, with the aim of identifying planes which could in principle meet the military requirements, and thus be submitted for pre-evaluation. On the basis of the information gathered, the Commission for National Defence picked out nine aircraft at the beginning of 1967, having first consulted experts from outside the department (industrialists and aeronautical experts). At the same time, as we have seen, it defined the fundamental requirements of the aircraft. Factories with an interest in the project were then invited to answer a questionnaire of about one-thousand questions. The data so gathered were processed by methods which we shall describe later. For the time being, it should be remarked that this treatment was carried out by the armaments section and by the Institute for Operational Research in Zurich, under the supervision of the Projects Center. At the same time and linked with this work, the military specifications were drawn up by the air force commander and approved by the chief of the general staff (February 1969). Lastly, during the pre-evaluation, the possibility of manufacture under licence was examined. The armaments section then contacted the Swiss Association for the aeronautical industry (a pressure group which includes all the main aeronautical industries), as well as the main industries interested in the project. On the basis of the results, the Projects Center submitted a proposition to the Committee for Coordination and to the Committee for Military Aircraft (CAM) for the benefit of the minister (July 1969). The government, informed of this by the minister, decided to concentrate on the A−7 Corsair (American) and the G−91Y (Italian) (August 1969). [18] Finally, it should be noted that the military commissions of the federal chambers were kept informed of the work by the Department of Defence, and in particular by the head of the project, Brigadier K. Bollinger.

(2) *Evaluation.* This phase, which began in September 1969, under the direction of the head of armaments finished towards the end of 1972. It involves the gathering of supplementary information which must be analyzed within the framework of analysis techniques perfected during the pre-evaluation. It will lead to a choice, which must be submitted to the government for approval.

(3) *The Parliamentary Phase.* After the government has come to a decision, the Department of Defence will prepare a request to parliament for the necessary credits. But it should be noted that this phase should not take too long, as the military commissions of the two chambers have already had the opportunity to follow the project since pre-evaluation, and a vast hearing was held at the beginning of the evaluation phase. In fact, at the beginning of September 1969, the two commissions in joint session (thirty-nine deputies in all) heard representatives of the Swiss aeronautical industry, science and the economy, officials in the Department of Defence, the Finance Department, the federal Office of Industry, the Arts and Professions and Labour (*l'Office fédéral de l'industrie, des arts et métiers et du travail* — OFIAMT — which deals in particular with foreign labour), and other officials.[19] It was essentially a question of deciding whether it was going to be possible to manufacture in Switzerland under licence.[20] The parliamentary commissions had clearly no decision to take. During the hearing it became clear what were the obstacles in the way of an affirmative answer. Manufacture under licence would (1) certainly delay deliveries and thus would not please the army which needed a tactical support aircraft with the least possible delay; (2) incur higher costs than in the case of pure and simple purchase and so would not please the members of the armaments section whose duty it was to find maximum efficiency at a given cost; (3) involve an increased call upon foreign labour and this would not please the OFIAMT; and (4) fail to guarantee independence from foreign sources as the Swiss industry was not able to manufacture the complete product. Lastly, the representatives of the aeronautical industry having "let it be known that purchase abroad would not plunge it into an insuperable crisis,"[21] it seemed that manufacture under licence would be the least probable outcome.[22]

Systems Analysis and Tree Analysis

Tree analysis (*strukturbaum analyse*) facilitates the presentation in a global table of the different criteria which form the basis of the choice and which must be applied using different techniques of analysis. Thus, for example, the technical and tactical qualities could be evaluated by means of systems analysis or operational research, while the politico-economic factors are evaluated on the

195

basis of the policy of neutrality and of policy towards European economic integration (EEC, EFTA, etc.).[23] In addition, a coefficient has been attributed to each sector. Thus, for example, a greater weight could be assigned to the tactical aspects in relation to technical maturity. By this is meant that one would be inclined to choose a relatively little developed aircraft, provided that it had great tactical efficiency (the development costs having been taken into consideration), rather than a more highly developed, but less efficient, one. These considerations enable one to see how necessary it is to establish an order of priorities (weighing up) between the objectives and the criteria of evaluation. This is the level at which systems analysis is used. It is a question, in effect, of taking into consideration nonquantifiable as well as quantifiable data by defining the objectives, searching for solutions (systems), evaluating these systems, and presenting the results to the decision-makers in such a form that they can make the decision by affixing their scale of value wherever the judgment of the analyst is insufficient. Tree analysis has precisely the virtue of facilitating these tasks.

The Application of Operational Research

It is at the level of the tactical and technical aspects of the project that operational research has been applied. In order to determine the efficiency of the aircraft under consideration an enormous mathematical apparatus was set up, in collaboration with the systems analysis team of the armaments section, the Zurich Institute for Operational Research, and the commander of the air forces and anti-aircraft artillery.[24] The aim of this work was to find out what chances (probability) of survival the aircraft had from the moment they left the airfield, throughout the attack, and during the return flight to their base. In addition to the information gathered from the manufacturers (weight, speed, load capacity, etc.), variables were introduced relative to the time,[25] the enemy potential,[26] the angle of attack, the point of dropping the bombs, etc. The variations of these data were tested by using mathematical models, with the help of computers. Thus, for example, 100,000 simulations of air combats were processed. The different phases of this work were presented on an *integral diagram* which gives a fair idea of the complexity of the problems. This diagram, dated June 1967, was later perfected by the addition of new analyses and by the integration of cost analysis.

The Application of Cost-Efficiency Analysis

Side by side with the determination of the efficiency of the aircraft under examination, work was done with the aim of discovering the most effective aircraft available within a budget of 1300 million Swiss francs. These studies were incorporated into the previous ones in a diagram called the *maxi-integral*, dated 15 September 1969, which gave the situation at the beginning of the evaluation phase.

We shall try to show the fundamental application of the cost-efficiency analysis by borrowing an example from Kohlas. [27] Suppose we are evaluating two types of aircraft A and B. The unitary cost of these aircraft varies, according to well-known economic laws, according to the volume of production. Let us then suppose that for the amount available (for example, 1300 million Swiss francs) the unitary cost of the two types of plane is such that 120 type A or 80 type B can be purchased. Having thus decided upon the number of planes which can be bought in each case, it remains to be seen what is the best solution. First, the chances of survival must be decided upon. [28] Suppose that these are 0.90 for A and 0.95 for B. We then include in the table the carrying capacity in tons of each aircraft. Suppose that it is 3.5 for A and 4.0 for B. It is thus possible to arrive at a significant representation of the two variants. In this case, variant B permits, with a smaller number of planes, a greater number of missions and a higher transport capacity.

In the case of the choice of a new aircraft, cost-efficiency analysis has made it possible to present the relevant facts clearly and completely to those responsible for the decision (the minister, and in the last instance, the government). Clear and complete that is as

TABLE 1

	Variant A	Variant B
Average number of missions n	9	19
Average capacity of transport in tons T	3780	6080

197

regards the aspects with which this technique of decision has dealt. In fact, other factors (political ones, for example) can affect the decision when the final choice is made. We have already seen how these other factors are taken into consideration and introduced in tree analysis.

Conclusion

In spite of the fragmentary nature of the information which we have managed to gather about the choice of the new aircraft, we think that it is, nevertheless, possible to draw some conclusions, which we shall present in two parts. The first relates to the organization of the work and to the use of techniques of decision, the second to the part played by the decision-makers in the process.

The Organization of the Work and the Application of Techniques of Decision

Contrary to what was done at the time when the Mirages were acquired, the organization set up to choose a new aircraft made it possible (1) to follow along parallel lines, from the outset, the analysis of the military, technical and economic aspects of the purchase; (2) to associate with the work, or to consult, experts outside the Department of Defence; (3) to ensure better coordination of the different tasks; (4) to exercise more effective control of the process; (5) to guarantee better circulation of information within the department; and (6) to supply better information to those outside the department, in particular to the government, the parliamentary commissions, and the public. In addition, the use of the most advanced techniques of decision-making made possible a more rational assembling of information, a more subtle, efficient treatment of the data, and a better presentation of the possible alternatives to those higher bodies upon which the final choice rests.

Finally, it should be noted that the application of a clearcut separation between development and acquisition had given rise to the sort of difficulties which are only to be expected when this principle is applied too rigidly. The work undertaken in this connection during pre-evaluation revealed that "this delimitation should not be operated in the sense of constructing a certain number of the two aircraft already in the developmental phase. It should rather be assured by means of a precise definition of the project before submitting to the federal houses of parliament the message on their acquisition. By calling attention to the repercussions of all the Swiss modifications to the original planes, it would be possible to recognize the extent of the risk." [29]

The Role of the Decision-Makers

The part played by the Department of Defence has undergone two major changes. The first has taken place within the department and corresponds to the greater importance given from the beginning to the technicians in the armaments section. The other took place at the level of relations between the department and outside experts. These latter participated in the evaluation of the new aircraft, whereas when the Mirages were chosen, it was not deemed necessary to associate independent experts with the work of evaluation. Nevertheless, it must not be thought, as some newspapers have understood, that these experts (especially those from the Zurich Institute for Operational Research) had a grip on the phase of pre-evaluation and will continue to dominate the evaluation. The independent experts have played an important part and in some partial analyses a preponderant one, especially for the mathematical model which enabled air combats simulation. But other partial analyses, just as important, were undertaken by the systems analysis team of the armaments section. It must be noted that the integration of partial analyses into a global diagram was the outcome of collaboration between experts in the department and external ones, under the supervision of the director of the project. Lastly, it must not be forgotten that this work, which calls upon operational research, is not concerned with all the aspects of a project on the acquisition of such a complex weapon as a fighter aircraft. Other factors (economic and political), which are outside the scope of these analyses, are brought to bear upon the choice. At this level, those who are making the decision can call upon other independent experts: the members of the Commission for Military Aircraft (CAM), who represent scientific, economic and industrial circles, and who can bring different criteria of judgment to bear.

The events leading to the purchase of the new aircraft also enabled some change in the part played by parliament. On the one hand, parliament was better informed about how the acquisition was developing, and on the other, took the initiative itself by deciding to gather supplementary information (hearing of September 1969), and by obtaining from the government the concession that some kinds of aircraft which had previously been out of the running should be submitted to a new analysis (June 1970, evaluation phase). It is open to question whether this initiative (taken also by some newspapers) will not be prejudicial in that it will undoubtedly prolong the phase of evaluation and, consequently, the delivery of the aircraft which is finally chosen. On the other hand, it must be noted that according to reliable witnesses, the hearing of September 1969 showed how difficult it is for most members of parliament to grasp problems relating to such a complex undertaking. Besides, the fact that the debate only dealt with the problem of manufacture under licence, which is more easily grasped than problems about the choice of a weapon system, is fairly significant. Clearly, it is difficult to draw definite conclusions about the ability of parliament to follow this affair knowledgeably and to wield effective control. It is, however, doubtful whether parliament can carry out these duties with the means presently at its disposal (an insufficiently equipped information service and nonprofessional members). Now that the administration has acquired more efficient means (more rational structure and rational decision-making techniques), parliament must ensure for itself the men (full time parliamentarians) and means (financial, auxiliary staff, full-time and/or occasional experts, and techniques for gathering, classifying, and analyzing information) which will enable it to better accomplish its tasks.

NOTES

[1] This is even truer for the choice of armaments in which tactical-technical factors of great complexity are added to economic, political, and ideological elements.

² See W. Geiger, "Der Mirage-Konflikt, eine Entstehung Lösung und grund-sätzliche Bedeutung" (*Annuaire Suisse de Science Politique*, 1965), pp. 90–99; P. Urio, "L'affaire des Mirages" (ibid, 1968) pp. 90–99; P. Urio, *L'Affaire des Mirages: décision administrative et controle parlementaire* (Genève: Ed. Médecine et Hygiène, 1972) 311 p.

³ For further details, see the works quoted in Note 2.

⁴ See, for example, R. Helg, "La haute surveillance du parlement sur le gouvernment et l'administration" (*Revue de droit suisse*, 1966, 11), pp. 95–164.

⁵ See *Message du Conseil fédéral à l'Assemblée fédérale concernant la réor-ganisation du Département militaire et la modification de la loi sur l'orga-nisation militaire* du 19 sept. 1966 (Berne: Federal Chancellory), 60 p.

⁶ These are notably planning, systems analysis, operational research, cost-efficiency analysis, PERT method, and decision trees.

⁷ Members of the general staff of direction are: the head of instruction, the head of the general staff, the head of armaments, and the director of the board of military administration. The general staff of direction is presided over by the head of the department of defence.

⁸ *Ordonnance du Département militaire fédéral concernant les modalités de l'armement* of 30 June 1969 (Berne: Federal Chancellory), 13 p.

⁹ It is to be noted that this process presents some analogies with the Ameri-can PPBS.

¹⁰ This consultative body of the head of the department is made up of the 4 corps commanders, the air force commander, the head of the general staff, the head of instruction and the head of armaments. The head of the department presides over it.

¹¹ The "messages" of the government are texts explaining the government's goals which accompany every bill submitted to parliament. They are pub-lished in the "Feuille Officielle fédérale" published by the Federal Chanc-ellory.

¹² See for example H. Wildbolz, *Fragen des Projektleitung in Zusammenhang mit der nächsten Flugzeuggeneration* (Berne, June 1967, roneotyped), *Verfahrensfragen zur Wahl des neuen Kampfflugseuges* (Berne, June 1968, 7 p., roneotyped); *Acquisition d'un nouvel avion d'appui tactique, état actuel du projet*, Press release from the Department of Defence (Berne, 27 August 1969, 9 p., roneotyped); *La préévaluation d'un nouvel avion de combat*, Department of Defence, press release (Berne, 16 December, 9 p., roneotyped); *Acquisition d'avions de combat*, Department of Defence press release (Berne, 15 July 1970, 1 p., roneotyped).

¹³ *Rapport du Conseil fédéral à l'Assemblée fédérale concernant la concep-tion de la défense nationale militaire* of 6 June 1966 (Berne: Federal Chancellory), pp. 12–13.

[14] The aims (1) and (2) are achieved by the Mirages III S and the Hunter; aim (4) is assured by the Mirages III RS and the helicopters Alouette 11 and 111. The Venoms, which date from the beginning of the 1950's, are no longer able to fulfill the objective satisfactorily.

[15] The Commission of National Defence was replaced in 1968 by the Commission of Military Defence. The two commissions have, by and large, the same tasks and the same composition, except that the CMD comprises also the head of armaments (see note 10 above).

[16] Press release put out by the Department of Defence on 27 August 1969, *Acquisition d'un nouvel avion*, p. 1.

[17] For various reasons, we stopped documenting this report on 31 December 1969. The parliamentary phase should probably come to an end towards the middle of 1973. We hope to present a report on the case as a whole during 1973.

[18] The following aeroplanes were involved: AJ-37 Viggen (SAAB), 'Jaguar' (Braguet/BAC), J-35X Draken (SAAB), A-4 Skyhawk (Douglas), G-91Y (Fiat), Mirage VS (Dassault), F-5 (Northrop), A-7 Corsair II (Ling-Temco-Vought), AA-7 et AR-7 (Altenrhein).

[19] See for example the *Tribune de Genève*, 11/12.9.1969, and the *Journal de Genève*, 12.9.1969.

[20] The Swiss plane AR-7 having been discarded during the preliminary evaluation, the possibility of granting aircraft construction to the Swiss industry was restricted to construction under licence.

[21] *Tribune de Genève*, 11/12.9.1969.

[22] This problem has concerned members of parliament since 1966. The head of the department, replying to the questions of three deputies (Schürmann, Keller, and Wüthrich) had even then held out very little hope of construction under licence (*Tribune de Genève*, 22.9.1966).

[23] It is to be remembered, moreover, that the Political Department and the Department of Finance and of Customs are called upon to give their opinion on problems of armaments which have an influence upon foreign policy.

[24] Two researchers in the Institute for Operational Research in Zurich have written their doctoral dissertations on these works: J. Kohlas, *Simulation von Luftkämpfen* (Zurich: Juris Druck + Verlag, 1967), 116 p.; and W. Glanzmann, *Die Entdeckungswahrscheinlichkeit von Flugzeugen unter visueller Beobachtung* (Zurich: Juris Druck + Verlag, 1969), 108 p.

[25] For example, time of parking on the runway, time used to reach the target, etc.

[26] In this case, different possible levels of the adverse defence have been

foreseen, for interception aircraft as well as for ground-air missiles and the anti-aircraft artillery in general.

[27] J. Kohlas, *Simulation von Luftkämpfen*, pp.9–14.

[28] The probability of survival q of an aircraft for n missions is given by the formula $q_n = q^n(1-q)$. From this can be deduced the average number of possible missions (n) until the aircraft is lost.

$$\bar{n} = \sum_{n=1}^{\infty} nq_n = \frac{q}{1-q},$$

as well as the average total transport capacity (T)

$$\bar{T} = Nt\bar{n} = Nt \frac{q}{1-q},$$

where N is the number of aircraft and t the bombing load in tons for each plane.

[29] Press release of the Department of Defence on 27 August 1969, *Acquisition d'un nouvel avion*, p. 4.

Decision-Making in Public Bodies of International Organizations (ILO, WHO, WMO, UN): A Preliminary Research Report

CHADWICK F. ALGER*

Public bodies in international organizations, like all organizations, make occasional decisions on issues of great import that receive wide attention. But most decisions are made on questions that are of minor consequence. While these minor decisions are inconsequential individually, their total impact over a long period of time is not negligible. Furthermore, these decisions help create the context in which occasional decisions recognized to be highly important are made. Because research on decisions in public bodies of international organizations has been confined almost exclusively to so-called "important" decisions, particularly as revealed in roll call votes, the research reported here has been carried out on the total population of decisions in certain organizations in the United Nations family. In order to encompass possible variation in so-called "less political" organizations, decisions have been selected not only from the United Nations but also from the International Labor Organization, the World Health Organization, and

* Ohio State University, Columbus, Ohio. David Johnson, Jennifer Lovald, Carol Soroos and Norman Walbek assisted in coding decisions. Michael Leavitt assisted in data processing. Lucille Mayer assisted at all stages of the research.

the World Meteorological Organization. In each organization all decisions have been analyzed in the plenary of the general assembly and in the executive body or council (with the exception of the World Meteorological Organization, whose Executive Committee proceedings do not provide adequate information for analysis). In contrast to the other organizations, which have only one council, the United Nations has three — Economic and Social Council, Security Council, and Trusteeship Council. Only one of these, the Security Council, was chosen for analysis.

Decisions made by these assemblies and executive bodies have been taken from their records, verbatim records for all four assemblies and summary records for the executive bodies, except the Security Council which provides verbatim records. Since it was a purpose of the research to obtain an overview of decision-making, including the apparently inconsequential, *all* decisions taken by these bodies as a whole have been included. Therefore, the total population ranges from procedural decisions, such as decisions to adjourn, to important program decisions, such as the adoption of a labor convention by the International Labor Organization. In order to obtain information on change across time, three years were selected — 1955, 1960, and 1965.

Before proceeding with discussion of a view of decisions in assemblies and councils of international organizations obtained from public records, it is important to emphasize that these records provide only a partial view of decision-making in these bodies. Activities related to these decisions also take place in private conversations during public meetings that are not placed in the record, and in a variety of kinds of negotiations and discussions that take place outside public meeting halls (both at the headquarters of international organizations and elsewhere). Writing on decision-making in the Executive Board of the International Monetary Fund, William Dale asserts:

> The crucial phase of decision-making in the Fund is not the phase of formal "decision-taking" which generally consists of hardly more than formal laying on of hands. Rather, the crucial phase of the process is "decision-shaping", which occurs (sometimes over a period of considerable length — months or even years) in advance of the formal recording of the decision. Everyone in the Fund — not least the Executive Directors — is well aware that he must act to shape a decision to be taken, not when it appears in dress of a formal proposal (by which time it is generally much

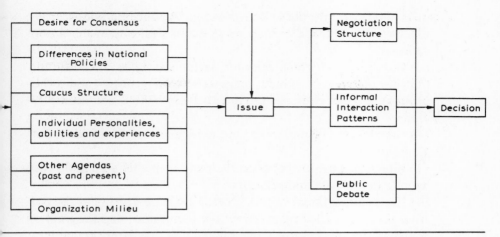

Fig. 1. Factors affecting international organization decision process.

too late to influence the outcome more than marginally), but when it is in process of being shaped and hammered and honed.[1]

Because it is recognized that the records of public bodies of international organizations only give one view of decision-making by these bodies, earlier research has been based largely on information collected through observation and interviews.[2] Therefore, the purpose of the research reported in this paper is methodological as well as substantive. It endeavors to explore what kinds of insights on decision-making can be obtained by systematic analysis of public records, realizing that no one methodology can answer all questions.

Figure 1 places public debate in international organization decision-making in context. On the right side, it shows that decisions are shaped not only by public debate, but also by negotiation outside the public arena and by more informal interaction patterns that develop in the headquarters, missions, and other places where delegates interact. The public aspect of decision-making may reflect some of the activity in negotiations and more informal interaction, but key actors in this activity may not be very active in the public arena, and some conflicts may never be brought out into the open. For example, conflicts between close allies tend to be acted out in private, whereas enemies are more likely to wage disputes publicly.

Figure 1 also identifies factors that affect the way in which an

207

issue is handled in the three activities that produce decisions:

(1) the intensity with which participants desire to reach a consensus;

(2) the degree to which relevant national policies are different;

(3) the manner in which regional caucus groups (and other groups) unify portions of the membership behind common positions;

(4) the abilities, experiences, and personalities of individual participants;

(5) interrelationships between the issue being debated and other agenda items, past and present;

(6) the organizational milieu created by such factors as the cultural setting of the organization, the secretariat, and the kind of social structure linking participants that has been created by past activities.

Number of Decisions

The seven bodies analyzed made a total of 5147 decisions in 1955, 1960, and 1965. In round numbers, there were 2000 in the UN, 1600 in the ILO, 1000 in WHO, and 500 in WMO. Table 1 provides a breakdown by years.

Those familiar with decision-making in public bodies would expect that decisions would not be spread evenly across meetings, and this is the case with the seven bodies being examined. Decisions tend to cluster at the end of the debate on a particular agenda item, with a decision to adjourn being the only decision made in some meetings. Table 2 reveals great disparity in the number of decisions made in individual meetings, ranging from

TABLE 1

Number of Decisions in Each Organization

Year	UN	ILO	WHO	WMO	Total
1955	450	584	384	184	1602
1960	828	536	407	204	1975
1965	723	454	248	145	1570
Total	2001	1574	1039	533	5147

TABLE 2

Number of Decisions Per Meeting (1955, 1960, 1965)

Body	No. of Meet-ings	No. of Deci-sions	Mean	Mode	Low	High
United Nations						
General Assembly	254	1230	4.8	1	1	46
Security Council	174	765	4.0	3	1	26
International Labor Org.						
Conference	94	440	4.7	3	1	78
Governing Body	61	1134	18.5	1	1	56
World Health Organization						
Assembly	37	303	8.2	1	1	38
Executive Board	76	730	9.9	6	1	32
World Meteorologi-cal Org.						
Congress *	52	532	10.2	12	1	24

* Figures are for 1955, 1959, and 1967 in all tables. No data available for Executive Committee.

one to a high of seventy-eight in a single meeting of the International Labor Organization Conference.

Subject of Decisions

Decisions were coded in five categories: (1) administrative, (2) budget-finance, (3) elections and appointments, (4) procedural, and (5) program. The administrative category includes decisions concerning the secretariat of the organization, except for budgetary and financial decisions, and the election and appointment of specific individuals. The budget-finance category includes all aspects of the organization's budget, as well as assessment of members and decisions relating to voluntary contributions of money by members. Elections and appointments include election and ap-

TABLE 3

Subject of Decisions for Each Body (1955, 1960, 1965)

Body	Adminis-tration	Budget/ Finance	Election/ Appoint.	Proced-ural	Pro-gram	Total
A. Number of Decisions						
United Nations						
General Assembly	30	51	116	640	399	123(
Security Council	0	0	244	452	69	76!
International Labor Org.						
Conference	0	7	86	117	230	44(
Governing Body	62	138	175	254	505	113⊲
World Health Org.						
Assembly	35	53	51	74	94	30?
Executive Board	24	175	59	194	280	732
World Meteorological Org.						
Congress	27	52	74	235	145	53⊰
Total	178	476	805	1966	1722	514⸀
B. Percent by row of above matrix						
United Nations						
General Assembly	2.4	4.1	9.4	51.8	32.2	
Security COuncil	0.0	0.0	31.9	59.1	9.0	
International Labor Org.						
Conference	0.0	1.6	19.5	26.6	52.3	
Governing Body	5.5	12.2	15.4	22.4	44.5	
World Health Org.						
Assembly	11.4	17.3	16.7	24.2	30.4	
Executive Board	3.3	23.9	8.1	26.5	38.3	
World Meteorological Org.						
Congress	5.1	9.8	13.9	44.1	27.2	
Total	3.5	9.3	15.6	38.2	33.4	

pointment of both administrative personnel and officers of the body making the decision, such as the election of a chairman. It also includes elections on the admission of new members. Procedural decisions are confined to decisions about the procedure of the body making the decision. Program decisions are made about the program of the organization except for the aspects of the first four categories that might be considered program.

Table 3 (A) provides the total number of decisions for each subject. It reveals that program and procedure account for approximately 2000 decisions each, or close to three-quarters of the total. Table 3 (B) reveals the percentage of decisions each body made in each subject. Particularly notable is the high percentage of procedural decisions in both United Nations bodies — 52 percent for the General Assembly and 59 percent for the Security Council. In contrast, ILO and WHO make more program decisions than any other kind. The percentage of procedural decisions in the WMO Congress, 44 percent, appears to be caused by the custom of making decisions in the Congress on procedural matters handled more routinely by the other bodies. For example, the Congress formally approved minutes of previous meetings, a practice not followed by other bodies.

Type of Discussion

Discussion for each decision was coded in three categories: (1) no discussion; (2) statements supporting the decision only; (3) debate on the decision, i.e., some disagreement. Occasionally there are statements and debate on issues other than the decision before the body. Two extra categories were established for this kind of discussion; (4) statements not on the decision; and (5) - debate about issues other than the decision. Table 4 indicates the type of discussion for each body. Part B reveals that 73 percent of the total decisions for all bodies were taken without discussion and only in 1 percent of the decisions was there any disagreement. The percentage of decisions in which there is disagreement is remarkably constant across the bodies, except the WHO bodies, varying only from 11 to 14 percent. The figures for the two WHO bodies are in sharp contrast, with the Assembly having an extremely low three percent and the Executive Board having a very high 22 percent. The figures suggest two hypotheses about disagreement in these bodies. First, debate in the Executive Board may

TABLE 4
Type of Discussion in Each Body (1955, 1960, 1965)

Body	No Dis-cussion	Discussion on Decision		Discussion not on Decision		Tota
		Agree	Dis-agree	Agree	Dis-agree	
A. Number of Decisions						
United Nations						
General Assembly	950	63	176	6	41	123€
Security Council	579	82	93	4	7	76!
International Labor Org.						
Conference	322	41	59	2	16	44(
Governing Body	793	172	132	14	23	113∢
World Health Organization						
Assembly	272	19	11	0	5	30⁷
Executive Board	444	108	165	0	15	73⁌
World Meteorological Org.						
Congress	402	47	66	5	13	53⌐
Total	3762	532	702	31	120	514⁷
B. Percent by Row of Above Matrix						
United Nations						
General Assembly	76.9	5.1	14.2	0.5	3.2	
Security Council	75.7	10.7	12.2	0.5	0.9	
International Labor Org.						
Conference	73.2	9.3	13.4	0.5	3.6	
Governing Body	69.9	15.2	11.6	1.2	2.0	
World Health Organization						
Assembly	88.6	6.2	3.6	0.0	1.6	
Executive Board	60.7	14.8	22.6	0.0	1.9	
World Meteorological Org.						
Congress	75.4	8.8	12.4	0.9	2.4	
Total	73.1	10.3	13.6	0.6	2.3	

substitute for debate in the Assembly, explaining why the two WHO bodies are extreme in both directions. Second, it would seem that a large amount of decisions with debate is not an indication that a body is fragmented and unable to work together. The WHO Executive Board is composed of medical doctors who seem to have considerable consensus on the mission of their organization and high esprit de corps. This suggests that this rather well-integrated group may feel more able to tolerate debate than the other bodies.

Table 5 reveals a gradual increase in the percentage of decisions made without discussion over the three years, with 69 percent in 1955, 74 percent in 1960, and 76 percent in 1965.

Table 6 indicates the relationship between type of discussion and the subject of decisions. Since 73 percent of decisions are taken without discussion, it is not surprising that more decisions in each subject are made without discussion than all other categories combined. But debate that does take place is concentrated highly on program issues, 57 percent (see Table 6C). Table 6A shows

TABLE 5

Type of Discussion Each Year

A. Number of Decisions	1955	1960	1965	Total
No Discussion	1101	1469	1192	3762
Supportive Statements Only	195	188	149	532
Disagreement	270	243	189	702
Statements not on Decision				
No Disagreement	6	10	15	31
Disagreement	30	65	25	120
Total	1602	1975	1570	5147

B. Percent by Column for Above Matrix				
No Discussion	68.7	74.4	76.0	73.1
Supportive Statements Only	12.2	9.5	9.5	10.3
Disagreement	16.9	12.3	12.0	13.6
Statements not on Decision				
No Disagreement	0.6	0.4	0.5	1.0
Disagreement	1.9	3.2	1.5	2.3

TABLE 6
Subject of Decisions and Type of Discussion (1955, 1960, 1965)

Type of Discussion	Adminis-tration	Budget/ Finance	Election/ Appoint.	Proced-ural	Pro-gram	Tot
A. Number of Decisions						
No Discussion	139	353	611	1664	995	376
Supportive Statements Only	27	35	121	85	264	53
Disagreement	7	77	59	163	397	70
Statements not on Decision						
No Disagreement	4	1	5	9	12	3
Disagreement	1	10	9	45	54	1
Total	178	476	805	1966	1722	514
B. Percent by Column from Above Matrix						
No Discussion	78.1	74.2	76.0	84.6	57.8	7
Supportive Statements Only	15.2	7.4	15.0	4.3	15.3	1
Disagreement	3.9	16.2	7.2	8.3	23.1	1
Statements not on Decision						
No Disagreement	2.2	0.2	0.6	0.5	0.7	
Disagreement	0.6	2.1	1.1	2.3	3.1	
Total	178	476	805	1966	2047	548
C. Percent by Row from Above Matrix						
No Discussion	3.7	9.4	16.2	44.2	26.1	
Supportive Statements Only	5.1	6.6	22.7	16.0	49.6	
Disagreement	1.0	11.0	8.3	23.2	56.6	
Statements not on Decision						
No Disagreement	12.9	3.2	16.1	29.0	38.7	
Disagreement	0.8	8.5	7.6	38.1	44.9	
Total	3.5	9.3	15.6	38.2	33.4	

contrast in the kind of discussion in the two most numerous sub-jects, procedure and program. Virtually all procedural decisions are made without discussion, 85 percent, whereas 58 percent of program decisions are made without debate.

How Decisions are Made

The way in which decisions are made can be classified in three categories: (1) a nonvoting consensus, (2) voting by show of hands, and (3) roll call vote. Two other forms are used occasionally, primarily for elections, (4) secret ballot, and (5) lot. One of the reasons the method of decision-making was coded was to place the roll call voting studies in the context of the total population of decisions. Another reason was to check an impression, gained while observing international organizations over a number of years, indicating that the percentage of decisions made by voting is declining.

In their analysis of General Assembly roll call votes Alker and Russett admit, in a footnote, that such analysis may not reveal "step by step consensus-building achievements of the United Nations". But they affirm, "just because roll calls more often express disagreements than agreements, they are useful summaries of voting alignments".[3] Whether roll call voting alignments really reflect alignments on all votes is a question which cannot be answered without having a team of observers collect data on show of hands votes. Even this might not be a reliable measure of show of hands votes, if delegates knew their votes were being recorded, because it might cause them to vote as they would in a roll call vote. But information can be given that indicates how voting is distributed between show of hands and roll call votes. Table 7 reveals that 477 votes were taken in the General Assembly in the three years under study 62 percent by show of hands and 38 percent by roll call. While the roll call could reflect alignments in all votes in the General Assembly, it is also quite possible that the approximately 39 percent of votes represented in roll calls could be a skewed sample. On the other hand, Table 7 (C) indicates that it is much less likely that roll call votes of the other organizations might reflect alignments in all votes. Show of hands votes in the bodies of these organizations ranged between 78 and 100 percent of total votes.

In the same footnote, Alker and Russett also assert that "the most controversial and important (decisions) will probably be *reflected* in roll call voting". In this assertion they extend the population of decisions whose alignments are being predicted from vot-

TABLE 7

Type of Voting in Each Body (1955, 1960, 1965)

Body	Hands	Roll Call	Other	Total
A. Number of Decisions				
United Nations				
General Assembly	297	180	759	1236
Security Council	2	167	596	765
International Labor Org.				
Conference	93	27	320	440
Governing Body	53	0	1081	1134
World Health Organization				
Assembly	19	4	284	307
Executive Board	81	0	651	732
World Meteorological Org.				
Congress	74	17	442	533
Total	619	395	4133	5147
B. Percent by Column from Above Matrix				
United Nations				
General Assembly	48.0	45.6		47.0
Security Council	0.3	42.3		16.7
International Labor Org.				
Conference	15.0	6.8		11.8
Governing Body	8.6	0.0		5.2
World Health Organization				
Assembly	3.1	1.0		2.3
Executive Board	13.1	0.0		8.0
World Meteorological Org.				
Congress	12.0	4.3		9.3
Total	619	395		1014

ing decisions alone to those that are "controversial or important". That is, including decisions reached by a consensus, if they are "controversial or important". Although they do not define "controversial" or "important", it seems quite plausible that roll call votes do include the most controversial issues. On the other hand,

TABLE 7 (continued)

Body	Hands	Roll Call	Other	Total
C. Percent by Row from Above Matrix				
United Nations				
General Assembly	62.3	37.7		477
Security Council	1.2	98.8		169
International Labor Org.				
Conference	77.5	22.5		120
Governing Body	100.0	0.0		53
World Health Organization				
Assembly	82.6	17.4		23
Executive Board	100.0	0.0		81
World Meteorological Org.				
Congress	81.3	18.7		91
Total	61.0	39.0		1014

unless "important" means the same thing as "controversial", the assertion that roll calls reflect alignments on important issues is less convinving.

A Dutch diplomat with long experience in UN organizations writes of decisions reached by consensus, indicating that they include the most routine and the most important and controversial. He divides decisions made by consensus into two categories, those formulated in a resulotion and those passed without a resolution. Every year, for example, most UN bodies, including the General Assembly, pass many routine resolutions that "take note of" or "approve" decisions of lower organs. Kaufmann also refers to cases where resolutions are passed by a consensus that has been "negotiated with so much difficulty, that the president himself is requested to propose it", although it would seem that this procedure is rarely used.[4]

Discussing consensus decisions without a resolution, Kaufmann writes that this is the procedure for agenda items which are either extremely routine, or so important and at the same time so controversial that delegations prefer to avoid both debate and the adoption of an explicit resolution. Decisions made by a consensus

217

TABLE 8

Type of Decision and How Decisions are Made (1955, 1960, 1965)

Type of Discussion	Non-vote	Hands	Roll Call	Secret Ballot	Lot	Total
A. Number of Decisions						
No Discussion	3287	301	91	78	2	3763
Supportive Statements Only	368	70	88	6	0	532
Disagreement	271	226	189	17	0	703
Statements not on Decision						
No Disagreement	25	2	3	1	0	31
Disagreement	72	20	24	2	0	118
Total	4023	619	395	104	2	5147
B. Percent by Column from Above Matrix						
No Discussion	81.7	48.5	23.0	75.0	100.0	73.1
Supportive Statements Only	9.1	11.3	22.3	5.8	0.0	10.3
Disagreement	6.7	36.6	47.8	16.3	0.0	13.7
Statements not on Decision						
No Disagreement	0.6	0.3	0.8	1.0	0.0	0.6
Disagreement	1.8	3.2	6.1	1.9	0.0	2.3
C. Percent by Row from Above Matrix						
No Discussion	87.5	8.0	2.4	2.1	0.1	
Supportive Statements Only	69.2	13.2	16.5	1.1	0.0	
Disagreement	38.5	32.2	26.9	2.4	0.0	
Statements not on Decision						
No Disagreement	80.6	6.5	9.7	3.2	0.0	
Disagreement	61.0	16.9	20.3	1.7	0.0	
Total	78.2	12.0	7.7	2.0	0.0	

without resolution sometimes are made without debate, avoiding discussion that might destroy a consensus. On the other hand, the consensus may follow debate which reveals that "the action to be taken is more or less agreed, but the drafting of a specific text would cause insurmountable difficulties. Summing up by the chairman in sufficiently vague or general language is then the way out".[5]

Table 8 sheds some light on the relationship between the character of discussions and the form of decision-making. As described above, type of discussion is divided into those cases where no speeches are made at all (except for the chairman), those in which supportive statements only are made, and those in which there is disagreement (debate). The last category could reasonably be construed as those cases in which there is controversy, although this is only a measure of controversy generated in public debate, and does not necessarily reflect controversy in other settings.

Table 8 (B) reveals that a higher proportion of roll call votes is made with debate than the other two categories (48 percent). But, combining the two "noncontroversial" categories, we find that almost as many roll call votes were taken without debate (45 percent) as with it. The same table also shows that a very small percentage of decisions reached without any vote are debated, only 7 percent. But, the actual number of decisions (271) are more "controversial" decisions than are involved in roll call votes.

TABLE 9

How Decisions Were Made Each Year (1955, 1960, 1965)

Form of Voting	1955	1960	1965	Total
A. Number of Decisions				
Nonvote	1164	1545	1318	4027
Hands	288	210	121	619
Roll Call	121	182	92	395
Secret Ballot	29	38	37	104
Lot	0	0	2	2
Total	1602	1975	1570	5147
B. Percent by Column from the Above Matrix				
Nonvote	72.7	78.2	83.9	78.2
Hands	18.0	10.7	7.7	12.0
Roll Call	7.6	9.2	5.9	7.7
Secret Ballot	1.8	1.9	2.4	2.0
Lot	0.0	0.0	0.1	0.0
Total	1602	1975	1570	5147

In percentage, 39 percent of decisions with debate are decided by consensus (see Table 8C), whereas only 27 percent are decided by roll call vote.

Table 9 provides figures on how decisions were made across the three years. Of the 5147 decisions, 4027 were made without voting (78 percent). Table 9B reveals that decision-making without voting has increased, indeed, from 73 percent in 1955 to 78 percent in 1960, and 84 percent in 1965. Voting has declined from 27 percent to 22 percent to 16 percent in these same years. Table 9B shows that the decline has come primarily in show of hands votes which have diminished from 18 to 11 to 8 percent. With no clear trend, roll call votes have varied between 6 and 9 percent of all decisions.

Since most decisions are made without voting, decisions on all subjects are made primarily without voting. Table 10B shows that decisions on all subjects are made by nonvoting in 68 percent or more of the cases. The 68 percent is program and elections, and appointments has the next highest percentage of voting, 30 percent. Procedural issues are least often voted upon — in only 10 percent of the cases.

All bodies under study make decisions without voting in over 78 percent of their decisions. Table 11 reveals, however, that there

TABLE 10

Voting and Subject of Decision (1955, 1960, 1965)

	Adminis-tration	Budget/ Finance	Election/ Appoint.	Proced-ural	Pro-gram	Total
A. Number of Decisions						
No Votes	147	383	562	1763	1172	4027
Votes	31	93	243	201	550	1122
Total	178	476	805	1966	1722	5147
B. Percent by Column from Above Matrix						
No Votes	82.6	80.5	69.8	89.7	68.1	78.2
Votes	17.4	19.5	30.2	10.3	31.9	21.8

TABLE 11

Voting and Nonvoting for Each Body (1955, 1960, 1965)

Body	Nonvote	Vote	Total
A. Number of Decisions			
United Nations			
General Assembly	715	521	1236
Security Council	592	173	765
International Labor Organization			
Conference	319	121	440
Governing Body	1080	54	1134
World Health Organization			
Assembly	280	27	307
Executive Board	650	82	732
World Meteorological Organization			
Congress	391	142	533
Total	4027	1120	5147
B. Percent by Row from Above Matrix			
United Nations			
General Assembly	57.8	42.2	
Security Council	77.4	22.6	
International Labor Organization			
Conference	72.2	27.8	
Governing Body	95.2	4.8	
World Health Organization			
Assembly	91.2	8.8	
Executive Board	88.8	11.2	
World Meteorological Organization			
Congress	73.4	26.6	
Total	78.2	21.8	

is considerable variation across these bodies. The General Assembly votes most often, in 42 percent of their decisions, and the bodies of WHO, ILO, and WMO vary between 5 and 28 percent.

A comparative view of voting across organizations will make it possible to put the studies of roll call voting in the United Nations

TABLE 12

How Decisions are Made for Each Body (1955, 1960, 1965)

Body	Non-vote	Hands	Roll Call	Secret Ballot	Lot	Total
A. Number of Decisions						
United Nations						
General Assembly	715	297	180	43	1	1236
Security Council	592	2	167	4	0	765
International Labor Org.						
Conference	319	93	27	1	0	440
Governing Body	1080	53	0	1	0	1134
World Health Organization						
Assembly	280	19	4	4	0	307
Executive Board	650	81	0	0	1	732
World Meteorological Org.						
Congress	391	74	17	51	0	533
Total	4027′	619	394	104	2	5147
B. Percent by Row from Above Matrix						
United Nations						
General Assembly	57.8	24.0	14.6	3.5	0.1	
Security Council	77.4	0.3	21.8	0.5	0.0	
International Labor Org.						
Conference	72.2	21.3	6.2	0.2	0.0	
Governing Body	95.2	4.7	0.0	0.1	0.0	
World Health Organization						
Assembly	91.2	6.2	1.3	1.3	0.0	
Executive Board	88.8	11.1	0.0	0.0	0.1	
World Meteorological Org.						
Congress	73.4	13.9	3.2	9.6	0.0	
Total	78.2	12.0	7.7	2.0	0.0	

in a broader context. Table 12 shows a remarkable difference in the use of roll call voting between the United Nations and the three specialized agencies. Over the three years, the WHO Executive Board and the ILO Governing Body had no roll call votes, the

WHO Assembly had only four, the WMO Congress, seventeen, and the ILO Conference only twenty-seven. The ILO Conference shows a steady decline in roll call votes from thirteen in 1955, to eight in 1960, and only six in 1965. While the WMO Assembly shows a steady increase from two to five to ten roll call votes in the same years, they are virtually all votes on amendments to the WMO Convention. The decline in ILO Conference votes is accounted for by a decline in votes related to East/West conflict which accounted for six of the thirteen votes in 1955. If votes on new members also are excluded, the ILO Conference has three or four votes each year on labor conventions and recommendations. The WHO Assembly has no constitutional requirement that it vote on certain issues, as the ILO Conference does. The four WHO Assembly votes were, with one exception, intrusions of "political" controversies external to WHO, two related to disarmament, and one to South Africa. Therefore, we see that roll call voting in the three specialized agencies occurs very infrequently and is confined, for the most part, to three kinds of issues: (1) "Political" controversies not directly related to items on agendas; (2) admission of new members; and (3) specific issues, such as charter amendments and conventions, for which organizational charters require roll call votes.

Turning to the United Nations bodies, all Security Council votes are automatically roll call votes, since national positions are inserted in the records for each vote.[6] This makes it impossible to make any differentiation between these two forms of voting. In order to get an overview of the content of General Assembly roll call votes, every tenth vote was selected, providing a sample of thirty-four votes. These tend to reflect the pattern observed in the ILO Conference, with one-third (11) related to East/West conflict, nine others concerned with conflicts between Cuba and the United States, the Congo, S. Africa, the Middle East, Aden, Cyprus, and Kashmir, and six related to admission of new members. These all are related directly to UN agenda items. But they reveal a very skewed sample of General Assembly agendas which include a wide range of subjects, including administrative, budgetary, economic, social, human rights, and legal questions.

Decision Paths

Figure 2 provides a map of the decision paths a decision may follow on the basis of the four decision-making variables: discussion, disagreement, voting, and roll call voting. Decisions can take nine paths:

Path No.	Discussion	Disagreement	Voting	Roll Call Voting
1	No	—	No	—
2	Yes	No	No	—
3	No	—	Yes	No
4	Yes	No	Yes	Yes
5	Yes	No	Yes	No
6	No	—	Yes	Yes
7	Yes	Yes	No	—
8	Yes	Yes	Yes	No
9	Yes	Yes	Yes	Yes

Figure 2 also recapitulates data presented in other tables in a different format, with one diagram for the General Assembly and Security Council, and another for the other three agencies. If the percentages at the four branch points are examined, it can be seen that:

(1) slightly more decisions are discussed in the agencies (6 percent more);

(2) more decisions produce disagreement in debate in the agencies (12 percent more);

(3) there is much more voting in the General Assembly and Security Council (21 percent more);

(4) there is much more roll call voting in the General Assembly and Security Council (37 percent more).

If the Security Council votes were subtracted from the total, the General Assembly alone would have much more roll call voting than the agencies (23 percent more).

Research in Progress

One of the objectives of this research was to compare roll call voting alignments in the General Assembly and Security Council

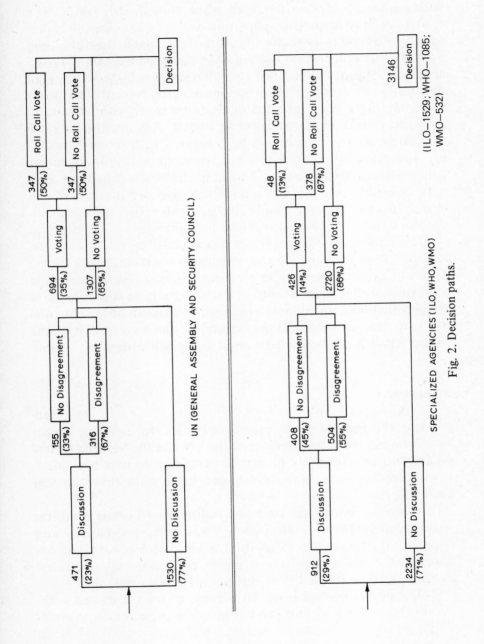

UN (GENERAL ASSEMBLY AND SECURITY COUNCIL)

SPECIALIZED AGENCIES (ILO, WHO, WMO)

(ILO—1529; WHO—1085; WMO—532)

Fig. 2. Decision paths.

225

with alignments in the specialized agencies of the UN family. The reason for making such a comparison would be to discern whether agency alignments crosscut those of the General Assembly and Security Council, thereby having an integrative effect on the global system. Unfortunately, not enough roll call votes were found in the agencies to make a comparison meaningful. Nevertheless, alignment data have been collected on decisions made without roll call votes by coding positions taken in debate. Alignment data gathered from agency debates will be compared with General Assembly and Security Council roll call votes. In addition, alignment data collected from General Assembly debates will be compared with Assembly roll call votes. This will give one measure of the degree to which Assembly roll call alignments reflect alignments in decisions on which roll call votes are not taken.

All decisions in the study are being coded again in order to identify those that provide task expansion for their organizations. This will make it possible to find out whether task expansion is associated with a specific kind of decision path. Task expansion is being coded on three dimensions: (1) the strength of the commitment to the decision, (2) the nature of the new activity, and (3) the kinds of participants involved in the new programs.

Summary

Using the records of the executive bodies and assembly plenaries of three specialized agencies of the UN and the Security Council and General Assembly plenary, 5147 decisions have been identified for the years 1955, 1960, and 1965, with the following findings:

1. When decisions were coded according to subject (administrative, budget-finance, election-appointments, procedural, and program), it was found that the UN General Assembly and Security Council make a much higher percentage of procedural decisions than the bodies of the specialized agencies.

2. The bodies studied make 73 percent of their decisions without any discussion. This percentage has been increasing gradually.

3. Only in 14 percent of decisions was there disagreement in debate.

4. Virtually all procedural decisions, 85 percent, are made without discussion, and 58 percent of decisions on programs are made without discussion.

5. In 39 percent of the cases where there is disagreement registered in debate, decisions are taken by consensus (i.e., no vote taken).

6. The General Assembly votes 42 percent of the time whereas voting in the bodies of the specialized agencies ranges between 5 and 28 percent.

7. In cases where disagreement is registered in debate, only 27 percent are decided by roll call vote.

8. When votes are taken in the General Assembly, show of hands is used 62 percent of the time and roll call 38 percent. This raises questions about the reliability of alignment studies based on roll call vote data.

9. Decision-making with voting has declined from 27 percent in 1955, to 22 percent in 1960, and 16 percent in 1965, but the percentage of roll call votes has remained rather constant, varying between 6 and 9 percent.

10. Alignment studies based on roll call vote data are of extremely limited value in the specialized agencies because roll call votes are taken very rarely.

11. Roll call voting in the specialized agencies is confined to three kinds of issues: (1) "political" controversies not directly related to items on agendas; (2) admission of new members; and (3) issues for which charters require roll call votes, such as charter amendments and conventions.

12. Roll call votes in the General Assembly are a skewed sample in which East/West, colonial, and border conflicts are highly represented, with economic, social, human rights, and legal questions rarely decided by roll call vote.

Conclusion

The decline in decision-making by voting suggests an increasing preference for consensual decision-making in international organizations. This is in accordance with personal discussions with participants in international organizations, in which they assert that voting is divisive and should be avoided if possible. The gradual increase in decisions taken without discussion also indicates that more consensual procedures are being developed — at least in the final stage of public decision-making. This may mean that increasing use is being made of committees and private negotiations for the reaching of decisions.

Another explanation could be that the content of decisions has become less divisive, possibly because decisions may now be involved only in the implementation of basic programs already underway. Additional research now in progress, discerning trends in decisions on task expansion and the way in which this kind of decision is made, may give more insight on this question.

Research underway on the generation of alignment data from debates may help to show alignments for decisions in problem areas that rarely require roll call decisions (economic, social, human rights, and legal) and in the specialized agencies (where roll calls are seldom used). But the decline in disagreement in debate will make this kind of analysis more difficult, although committee records may be helpful.

NOTES

[1] William Dale, "Decision-Making in the International Monetary Fund", paper presented at Conference on Decision-Making in International Management Systems, University of Chicago Graduate School of Business, June 1968, pp. 44–45.

[2] See for example, Chadwick F. Alger, "Personal Contact in Intergovernmental Relations", in Herbert C. Kelman, Ed., *International Behavior* (New York: Holt, Rinehart, and Winston, 1965), pp. 523–547; "Interaction and Negotiation in a Committee of the United Nations General Assembly", *Peace Research Society (International) Papers (Philadelphia Conference, 1965)* (V, 1966), pp. 141–159; "Interaction in a Committee of the United Nations General Assembly", in J. David Singer, Ed., *Quantitative International Politics: Insights and Evidence, International Yearbook of Political Behavior Research,* VI, Heinz Eulau, General Editor, (New York: The Free Press, 1968), pp. 51–84.

[3] Hayward R. Alker, Jr. and Bruce M. Russett, *World Politics in the General Assembly* (New Haven and London: Yale University Press, 1965), p. 19.

4 Johan Kaufmann, *Conference Diplomacy* (New York: Oceana; Leyden: A.W. Sijthoff, 1968), p. 42.

5 Ibid., p. 44.

6 With the exception of two cases where results were not given in the official records of the Security Council and four cases which were secret ballots for election to the International Court of Justice.

Author Index

Danquah, J.B., 57
Davenport, William, 54
Dawson, R.M., 109
Deutsch, Karl, 5
Duwuona-Hammond, A.J., 84
Due, Jean M., 84

Easton, David, 5, 10, 22–23, 32, 36–
  37, 52, 139
Edding, Friedrich, 139
Edusei, Krobo, 77
Emery, F.E., 33–34, 48, 53
Eulau, Heinz, 228

Fagen, Richard R., 81
Farrell, R. Barry, 180
Finer, S.F., 8
Finlay, David J., 81, 85–86
First, Ruth, 83
Fisherman, Joshua A., 53
Fitch, Bob, 81
Friedland, William H., 85–86
Friedrich, Carl J., 83

Gbedemah, Komla, 61, 74–76, 84
Geertz, Clifford, 139
Geiger, W., 201
Genoud, Roger, 81
Gerth, H., 109
Glanzmann, W., 202
Goody, Jack, 80, 86
Gournay, B., 52
Groth, Alexander J., 9, 13, 111
Gurvich, George, 52
Gutteridge, William, 85

Haas, Ernst B., 181
Hadwen, John G., 180
Halpern, Ben, 83
Harbison, Friederich, 139
Harvey, W.B., 84
Helg, R., 201
Hodge, Peter, 84

Hoffman, David, 94, 109
Holsti, Ole R., 81
Homans, George C., 90, 99–100, 103,
  108–109

Ikle, Fred C., 180
Ikoku, Samuel G., 64

Jacobson, H.K., 9, 13, 15, 143–144
Jamous, Haroun, 28, 52
Johnson, David, 205

Kaplan, Morton A., 172–173, 181
Kaufmann, Johan, 180, 217, 228
Kautsky, John H., 142
Kelman, Herbert C., 228
Kohlas, J., 197, 202–203
Kornberg, Allan, 109
Kraus, Jon, 81, 86

Leavitt, Michael, 205
Lee, J.M., 84, 86
Legum, Colin, 85–86
Lewis, W.A., 83
Lijphart, Arend, 180
Lloyd, C., 84
Lovald, Jennifer, 205
Lowi, Theodore J., 180

Machlup, Fritz, 141
MacRae, Donald G., 83
Madge, Charles, 83
Madjitey, Eric, 85
Mahoney, William P. Jr., 83
Malinowski, Bronislaw, 50, 54
Marcelles, J.B., 53
March, James G., 52, 180
Maris, Ronald, 108
Maruyama, Magoroh, 53
Mayer, Lucille, 205
Meehan, Eugene J., 39–42, 51, 53
Meisel, James H., 82
Mélèse, Jacques, 47, 54

Subject Index